20
Literacy Strategies
to Meet the
Common Core

INCREASING RIGOR IN MIDDLE & HIGH SCHOOL CLASSROOMS

Elaine K. McEwan-Adkins
Allyson J. Burnett

Solution Tree | Press

a division of

Solution Tree

555 North Morton Street
Bloomington, IN 47404
800.733.6786 (toll free) / 812.336.7700
FAX: 812.336.7790

email: info@solution-tree.com
solution-tree.com

Visit **go.solution-tree.com/commoncore** to download the reproducibles in this book.

Printed in the United States of America

16 15 14   4 5

Library of Congress Cataloging-in-Publication Data

McEwan-Adkins, Elaine K., 1941–

20 literacy strategies to meet the common core : increasing rigor in middle & high school classrooms / Elaine K. McEwan-Adkins, Allyson J. Burnett.

p. cm.

Includes bibliographical references and index.

ISBN 978-1-936764-28-0 (perfect bound)   1. Language arts (Middle school)--United States. 2. Language arts (Secondary)--United States. 3. Language arts--Standards--United States.   I. McEwan-Adkins, Elaine K., 1941- II. Burnett, Allyson. III. Title. IV. Title: Twenty literacy strategies to meet the common core.

LB1631.M3943 2013

428.0071'2--dc23

2012032637

Solution Tree

Jeffrey C. Jones, CEO
Edmund M. Ackerman, President

Solution Tree Press

President: Douglas M. Rife
Publisher: Robert D. Clouse
Editorial Director: Lesley Bolton
Managing Production Editor: Caroline Wise
Proofreader: Elisabeth Abrams
Cover Designer: Amy Shock
Text Designer: Jenn Taylor

ACKNOWLEDGMENTS

Solution Tree Press would like to thank the following reviewers:

Steve Bowen
Retired English Language Arts
  Teacher and Coach
Red Oaks, Texas

Val Bresnahan
Sixth-Grade Teacher
Franklin Middle School
Wheaton, Illinois

Morgan Cuthbert
Mathematics and Science Teacher
Frank Harrison Middle School
Yarmouth, Maine

Johnnalyn Davis
Secondary Reading Specialist
West Virginia State Department
  of Education
Hurricane, West Virginia

Frank Iannucci, Jr.
Supervisor of Mathematics, 6–12
Orange High School
West Orange, New Jersey

Kristina McLaughlin
Classroom Teacher
Leetonia, Ohio

Christopher D. Schmidt
Secondary English Teacher
Dallas, Texas

Tracy Scholz
9–12 English Language Arts and
  Reading Interventionist
Alief ISD
Houston, Texas

Shekema Silveri
AP English / Language Arts Teacher
Mt. Zion High School
Jonesboro, Georgia

Kelly Tumy
K–12 District Writing Coordinator
Crosby ISD
Crosby, Texas

Rebecca Wade
Lead Reading Teacher
Giddings State School
Giddings, Texas

Visit **go.solution-tree.com/commoncore** to download
the reproducibles in this book.

TABLE OF CONTENTS

ABOUT THE AUTHORS

Elaine K. McEwan-Adkins, EdD, is a partner and educational consultant with the McEwan-Adkins Group, offering professional development in literacy and school leadership. A former teacher, librarian, principal, and assistant superintendent for instruction in several suburban Chicago school districts, Elaine was honored by the Illinois Principals Association as an outstanding instructional leader, by the Illinois State Board of Education with an Award of Excellence in the Those Who Excel Program, and by the National Association of Elementary School Principals as the 1991 National Distinguished Principal from Illinois.

Elaine is the author of more than thirty-five books for parents and educators. Her most recent titles include *40 Reading Intervention Strategies for K–6 Students: Research-Based Support for RTI, Teach Them All to Read, Ten Traits of Highly Effective Schools, Literacy Look-Fors: An Observation Protocol to Guide K–6 Classroom Walkthroughs,* and *Collaborative Teacher Literacy Teams, K–6: Connecting Professional Growth to Student Achievement.* To learn more about McEwan-Adkins's work, visit www.elainemcewan.com.

She received an undergraduate degree in education from Wheaton College and a master's degree in library science and a doctorate in educational administration from Northern Illinois University.

Allyson J. Burnett is a retired teaching veteran with twenty years of experience in the classroom and ten years in instructional leadership. A reading specialist and independent consultant, she presents at regional, state, and national conventions. Through her work, Allyson shows content teachers how to use strategies to help students master the College and Career Readiness Anchor Standards for Grades 6–12.

Allyson has traveled all over the United States to consult with schools in a variety of areas. She specializes in helping schools implement literacy strategies into *all* classrooms by creating and building the capacity of a cross-curricular literacy cohort. Her expertise is in helping these cohorts become experts at making text accessible to students and guiding the cohorts as they become presenters to and peer coaches for their content colleagues.

Allyson has coauthored a comprehension workbook for grades 4–8 and has published articles in *Principal Leadership* and the *Texas Study of Secondary Education*.

To book Elaine McEwan-Adkins or Allyson J. Burnett for professional development, contact pd@solution-tree.com.

I met Allyson Burnett for the first time in 2002 when I made a presentation based on my book *Raising Reading Achievement in Middle and High Schools: 5 Simple-to-Follow Strategies for Principals* (McEwan, 2001) to central office administrators, secondary principals, and teacher leaders of the Alief Independent School District (Houston, Texas). One of the five strategies focused on content literacy: *Teach every student how to read to learn*. Although this big idea is simple enough to grasp, in reality, implementing secondary content literacy is often messy, time-consuming, and abandoned in frustration for its lack of teacher buy-in and instant results.

As an author and consultant, I do not always know how my ideas are received, but since my presentation was more in the way of an exploration of the topic I did not expect to hear further from anyone. However, when I contacted Allyson in 2005 to interview her for the second edition of the book, I was delighted to learn that some of the seeds I planted in 2002 had germinated in the minds of key teachers and administrators. I discovered that Allyson was a key member of a highly successful literacy cohort at Hastings High School called the Textperts. She explained to me that the Textperts at Hastings were "experts at making text accessible to students." I subsequently visited the Hastings' campus and interviewed many of the Textperts, describing their journey from a fledgling building literacy committee to a high-functioning professional learning community in my book.

—Elaine McEwan-Adkins

One of my most memorable experiences as an educator was simultaneously serving as an interventionist and literacy coach at Hastings as we worked to develop the Textperts model. The most remarkable thing about the Textperts is that to the date of this writing, the cohort is still constituted and functioning as a way of facilitating content literacy in all classrooms. Generally, in districts and schools where administrators are regularly coming and going and instructional priorities are constantly shifting, experienced teachers often adopt the "this too shall pass" philosophy. They ride out the storms that inevitably result from yet another initiative or a new supervisor and rarely pay more than lip service to a reform. In contrast, literacy leaders at Hastings have hung on through the storms, anchored in two beliefs: (1) content literacy is essential to meaningful and long-lasting learning, and (2) a teacher cohort to facilitate subject-specific professional learning through teaching and modeling research-based literacy strategies is the only way to transmit those strategies into the instructional practices of all teachers.

I was thrilled when Elaine approached me with the idea of writing a book together that would meld our experiences and passion for secondary literacy into a set of strategies to help teachers meet the Common Core State Standards for English Language Arts (ELA) and Content Literacy in Grades 6–12. With our shared vision, we have merged our efforts to create a united voice for secondary literacy.

—Allyson J. Burnett

Our View of Secondary Content Literacy

Although content literacy as a semester course has been taught in preservice teacher training for decades, implementation for many novice teachers has been frustrating. Often their dreams of becoming skilled content facilitators became mired in the boring but more manageable role of a "talking textbook." Regrettably over the years, even experienced teachers, faced with too many struggling students, have become like the swimming coach who conducts class from the side of the pool with her athletes on the stands. Neither the coach nor the kids get into the water. They don't get in the shallow end, where students could safely learn the basic elements of swimming—how to hold your breath and put your face in the water—and therefore, not surprisingly, they never get to the deep end either. When faced with summative assessments that expect students to read and write in response to reading, they are in over their heads.

The rigorous Common Core State Standards for English Language Arts and Literacy in History/Social Studies, Science, and Technical Subjects for Grades 6–12 call for students to independently read and comprehend literary and informational texts in their English courses and content-specific textbooks and supplementary materials in history, social studies, science, and technical subjects.

We have chosen to focus exclusively on *informational text*, believing that ELA teachers have a wealth of knowledge when it comes to teaching literary texts but may welcome support in teaching literary informational texts, particularly when it comes to meeting the College and Career Readiness Anchor Standards for Reading. This book provides the scaffolding and expertise that teachers need to introduce literacy strategies into your content instruction—models, detailed lesson plans, and reproducible graphic organizers.

Our Goals in Writing This Book

We have three major goals in writing this book:

1. To facilitate the reading of informational text in secondary class-rooms by offering a set of strategies that are individually aligned to the College and Career Readiness Anchor Standards for Reading found in the Common Core State Standards (Common Core State Initiative, 2010a) while at the same time responding to the recommendations from the authors of the Common Core State Standards in English Language Arts and Literacy for Instructional Materials as described in figure 1

2. To encourage and support secondary teachers in the challenging task of teaching all of their students how to read to learn

3. To provide the basis for discussion and reflection in PLCs and departmental teams who desire to make the standards and strategies content-specific

FIGURE 1: Features of the 20 Literacy Strategies That Support the Common Core State Standards

Recommendations From the Authors of the Common Core State Standards in English Language Arts and Literacy for Instructional Materials	Features of the 20 Reading Strategies
Eighty to ninety percent of standards require text-dependent analysis.	One hundred percent of the literacy strategies require text-dependent analysis and provide informational texts such as might be found in content textbooks as well as literary informational texts such as opinion and journalistic pieces and memoirs.
Students need support to read more complex texts.	The lesson plans offer support for students in executing text-dependent reading.
Materials should include specific models.	Every strategy includes sample texts and completed model organizers to support teachers in showing their students how to execute the strategy.
Students should be required to return to the text to check the accuracy of their answers.	The strategies contain built-in steps that take students back to the text to both write and check the accuracy of their answers.

continued →

Recommendations From the Authors of the Common Core State Standards in English Language Arts and Literacy for Instructional Materials	Features of the 20 Reading Strategies
Texts should be short enough to encourage careful examination.	The strategies are designed to be used with a short piece of content text that can easily be chunked into three sections: one for teacher modeling, one for scaffolding the text, and one for student pairs or individual students to independently process.
Students should first be required to demonstrate an understanding of what they read before producing opinions and interpretations. Before being asked to go beyond the text, they should demonstrate their grasp of the specific ideas and details of the text.	The strategies are designed with steps that lead students to a full understanding of the text before they are expected to summarize, draw conclusions, make inferences, or analyze text.

Source: Information in column 1 is summarized from Coleman & Pimentel, 2011.

How to Use This Book to Advance Schoolwide Content Literacy

There are multiple ways to use this book to advance the goal of content literacy in more manageable increments, including the following activities:

- Use the book as part of a pilot program in a content department.

- Use the book for a whole-faculty book study to increase background knowledge and understanding of the Common Core content literacy standards.

- Use the book to stimulate conversations among members of a PLC regarding the quality or effectiveness of the current strategies they use and whether those strategies will help students be successful with the new standards.

- Use the book as a vehicle to discuss how the faculty can systematically address the gap between what students need to be able to do and what they can do.

- Use the book to spur a discussion of how and in what ways educators are currently teaching the skills required by the standards to their students and how their instruction may need to change.

- Use the book to review and discuss examples of current student products in relation to the products the standards will require.

- Use the book to begin conversations about the scaffolding that may need to be put in place in order to help students be successful with the new standards.

The Audience for This Book

We have written this book for all grades 6–12 teachers who want to become more effective but are sometimes frustrated by their students' seeming inability to read and respond in writing to grade-level materials. The following individuals may also benefit from the book's more intensive and research-based approach to content literacy:

- Literacy coaches, interventionists, and instructional content specialists who are supporting secondary teachers in their classrooms

- Special education, English learner (EL), and Title teachers who need resources to help teachers meet the needs of their specialized groups of students

- College and university professors who are looking for a research-based collection of literacy strategies that are closely aligned with the Common Core Content Literacy Standards, Grades 6–12, to use as a resource in their courses

- Secondary administrators who are contemplating the implementation of a buildingwide content literacy initiative in anticipation of the adoption of more stringent reading and writing standards

INTRODUCTION

Close strategic reading is one of the most powerful and enjoyable
ways to develop the ability to think critically and evaluate
information—to literally become smarter. Students should
therefore have abundant daily opportunities to carefully read and
reread texts for intellectual purposes—and with a pen in hand.

—SCHMOKER (2006, P. 59)

This introduction contains background information on topics germane to your successful implementation of the twenty literacy strategies found in this book. The topics are listed here and then explained in greater detail.

- A description of the Common Core State Standards for English Language Arts and Literacy in History/Social Studies, Science, and Technical Subjects (Grades 6–12) and its implications for secondary teachers

- How this new approach to literacy differs from previous content literacy models

- The nature of skilled reading and how it looks in the minds of skilled readers

- The role that teachers' modeling plays in students' acquisition of content literacy

- Guidelines for accessing and utilizing the twenty literacy strategies

Figure I.1 (page 2) defines documents and concepts that may be unfamiliar to readers. While there is a complete glossary that comprises the student-friendly definitions found in each strategy, it does not contain the terms and concepts found in this figure.

FIGURE 1.1: Definitions of Key Concepts

Term	Definition
Literacy rehearsal	The sustained practice of various reading and writing processes shown by research to develop the reading and writing proficiencies that enable students to eventually read and comprehend complex literary and informational texts independently and proficiently.
Content literacy	"The ability to use reading and writing for the acquisition of new content in a given discipline" (McKenna & Robinson, 1990, p. 184). As defined in the CCSS, literacy encompasses the abilities to read, write, speak, listen, and use language effectively in a variety of content areas.
Flesch-Kincaid Grade Level	The scale is derived from a formula based on the total number of sentences and the total number of multisyllabic words in a specific passage. Roughly, passages with more sentences and a greater number of multisyllabic words are considered to be written at a higher grade level, making them more difficult to read. Flesch-Kincaid Grade Level designations are assigned to the text samples in this book.
Content	The specific outcomes that students are expected to master in a discipline. For example, the content of ELA will focus on literacy specifically throughout its sequence of courses.
Content standards	Standards that generally contain a K–12 scope and sequence of learning outcomes for a specific subject. The CCSS for ELA and Mathematics are the only "content subjects" that are fully treated by the CCSS.
Literacy cohort	A group of teachers serving as literacy leaders and professional developers for their colleagues.
Embedded professional development	Professional development that is directly related to the specific needs and goals of a team, department, or a whole school faculty and is carried on and acted on in a collaborative team meeting.
Student-friendly language and definitions	Definitions reduced to their essence using simple words that students are more likely to understand.
Professional learning community	A teacher work group having the characteristics of trust, self-reflection, support, communication, shared mission, and conflict resolutions skills.
Common Core State Standards for English Language Arts and Literacy in History/Social Studies, Science, and Technical Subjects	The official name of the standards document developed by the Common Core State Standards Initiative (CCSI), the goal of which is to prepare America's students for college and career. The standards encompass grades K–12 for the ELA standards and grades 6–12 for the content literacy standards (Common Core State Standards Initiative, 2010a). This book focuses specifically on the ELA Standards and content literacy standards for grades 6–12.
College and Career Readiness (CCR) Anchor Standards	The broad statements that incorporate individual standards for various grades levels 6–12 and specific content areas (English language arts and other content subjects). There is a specific set of Anchor Standards for reading, writing, and listening/speaking.

literacy strategy	A routine, activity, process, set of prompts, graphic organizer, or complete lesson used to facilitate skilled reading and writing in response to reading or writing in the service of reading comprehension in secondary ELA, history, social studies, science, and technical subjects.

The Common Core State Standards

In anticipation of implementing the literacy strategies in this book, you need an understanding of the standards on which they are based: the Common Core State Standards for English Language Arts and Literacy in History/ Social Studies, Science, and Technical Subjects, Grades 6–12 (CCSSI, 2010a), the official but very long name of the standards document developed by the Common Core State Standards Initiative, the goal of which is to prepare students in the United States for college and career (CCSSI, 2010a). This document is one of two broad sets of standards: one for language arts and literacy and a second for mathematics. We focus solely on the document that spells out standards for language arts and literacy. It has three parts: (1) K–5 language arts and literacy, (2) 6–12 language arts, and (3) 6–12 literacy.

We are interested in only two of the three aforementioned parts: (1) 6–12 language arts, the content taught by English language arts teachers; and (2) 6–12 literacy, taught by content teachers. If you are a secondary teacher, there is no doubt that these two sets of standards will impact your classroom practice. The question is how.

Most ELA teachers will be familiar with many of the grade-specific standards and may in fact be held to higher standards in their schools and districts. However, many ELA teachers will be surprised and perhaps shocked by the seismic shift the standards require in terms of the kinds of text students should be reading during the process of meeting those standards. You are being asked to use far more literary informational text than you previously have. We have designed the strategies in this book to scaffold that process for you, particularly if you have never had specific training in teaching reading comprehension.

Content teachers are about to move into what may be brand-new territory for many—showing students how to engage with informational text both from grade-level content textbooks and a wide range of literary informational texts such as historical documents and scientific writing.

The 6–12 standards for language arts and the 6–12 literacy standards for the content areas provide detailed expectations for each grade level or in some cases, a span of grade levels. These standards are based on a set of broad expectations called the College and Career Readiness Anchor Standards. Think of these anchor standards as the backbone of the more detailed and specific standards that apply in various grade levels. The specific grade-level standards are designed to work in tandem with the anchor standards. There is a specific set of anchor standards for both reading and writing, and these apply equally to ELA and content teachers. There are also sets of anchor standards for listening and speaking, as well as language, that apply only to ELA teachers.

The on-ramp to success at every grade level and beyond is reading, and that is why we have selected the Common Core College and Career Readiness Anchor Standards for Reading in Grades 6–12 on which to base our book. The CCR Anchor Standards for Reading apply to reading text in every course and classroom, except perhaps in mathematics. Teachers in all content areas (except math) must understand the anchor standards in reading before they a deal with the more specific standards as they relate to each content and grade level. The CCR Anchor Standards for Reading are shown in figure I.2. This was our road map as we developed the strategies, and it will be your road map as you implement. The standards are numbered from one to ten, and we will refer to the standards throughout the book. Our strategies and the anchor standards are not specific to various disciplines or specific courses. Making the standards and strategies content-specific will be a part of what teachers initially do as they select content or literary informational text and determine how best to use the strategies with their texts. Eventually, departmental teams and PLCs should tackle this task collaboratively.

FIGURE I.2: College and Career Readiness Anchor Standards for Reading in Grades 6–12

Key Ideas and Details
1. Read closely to determine what the text says explicitly and to make logical inferences from it; cite specific textual evidence when writing or speaking to support conclusions drawn from the text.
2. Determine central ideas or themes of a text and analyze their development; summarize the key supporting details and ideas.
3. Analyze how and why individuals, events, or ideas develop and interact over the course of a text.
Craft and Structure
4. Interpret words and phrases as they are used in a text, including determining technical, connotative, and figurative meanings, and analyze how specific word choices shape meaning or tone.
5. Analyze the structure of texts including how specific sentences, paragraphs, and larger portions of the text (e.g., a section, chapter, scene, or stanza) relate to each other and the whole.
6. Assess how point of view or purpose shapes the content and style of a text.

Integration of Knowledge and Ideas
7. Integrate and evaluate content presented in diverse formats and media, including visually and quantitatively, as well as in words.
8. Delineate and evaluate the argument and specific claims in a text including the validity of the reasoning as well as the relevance and sufficiency of the evidence.
9. Analyze how two or more texts address similar themes or topics in order to build knowledge or to compare the approaches the authors take.
Range of Reading and Text Complexity
10. Read and comprehend complex literary and informational texts independently and proficiently.

Source: © 2010. National Governors Association Center for Best Practices and Council of Chief State School Officers. All rights reserved.

To recap, the focus of this book is secondary content literacy—the abilities of students to read and write in a variety of content areas (disciplines) to include English language arts. The literacy strategies in this book are not magical. They consist of routines, activities, processes, prompts, organizers, and lesson plans for facilitating skilled reading and writing in the service of reading comprehension in secondary English language arts, history, social studies, science, and technical subjects. Although we do not specifically focus on writing skills as we do reading, nearly every strategy includes activities in which teachers will model writing in response to text and students will be expected to respond in writing to what they have read. Teachers who primarily cover content by lecturing to students will need to shift their paradigms. Teachers who prefer literary text to informational literary text will also need to rethink how they are selecting texts for students. These shifts will be difficult. However, the strategies you find just ahead will show you how. Figure I.3 compares the prevalent content literacy model with the more rigorous approach demanded by the standards.

FIGURE I.3: Traditional Content Literacy Compared to Effective Content Literacy

Characteristics of Traditional Content Literacy	Characteristics of Effective Content Literacy as Required by the CCSS
Teacher determines in advance that students are incapable of independently reading the text and consequently prepares PowerPoint presentations and then talks or tells the big ideas of the text while students copy notes from the screen as the teacher elaborates on the information.	Close and careful reading of content text is a central part of classroom activities. Teacher selects content-specific text and appropriate scaffolding strategies to enable students to rehearse close and careful reading of content-specific text.
Teacher uses activities to teach and reinforce learning that require as little independent reading and writing as possible.	Teacher designs questions, tasks, and activities that require students to be cognitively engaged in reading and writing in response to reading content text.

continued →

Characteristics of Traditional Content Literacy	Characteristics of Effective Content Literacy as Required by the CCSS
Teacher does the majority of thinking for students, telling them what the big ideas are and providing a list of facts they need to learn (memorize) for the test.	Students are expected to find evidence in content text to support their inferences, assertions, and arguments.
Literacy strategies are decontextualized from the content textbook and are often introduced and practiced in noncontent text materials or in isolated instances where they are learned and never applied, or where they are modeled once and never used again. Or students see a strategy introduced in one content area instead of seeing how that strategy travels from class to class.	Reading the content textbook is an essential part of content learning, and strategy learning is embedded in the context of content learning in all classrooms.
Teacher provides students with the inferences and insights while students simply listen and take notes.	Students are expected to read like detectives, combing the content text for evidence to support their inferences and writing in defense of their conclusions with evidence from the text.
Teacher summarizes the content text for students, deciding for them what is relevant, important, and worth knowing. Even if students do read a text, they are asked only basic knowledge and comprehension questions about it.	Students are expected to read the content text and write their own summaries of the text, offering evidence to support their assertions.
Literacy strategies are selected based on their appeal to individual teachers and ease of use, without efforts to coordinate such strategies either departmentally or schoolwide.	Literacy strategies are selected on the basis of their research-based effectiveness in supporting content learning, are implemented schoolwide, and are focused on and supported in PLCs.
Students are frequently assigned tasks for which the teacher has provided insufficient instruction, modeling, or high-quality samples of proficient student responses.	When students are assigned a text-dependent task, the teacher provides instruction, modeling, and high-quality samples of proficient student responses.
Teachers have low expectations for struggling students and rarely provide scaffolded instruction or materials for those students that show them how to execute specific literacy strategies.	Teachers are cognizant of struggling students and their needs for scaffolded instruction and provide materials designed to show them how to execute specific strategies.

Embracing the standards might well be a challenge for some content teach-ers who in their desire to cover the course content have replaced textbooks with PowerPoint slides and lectures. They will also be a challenge for ELA teachers who have focused primarily on reading fiction. In our opinion, how-ever, the standards cannot be ignored. David Coleman (2011), leading author of the Common Core Standards, explains that the standards "demand, they do not request, that the building of knowledge through reading text plays a fundamental role in [all] disciplines." Close, personal, and eventually independent encounters with content text will be required of all students who live in states that have adopted the standards.

In spite of our recognition of the power these standards and strategies hold to improve literacy if faithfully implemented, we understand the realities in your classroom—poorly written textbooks, struggling readers, and too many mandated outcomes. We recognize that these roadblocks to student learning have thwarted your efforts to be the teacher you dreamed of being. We are aware that you may have acquired some unproductive habits in your efforts to cope with these challenges. Our goal is to help you adopt a set of more productive strategies that will in turn empower your students to meet the standards. Undeniably, this transformation cannot happen all at once. But, change can begin with one teacher or one department. If not you, then who will begin the change process? And there's no better time than right now.

In the following section, we move the spotlight from the standards to the critical role that students must play in the implementation of content literacy.

Skilled Readers Are Strategic Readers

You can likely identify students in your classes who mistakenly believe they are reading when they are actually engaged in what researchers call "mindless reading" (Schooler, Reichle, & Halpern, 2004), zoning out while staring at the printed page. One writer calls mindless reading "the literary equivalent of driving for miles without remembering how you got there" (Feller, 2006, online). Strategic readers monitor their reading and know what to do if they wander off the reading road while attempting to read difficult text. Strategic readers draw on a variety of literacy strategies as they process the information and ideas found in text and are able to extract meaning, even from challenging text. Struggling students just give up. Figure I.4 draws a comparison between these strategic readers and their nonstrategic counterparts.

FIGURE I.4: A Comparison of Strategic and Nonstrategic Readers

Strategic readers . . .	Nonstrategic readers . . .
Know why they are reading text and adjust their purpose and reading speed to accomplish their goals	Understand reading to be a single attempt to accurately identify the words on the page and not a concentrated focus and effort to wrestle with the meaning of the text
Ask questions from multiple perspectives while they are reading (for example, asking the author, asking a question to motivate further reading, or asking a peer or the teacher about the meaning of something that is confusing in the text)	Do not understand the value of and the necessity for asking questions in order to understand and remember important information

continued →

Strategic readers . . .	Nonstrategic readers . . .
Activate relevant and accurate prior knowledge and experiences, connecting what they know to what they are reading	Attempt to make connections with prior knowledge and experiences that are irrelevant, or do not know they should be making connections at all
Make inferences based on evidence in the text, both stated and unstated, combined with their own experiences and background knowledge	Make wild guesses about what the text means or what the author's purpose for writing is
Are able to adjust their reading speed to skim and scan text they have already read to find information in the text needed to make an inference, answer a question, solve a problem, or write a response to what is read	Do not retain an overall sense of what the text means after a first reading and, even if they choose to reread, are not able to deepen their understanding with multiple rereadings
Monitor their understanding while they are reading, stopping, if needed, to clarify what they don't understand before continuing	Read mindlessly without regard for the need to understand, summarize, and connect what they are reading to what they already know while they are reading
Are persistent about extracting and constructing meaning from text, taking time to reread what they do not understand, look up unfamiliar terms, ask questions of peers or the teacher, or search for an easier more accessible text that contains similar information	Give up easily when they don't understand what they are reading
Are able to identify key ideas and details and write a summary statement or paragraph in their own words	Do not have the skills to identify what is most important in a text and become bogged down in insignificant details
Recognize the value of creating graphic representations of the text to aid in understanding and remembering the big ideas and use a variety of such organizers when they are reading for understanding and retention	Have not learned how to create simple graphic organizers to help them understand and remember content and do not understand the importance of annotating as they read

According to Mortimer Adler (1940), reading is thinking, while William Thorndike (1917) described reading as problem solving. Adler and Thorndike were right, to a point, but more contemporary scholars focus their definitions of reading on meaning, most particularly the construction of meaning by the reader. The RAND Reading Study Group (2002) defined reading comprehension as "the process of simultaneously extracting and constructing meaning through interaction and involvement with written language" (p. 11). This meaning as stated, however, makes it seem as though these processes, extracting and constructing, are concurrent and inextricable. They are not, particularly for students who have majored in making their own meaning from text, rather than finding meaning in the text as it is written. Our strategies begin with the text and expect that you and your colleagues will lead your students to the close reading and analysis of text.

The most informative descriptions of what happens in the minds of skilled readers as they process text can be found in a type of research called *verbal protocols*. Verbal protocols are verbatim self-reports that people make regarding what is happening in their minds as they read (Pressley & Afflerbach, 1995). These transcripts are then analyzed to determine the discrete thinking processes employed by the expert readers. As subjective as a verbal protocol might seem, it is a valid and useful tool for helping us get inside the minds of skilled readers during the act of reading.

The strategies in this book are designed to help you show your students how to employ the thinking processes employed by expert readers. Think of strategies 1–19 as a spiraling curriculum that depends on the beginning strategies to lay a sound foundation for students grappling with the key ideas and details in the text, moves on to explore the various ways in which authors demonstrate their unique styles in different kinds of text, and builds to three challenging standards that expect students to evaluate and analyze texts to build their content knowledge. The success of your students depends on recursive instruction—instruction that comes back again and again to various thinking and writing processes in successively more challenging texts.

The Role of Teacher Modeling

The key to becoming a skilled content facilitator lies in the modeling of your own thinking processes as you read text—thinking aloud. Despite the research showing the power of teacher modeling to engage students in the difficult tasks of reading content text, we seldom see it in secondary classrooms. In a study of the frequency of general education teachers' classroom behaviors, modeling was observed less than 5 percent of the time. At the other end of the frequency continuum, lecturing (the talking-textbook mode) was observed slightly more than half the time while giving directions took up 25 percent of the time (Schumaker et al., 2002). Teacher modeling is a central component of content literacy implementation and the only way to show your students how to access and employ literacy strategies.

Modeling literacy strategies for students involves "showing students exactly how a good reader would apply [a particular] strategy" (Pressley, El-Dinary, & Brown, 1992, p. 112). If you have never engaged in thinking aloud for students, your initial attempts may seem awkward and artificial, but with practice, you can make mental modeling a part of nearly every class period (Davey, 1983).

Thinking aloud requires doing three things simultaneously: (1) comprehending the text, (2) figuring out just what you did to understand it (since the cognitive processing happens in split seconds), and then (3) articulating for students what was going on in your mind. Thinking aloud refers to the "artificial representation[s] of a real experience; a contrived series of activities which, when taken together, approximate the experience of the process that ultimately is to be applied independently" (Herber & Nelson, 1975, as quoted in Herber & Herber, 1993, p. 140). Some teachers pair up with a colleague, combine their classes, and alternate reading and thinking aloud from the same text to show students that different readers process text in unique ways based on their backgrounds, experience, and strategy usage.

Here are some guidelines to help you prepare for thinking aloud for students. Choose one to three sentences in a short chunk of content text. Read the text with pen in hand so you can quickly jot down the first thoughts that come to you.

- In order to convey the purpose of the think-aloud to students, write "I" statements that answer one or two of the following prompts:

  + What connections did you make between the text and your prior knowledge or experience?

  + What part of the text did you find confusing, and what did you do to fix-up your mix-up?

  + What words did you encounter that were unfamiliar, and how did you figure out what they meant?

  + What inferences (predictions, explanations, or conclusions) did you make as you read?

  + What questions do you have for the author of the text?

- Orally rehearse your think-aloud so that it sounds natural. Recall from an earlier definition that you are creating an artificial representation of what happened in your brain from the first moment you began to read the text. With practice, you will be able to think aloud fluently.

- Be careful to keep the following nonexamples of thinking aloud from sneaking into the statements you make to students:

  + Explaining what the text means

  + Giving a short synopsis of the text

  + Teaching the meaning of a concept or idea in the text

  + Giving the impression that you never have any comprehension problems when you read

To recap, the purpose of thinking aloud is to show students how you personally process and respond to what you read. In so doing, you become the master reader or cognitive mentor and your students serve as cognitive apprentices (Collins, Brown, & Holum, 1991). In addition to thinking aloud about your processing of text, plan to show students how you respond to the completion of an organizer or write a constructed response.

The Components of Each Strategy

The twenty literacy strategies in this book (with the exception of Strategy 20) are formatted similarly. Once you grasp the organizational structure, you can readily introduce, explain, and model any specific strategy for students. Following is a detailed description of the components of each strategy.

The Strategy Name and Number

Each literacy strategy is designated by a number to help you quickly locate the strategy as you page through the book. The first strategy is number 1, and the remaining strategies follow in numerical order. We have also given each strategy a short name to help you and your students remember what it is designed to accomplish during the reading of text.

The Gist of the Strategy

Each strategy is introduced with a brief description that gives you the gist of what your students will be doing as they apply this strategy to reading informational text such as textbooks and supplementary materials, as well as literary nonfiction text that includes "the subgenres of exposition, argument, and functional text in the form of personal essays, speeches, opinion pieces, essays about art or literature, biographies, memoirs, journalism and historical, scientific technical or economic accounts (including digital sources) written for a broad audience" (CCSSI, 2010a, p. 57).

Note that the gist also refers to a part of the strategy called the *+feature*, an extension or enhancement of the strategy lesson in which students are generally expected to engage in higher-level thinking and writing in response to what they have read. We have embedded this feature into the strategy lesson plan because we see it as the next step for students to become proficient in the application of the strategy and as a way to increase the rigor of the work products you expect your students to produce.

The College and Career Readiness Anchor Standards Addressed in the Strategy

This section of the strategy lists the CCR Anchor Standards for Reading that are specifically addressed in both the strategy lesson and in the +feature. These standards are quoted verbatim from figure I.2 (page 4) and are packed with technical terms. In some instances, only one aspect of a standard will be featured in a strategy. In that case, we italicize only the part of the standard that is aligned to the strategy.

Background Knowledge About the Strategy

This section provides background information about the processes used in the strategy and its underlying research base, where applicable. While this information may not be essential to your implementation of the strategy, having it will help you make connections to things you have read about and done in the past.

Understanding How the Strategy Works Through Models and Samples

Each strategy contains two samples: (1) a sample resource text to read and process as you walk through the strategy before showing your students how to execute the strategy, and (2) a sample organizer demonstrating how the strategy was used in processing the sample text. These resources are intended for you, not your students. They give you an opportunity to test-drive the strategy and figure out how it works before you stand in front of your students.

Items to Prepare Before Showing Your Students How to Use the Strategy

This section of the strategy explains the materials you need to prepare before you use the strategy with students for the first time: your chosen content text from which to model the strategy for your students, copies of the content text for students, a set of student-friendly definitions of terms used in explaining the strategy, copies of the reproducible organizer for students, and copies of other supportive resource material as provided. This information is also noted in the first step of the strategy's lesson plan. Depending on the strategy, you may be asked to write essential statements or questions that align with your content text. The two most challenging tasks to complete before you will be fully prepared to teach the strategy are these: (1) selecting content-related text for your students and (2) completing the sections of the organizer based on your reading of the text in order to model for your students.

Finding and selecting text to show students how to apply the strategy is the first task. Select text that is related to a specific content standard, is accessible to most of the students in the class, and works with the strategy you have selected. Some texts may already have subtitles that summarize each section, making them inappropriate for a strategy that expects students to write a key phrase or summary sentence. Other texts may not contain the specific text features you are asking students to find. Walk through your selected text using the strategy to make sure you have a good fit.

We recommend using easier text as you model how to use the strategy for the first time. It will be less stressful for both you and your students. The overall objective of strategy usage is to enable as many students as possible to independently extract content meaning from the text. The information processing that occurs when students struggle to extract meaning from text is the only path to deep and long-lasting learning. Lay aside your desire to simply tell them what it means so you can move on and cover more content. You are shortchanging all of your students—those who will easily memorize what you tell them, only to forget it after the test is over, and those who will be completely deprived of opportunities for scaffolded learning in your classroom.

A Lesson Plan for Showing Students How to Use the Strategy

Figure I.5 provides an annotated version of the lesson plan. As you review the lesson plan, you will no doubt wonder about the timing and pacing of strategy lessons. The regular lesson without the +feature can probably be completed in a class period of about fifty-five minutes. If you have a longer class period, you may well be able to teach the entire lesson including the +feature. The +feature is designed to challenge students to produce a more rigorous work product. It is highlighted to distinguish it from the regular lesson plan and is found immediately after Lesson Step 5.

Take time to carefully read through the annotated plan in preparation for using the first lesson plan in Strategy 1. The first column on the lesson plan enumerates the seven steps of the regular lesson. The annotations in the second column describe what each step contains including reminders about materials to prepare, a suggested advance organizer that fits the strategy, and scaffolded lesson steps that lead students from watching the teacher use the strategy to working with peers to eventually working independently.

FIGURE I.5: Annotated Lesson Plan

Lesson Step	Explanatory Notes for the Teacher
1. Teacher prepares and assembles the necessary materials.	1a. Choose a content-related and standards-aligned text to use for teacher modeling and student reading, then: • Chunk, highlight, or number sentences in the text as directed in the lesson plan • Write questions or essential statements as directed in the lesson plan • Complete the graphic organizer to use when you think aloud for students

continued →

Lesson Step	Explanatory Notes for the Teacher
1. Teacher prepares and assembles the necessary materials. *(continued)*	1b. Prepare photocopies for students of the selected text, the strategy's reproducible graphic organizer, the student-friendly vocabulary definitions, and any other resources provided for the lesson. 1c. As appropriate, assemble technology to use in modeling the strategy for students (for example, document camera, PowerPoint [PPT] slides, SMART Board, overhead transparencies, or an enlarged poster version of the vocabulary).
2. Teacher identifies the content standard from the state or district standards.	In this section, you will identify a content standard from your district, state, or Common Core State Standards for your discipline. The purpose of all of the literacy strategies is to scaffold the understanding and retention of course content. If you use the strategy without content, you have missed the point, and so will your students.
3. Teacher shares an advance organizer, reviews the student-friendly definitions, and distributes teacher-prepared materials.	The advance organizer should engage your students by connecting what you will be doing to some background knowledge you believe they have.
4. Teacher models and provides rehearsal opportunities, gradually releasing responsibility to students for doing more of their own thinking and writing.	This section of the lesson encompasses modeling (the teacher), scaffolding (the teacher supporting students), and a gradual release of responsibility to students for doing the work—collaboratively at first and then independently. The amount of time that you and your students will need to move through all of these steps will vary according to your comfort levels with modeling and scaffolding and the speed with which your students pick up on how to employ the strategy.
4a. Teacher models thinking and or writing.	In this part of the lesson, show your students how the strategy works and demonstrate for them how you process information when you read text.
4b. Students work with teacher.	After your modeling, begin to enlist students to do the work required by the strategy independently before formatively assessing their work during an informal whole-group discussion.
4c. Students work with peers.	Once students seem to be getting it as you have worked with the whole group, gradually transition them to working with their peers. If you have not previously engaged in cooperative groups in your classroom, you may want to spend a class period teaching students how to work in such groups.

5.	Teacher formatively assesses student work.	At this point in the lesson, begin to check for understanding to see if students are adequately processing the text and gaining the content meaning that was stated in your original objective. NOTE: At this point, you have two options: (1) conclude this lesson by going directly to steps 6 and 7, temporarily skipping the +feature (schedule the +feature for a later class period using the same text and organizers students have completed up to this point), or (2) extend this lesson by incorporating the +feature followed by steps 6 and 7.

+Feature
The +feature of the lesson contains either a directed writing activity or a constructed response in which students create a work product that requires a higher level of cognitive processing that will lead to deeper understanding and retention of content concepts.

6.	Teacher returns to the content objective to identify progress in understanding and retaining new content.	In order to show what they learned from the text, ask students to write an exit ticket in response to this stem: In what ways did the reading, thinking, and writing you did today help you understand the content standard? Explain.
7.	Closure	Ask students to reflect on their current level of understanding of the content standard(s) and the literacy skill(s) they worked with today by using "fist to five" hand signals to the following questions as you display them, read them aloud, and ask for student responses: On a scale of fist to five, where making a fist means not at all and holding up all five fingers means so completely that you could be the teacher, rate your understanding of the following content standard: _____ On a scale of fist to five, where making a fist means not at all and holding up all five fingers means so completely that you could be the teacher, rate your level of understanding of the following CCSS literacy skill: _____

Begin With the End in Mind

Stephen Covey (1989) recommends that we "begin with the end in mind" (p. 95). The word *end* has various meanings in the context of our use of Covey's words:

- The final strategy in the book

- An implementation target for teachers

- The ultimate goal for students

We feel compelled to reveal to you where we're heading before you pack your bags.

The Final Strategy

Strategy 20 in the book is titled Literacy Rehearsal. It is aligned with Anchor Standard 10 in the CCR Anchor Standards for Reading in Grades 6–12: *Read and comprehend complex literary and informational texts independently and proficiently.* This standard and the strategy we have aligned to help you reach this goal represent the end you should keep in mind as you begin to implement these strategies. Once you have completed what remains of this introduction, we suggest that you take a look at the final strategy on page 277.

An Implementation Target

One reason to begin with the end in mind is to make a journey more successful. How often have we said to ourselves, "If I'd only known then what I know now" to describe an implementation that failed because we didn't do our homework ahead of time? We aim to reduce the likelihood of that happening as you implement content literacy. The research tells us that when teachers collaborate around meaningful and measurable goals, there are documented results for both teachers and students (Hord, 1997; McEwan-Adkins, 2010). Our hope is that you will use collaboration as the engine to power your implementation of the Anchor Standards in Reading. Figures I.6 and I.7 are reproducible resources to use in PLCs or collaborative teams to guide your work. Figure I.6 is designed to use in your team as you contemplate implementing a strategy. If your school or district does not support a collaborative structure that provides time for teams and departments to work together, you can still implement the strategies in this book. However, you will lose the synergy and energy that is produced when teachers collaborate on issues of teaching and learning.

FIGURE I.6: Pre-Implementation Planning Form

Question	Notes From the Discussion
1. What do you understand (and not understand) about the standard and the strategy?	
2. How does the anchor standard lead to (or relate to) the CCSS grade- and content-specific standard you must teach?	
3. What content text should you use with the strategy?	
4. Who will be responsible for completing the reproducible organizer to serve as a model for thinking aloud and showing students how to employ the strategy?	

5.	Is there anyone on the team who feels confident about teaching the strategy to the team or who is willing to teach the strategy to a class of students for team observers?	
6.	What are the possible challenges you might encounter?	
6a.	Is the level of text too challenging (or not challenging enough)?	
6b.	Do you have enough time allotted to teach this well during students' first encounter with this strategy? How many days do you think it will take?	
6c.	Can you find text that relates specifically to your content standard?	
6d.	How can you make copies for all of your students? Who will make the copies?	

Visit **go.solution-tree.com/commoncore** to download and print this figure.

After you and your team members have implemented a strategy with your students, figure I.7 provides a structure for reflecting about how the process went in your classrooms and what your next steps will be.

FIGURE I.7: Post-Implementation Evaluation Form

Questions for Reflection Discussion	Notes From the Discussion
1. Reflect on how the process went (or is going) in your classroom.	
2. Discuss the benefits and challenges of the strategy.	
3. Think about how to ramp up the rigor the next time you use the strategy and identify where and when the next time might be.	
4. Think about the connections you can make between this strategy and prior strategies in the book or connections you can make between this strategy and previous or similar strategies you have used in your classroom.	

continued →

Questions for Reflection Discussion	Notes From the Discussion
5. Reflect on how you can increase students' independent use of the strategy.	
6. Discuss variations of the strategy that have recently occurred to you. Share them with the team.	

Visit **go.solution-tree.com/commoncore** to download and print this figure.

The Ultimate Goal for Students

Keep in mind that your ultimate goal is not to "teach" all of the strategies. The pot of gold at the end of the rainbow of strategies is your students' acquisition of the ability to read and comprehend complex informational texts independently and proficiently. Making progress toward this goal each day is essential. That is why literacy rehearsal, first engaging in reading, comprehending, and writing in response to easier informational texts independently and proficiently, is so important. Begin where you are, but never lose sight of where you and your students are headed.

What's Ahead?

Just ahead you will find the twenty literacy strategies categorized in four topical sections that align with the sections of the Common Core State Standards Content Literacy Anchor Standards for Reading (figure I.2, page 4):

- Part I contains eleven strategies aligned to Key Ideas and Details.

- Part II contains five strategies aligned to Craft and Structure.

- Part III contains three strategies aligned to the Integration of Knowledge and Ideas.

- Part IV contains just one strategy designed to help you develop a schoolwide program to infuse literacy rehearsal in every aspect of your academic program.

PART I:
Overview of Key Ideas and Details

The Common Core State Standards demand, they do not request, that the building of knowledge through reading text plays a fundamental role in [all] disciplines.

—COLEMAN (2011)

Part I presents a set of literacy strategies designed to help your students meet the standards found in the first section of the Common Core College and Career Anchor Standards for Reading titled *Key Ideas and Details*. It is one of four broad categories set forth in the CCR Anchor Standards for Reading to describe the critical skills of reading comprehension that independent and highly proficient readers use during the reading of complex informational literary and informational texts. This first section of the CCR Anchor Standards for Reading contains more strategies than the remaining three categories combined. The reason for this seeming imbalance is that each of the CCR Anchor Standards in Key Ideas and Details contains several foundational reading skills. This necessitates teasing out each of these more discrete skills before we reassemble and apply them in later more complex standards and strategies.

Mini-Lessons for Reading-Thinking Processes in Key Ideas and Details

The big idea of the Key Ideas and Details category is this: *Students cannot understand and master content unless they are able to closely read the text, determine its explicitly stated meaning, infer more implicit (unstated) meanings, and then summarize and support their conclusions with evidence from the text.* This may sound like an impossible undertaking if you have never demanded this kind of reading from the majority of your students in the past. We are going to show you (and your students) how to do it step by step.

Figure P1.1 provides sample text on which the four reading-thinking models (illustrated in figure P1.2, page 23) are based. Figure P1.2 is a comprehensive figure to help you and your students nail down four reading-thinking processes that are found throughout the strategies in part I: (1) identifying the central idea of a text, (2) writing a summary of the central idea and key supporting details, (3) drawing a conclusion, and (4) making inferences. The figure defines and describes these four processes and provides an example of each based on the short sample text in figure P1.1. These two figures are primarily for teacher use but could be adapted.

FIGURE P1.1: Sample Text to Illustrate Figure P1.2

"The Coyote"
Chunk 1
I often wander around in the desert by myself and have been very fortunate in seeing lots of wildlife and in observing many of the miracles that happen every day in nature.
One of my favorite memories is of an encounter with Coyote.

continued →

Chunk 2

I was walking up a lushly vegetated wash at dawn one summer morning. A coyote started ambling across the wash, then suddenly realized I was there. He began to trot away, so I sat down on the sand. That immediately aroused his interest since it's not a typical reaction from people, and it's also a very non-threatening gesture. So the coyote stopped and sat down, watching me. I simply sat, waiting for him to make the next move. He did. He lay down and put his head on his paws, still watching and assessing me. I lay down resting my head on my hands staring into those intelligent brown eyes. After a minute he rolled on his side, so of course I did too. We spent several wonderful minutes changing positions and rolling around.

Chunk 3

Suddenly Coyote sat up cocking his ears around. He glanced at me one last time as if to say goodbye, then moved off into the brush, just before a horseback rider came into view down the wash. It was an incredible, magical feeling staring into the soul of Coyote and finding myself judged worthy of a few private moments of play.

Source: Merlin, P. © 2000. Reprinted by permission of the Arizona-Sonora Desert Museum, from A Natural History of the Sonoran Desert.

Figures P1.1 (page 21) and P1.2 illustrate the importance of using content text whenever you are engaged in strategy instruction. For maximum benefit, always provide students with text to read, models of constructed responses, and think–alouds about how you are processing a piece of text.

Types of Informational Text

In the pages ahead, you will find eleven literacy strategies designed to facilitate your students' reading, understanding, and retention of the ideas and concepts found in the informational text that supports your particular discipline or content course. Informational text is comprised of the following categories:

- Literary informational text such as biography, memoirs, and essays studied in English language arts classes

- Primary historical sources such as documents, speeches, letters, and laws along with history textbooks such as those used in typical secondary history classes

- Social studies texts to include material from the disciplines of geography, anthropology, sociology, psychology, and economics

- Science texts used in any science classes to include biology, zoology, chemistry, and physics

- Technical texts used in high school elective courses

Figure P1.3 (page 25) further describes the two types of informational text you will encounter in the sample texts throughout this book.

FIGURE P1.2: Comparing a Central Idea, Summary, Conclusion, and Inference

Reading-Thinking Process	How It Is Defined	Description of the Process for Texts That Are Chunked	A Sample Response From "The Coyote"
Identifying the Central Idea	The central idea is what the text is mainly about. It is also known as the main idea. It can usuallly be expressed in a phrase or short sentence.	**How to identify the central idea:** 1. Read the first text chunk. 2. Make (or highlight) a list of words and phrases that contain the most important information in that chunk. 3. Identify the connection among the words and phrases. 4. Based on the connection, identify what the text s mainly about and write the central idea. 5. Repeat steps 1–4 for all remaining chunks. 6. Identify the connection among the central ideas for each chunk and write the central idea for the entire text. Ask: What is the text mainly about?	**Central Ideas of the Three Chunks of Text:** Chunk 1: The author reflects on the miracles o⁻ the desert. Chunk 2: The author interacts with a coyote. Chunk 3: The author judges the encounter as magical. **Central Idea of the Whole Text:** The author reflects on a memorable and magical encounter with a coyote.
Summarizing the Text	A summary is a short, written synthesis of the most important information (central idea and key supporting details and ideas) in your own words.	**How to write a summary:** 1. Read the first text chunk. 2. Identify the central idea and list the key supporting details. 3. Succinctly combine or blend the most important information in your own words. 4. Repeat this process for all remaining chunks. 5. Write a short statement that compiles the information from all of the summary sentences from each chunk. Ask: What is this text most importantly about?	**Summary of the Three Chunks of the Text:** Chunk 1: The author, who often wanders the desert, reflects on a favorite memory. Chunk 2: The author watches and interacts with a coyote by imitating his movements. Chunk 3: The startled coyote flees, leaving the author to consider the magic of the encounter. **Summary of the Whole Text:** In an unexpected encounter with a coyote, a desert hiker discovers the curious and playful side of the wild creature.

continued →

Reading-Thinking Process	How It Is Defined	Description of the Process for Texts That Are Chunked	A Sample Response From "The Coyote"
Drawing a Conclusion	A conclusion is an important decision the reader makes about the information in the text by identifying and connecting the explicit evidence in the text.	**How to draw a conclusion:** 1. Read the entire text. 2. Make a list of the important evidence used to support the central idea of the text. 3. Identify and connect the most important and relevant evidence. 4. Make a decision (draw a conclusion) about what the evidence means about the people, events, or ideas in the text. Ask: What important decisions can I make based on the evidence?	**Conclusion About the Whole Text:** The author's "magical" encounter with the coyote is safe and successful because he applies his knowledge about wildlife as he interacts with the animal. **Evidence:** Often wanders alone in the desert Observes the miracles every day Knows the difference between threatening and nonthreatening movements when animals are present
Making an Inference	An inference is a type of conclusion based on explicit evidence from the text and the reader's own reasoning and background knowledge. Synonyms for *infer* include: *think, believe, assume, deduce, conclude, judge, surmise, predict,* and *hypothesize.*	**How to make an inference:** 1. Read the entire text. 2. Make a list of the important evidence used to support the central idea of the text. 3. Identify and connect the most important and relevant evidence. 4. Apply your own reasoning (analyze, evaluate, and predict) to the connections based on the evidence. Make an informed judgment (inference) based on your own reasoning. Ask: What decisions can I make based on the evidence (in the text) and my own reasoning (in my head)?	**Inference About the Whole Text:** Because of the author's knowledge and behaviors, the coyote was ultimately more curious than scared. **Evidence:** The author knows the difference between threatening and nonthreatening movements when animals are present. The author sits down. When the coyote hears the horseback rider approaching, he moves into the brush. **My Reasoning:** When animals are scared, they either attack or run away (fight or flight), and the coyote did neither until the rider entered the wash.

FIGURE P1.3: Types of Informational Text

Types of Informational Texts	Purposes* for Writing Informational Text	Varied Text Structures* Used in Writing Informational Text	Features of the Text

1. Informational (non-fiction)*
   a. Content textbooks
   b. Supplementary materials
   c. Encyclopedia articles (reference books or online sources)
   d. Non-fiction single-concept books
 *Referred to as expository text in some sources.
	1. Inform or teach
	 2. Explain
	 3. Entertain
	 4. Describe or give an account of
	 5. Present
	 6. Persuade or convince
	 7. Show or prove
	
	 *Purpose: Why the author is writing a text or what the author hopes to accomplish in the text
		1. Descriptive
		 2. Comparison-Contrast
		 3. Cause-Effect
		 4. Problem-Solution
		 5. Time-Sequence-Order
		 6. Argument or Persuasion
		
		 *Text structure: The way a specific text is organized by the author
			Features of Expository Informational Text
			 1. Table of contents
			 2. Headings and sub-headings
			 3. Glossary and Index
			 4. Chapter divisions
			 5. Charts, graphs, diagrams, or maps

2. Literary Informational (literary non-fiction)
   a. personal essays
   b. speeches
   c. opinion pieces
   d. essays about art or literature
   e. biographies
   f. memoirs [autobiographies]
   g. journalism
   h. historical, scientific, technical or economic accounts written for a broad audience (including digital sources)
 (CCSSI, 2010a)
			Features of Literary Informational Text
			
			 The text generally has a more recognizable and noteworthy author's style* (see figure P2.1 on page 147 for further information).
			
			 *Author's style: How the author uses language (words, phrases, and sentences)

Note: This set of text structures is not intended to be comprehensive. Various authors or resources may suggest additional text structures or provide alternative names for similar text structures. This list was designed to provide support to the various types of text structures found in the informational text in this book.

If you have not already read the introduction, please do so before you check out the strategies. There are five sections in the introduction—all essential for maximizing your effectiveness as you show your students how to process the information, ideas, and concepts that are the essence of your discipline. Critical to implementation is your understanding of the rationale underlying the strategies and their suggested lesson plans. The final section of the introduction provides a road map for navigating the twenty strategies found in the book. They are similarly configured and once you understand the basic template, you can readily begin to adapt these strategies to better meet the needs of your students and mesh with the content of your specific discipline.

Read-Decide-Explain

The Gist of Read-Decide-Explain

Students are asked to decide whether each sentence in the text contributes to answering a teacher-generated question and explain why it does or does not. In the +feature of the lesson, students are asked to write summaries of the relevant sentences.

CCR Anchor Standard 1 for Reading: *Read closely to determine what the text says explicitly* and to make logical inferences from it; cite specific textual evidence when writing or speaking to draw conclusions from the text.

CCR Anchor Standard 2 for Reading: Determine central ideas or themes of a text and analyze their development; *summarize the key supporting details and ideas.*

The Read-Decide-Explain strategy consists of a three-step process to scaffold the close reading of text to determine what it explicitly says or means. The strategies found later in part I will tackle the challenging task of making inferences during reading. In this strategy, however, focus your students' attention on a close reading of the facts. This strategy is designed to hold students accountable for cognitively processing a text in a sentence-by-sentence fashion.

You may have students who have fallen into haphazard reading habits that lead to confusion rather than comprehension. To the extent that these bad habits have been entrenched for two or more years, some students will have given up on the hard work of extracting meaning from text. These students will have become accustomed to relying totally on their teachers' interpretation of the text or on answers given by other students that may or may not be accurate. While these sources for understanding what a text means are not to be totally discounted in the learning process, too many students never have an opportunity to actually decide for themselves what a given text means. They are totally dependent on others—a state of affairs that is frustrating for both students and teachers.

Reading text closely to see what it explicitly says is a challenge for many students, some of whom are only too happy if their teachers ignore their inability to get meaning from text, an approach that may seem to save time so that the necessary content can be covered. In the long run, however, this approach leaves far too many students with little solid content knowledge and without the tools to comprehend independently.

Background Knowledge

This strategy is all about comprehension—understanding what is read. Mortimer J. Adler (1940) defines comprehension as reading with "x-ray eyes." Comprehension has two facets: extracting meaning and constructing meaning. Extracting meaning from text at the most basic level—literal comprehension—involves enumerating the key facts, opinions, or ideas in expository text or retelling a narrative. Extracting meaning enables students to come up with answers to questions like: What does the text explicitly say about . . . ? The second facet of comprehension is constructing meaning, a process whereby the reader brings a unique set of experiences and knowledge to the text and, from reading and interacting with peers and teachers, develops new (to the reader) insights and ideas that help affix the reading experience in long-term memory. Both of these facets of comprehension should be introduced and rehearsed in preschool and kindergarten as teachers use read-alouds of both narrative and expository texts and engage in wide-ranging discussions of meaning. At the same time, all students should have opportunities to learn the sound-spelling correspondences that enable them to decode simple texts on a daily basis so as to acquire the vast number of sight words through multiple decoding rehearsals with an increasing number of words.

You are no doubt asking yourself: "Why are we still working on reading comprehension at the secondary level?" This question has several answers. First, some students have difficulty in word identification and lose the thread of comprehension because they cannot automatically and accurately identify words. Their working memories become so focused on figuring out the words that they are unable to simultaneously comprehend the meaning of the text. If they have not had the opportunity to acquire phonemic awareness and word identification skills, their independent reading will be less fluent. These are issues of curriculum and instruction in the primary grades.

The second answer to the question is more complicated. Some readers (inadvertently led by their teachers) become so enamored by their own experiences and creative thoughts that they fail to recognize that comprehension is about getting meaning from the text—particularly when that text requires a response in writing.

In a fascinating qualitative study of students who, despite their abilities to read grade-level text with fluency, persisted in missing the point of what they were reading, Peter Dewitz and Pamela K. Dewitz (2003) probed students' thinking to find out exactly where they had gone wrong. Students encountered the following difficulties:

- They often had difficulties with comprehension at the sentence level because of the syntax (how the words and phrases are arranged in the sentence).

- They made excessive elaborations with their own experiences, confusing them with what actually took place in the text.

- They failed to make causal inferences that required them to follow a chain of events throughout the narrative to identify a cause and effect.

- They failed to make causal inferences that required them to add some kind of background knowledge to what they read in the text.

- They had difficulties with relational (anaphoric) inferences, failing to determine how pronouns in the text matched up to actual people, thereby losing track of who did what and when.

- Their lack of vocabulary knowledge kept them from fully understanding certain parts of the text, leading to confusion even in parts of the text that they could have understood.

Read-Decide-Explain addresses comprehension at the sentence level, holding students accountable for intentionally attending to how the words and phrases are arranged in a sentence and what they explicitly mean absent any excessive elaborations from students' experiences. Without the discipline required to engage in a close reading of text to determine what it explicitly says, there is little hope that students will be able to determine the central ideas of a text and construct a written summary of it.

Understanding How the Strategy Works

In order to appreciate how the Read-Decide-Explain strategy works, spend some time with the sample text in figure 1.1 on page 30 (Flesch-Kincaid grade level 7.9) and the completed organizer to follow that replicates the process you and your students will use. The text is divided into three chunks and the sentences are numbered in order to make the Read-Decide-Explain steps more manageable.

FIGURE 1.1: Sample Text for Read-Decide-Explain: The Changing Earth

"A Changing Land"
Chunk 1
(1) The land surface of the earth has not always looked as it does today. (2) In fact, the continents are constantly moving very slowly. (3) In a process that takes many millions of years, they pull apart and merge together over and over.
Chunk 2
(4) Almost three hundred million years ago, the land of Earth's surface was made up of a single supercontinent. (5) Over time, geological forces split the giant continent into the multiple continents we know today. (6) The Great Rift Valley of East Africa is one of the few places on dry land where people can observe these geological forces at work.
Chunk 3
(7) About twenty million years ago, in what is now East Africa, magma thrust its way upward. (8) The land above the magma lifted and commenced to split and crack, creating a fissure that would extend over two thousand miles. (9) As the rift opened, it fashioned fantastic valleys bordered by towering cliffs. (10) In some places, the cliffs soar two thousand feet straight up from the valley floor.

Source: McEwan, Dobberteen, & Pearce, 2008, p. 73.

Visit **go.solution-tree.com/commoncore** to download and print this figure.

Figure 1.2 is a completed organizer based on the text. Note the highlighted Read-Decide-Explain +feature. This optional component of the lesson provides a differentiated challenge for students who are ready to produce a more rigorous work product. The lesson plan that accompanies this strategy will lead you and your students through this optional part of the lesson.

FIGURE 1.2: Sample Organizer for Read-Decide-Explain

Text title: "The Changing Earth" Name:			
Directions: Read each sentence in the text to decide if it answers this question: What does the text explicitly say caused the land surface of the earth to change? Explain your answers.			
Chunk	**Read (sentence number)**	**Decide**	**Explain**
Chunk 1	1	No	Introduces us to the topic of the text but doesn't identify causes
	2	Yes	Identifies a cause: constantly moving
	3	Yes	Identifies a cause: pull apart and merge together over and over
Read-Decide-Explain+ Directions: Write a one-sentence summary of how the text in this chunk explicitly answers the question.			
Chunk 1—Answer: The land surface changed because the constantly moving continents pulled apart and merged together.			

Chunk 2	4	No	Shares interesting facts that will help us understand the causes but does not identify causes
	5	Yes	Identifies a cause: geological forces
	6	No	Shares interesting facts that will help us understand the causes but does not identify causes

Read-Decide-Explain+ Directions: Write a one-sentence summary of how the text in this chunk explicitly answers the question.

Chunk 2—Answer: Geological forces resulted in the multiple continents we have today.

Chunk 3	7	Yes	Identifies a cause: magma thrust its way upward
	8	Yes	Identifies a cause: magma lifted and commenced to split and crack
	9	Yes	Identifies a cause: rift opened
	10	No	Shares interesting facts that help us see the results but not the causes

Read-Decide-Explain+ Directions: Write a one-sentence summary of how the text in this chunk explicitly answers the question.

Chunk 3—Answer: Valleys bordered by towering cliffs are the result of magma thrusting its way upward and impacting the land above it.

Items to Prepare

There are two reproducible figures that support the Read-Decide-Explain strategy. Figure 1.3 is a poster with student-friendly definitions of the terms you will explain as you show your students how to execute this strategy during their reading. You can create a poster-size version of the definitions, provide copies for your students, have students add them to a personal glossary, or make these terms part of an ongoing word wall in your classroom. Many of the terms will be encountered in subsequent strategies, so there will be opportunities to reteach and remind students of the definitions in the context of acquiring other strategies.

FIGURE 1.3: Student-Friendly Definitions for Read-Decide-Explain

Explicit: Clearly stated in the text, leaving no doubt as to meaning

Text: In the context of classroom instruction, any printed material you are expected to read and understand

Read: Get meaning from the text

Decide: Make up your mind about something

Explain: Make something clear to someone

Summarize: Write or explain the meaning of what you have read in your own words

Summary: A statement in your own words that tells the central idea and key supporting details of the text you have read

Visit **go.solution-tree.com/commoncore** to download and print this figure.

The second reproducible, figure 1.4, is an organizer for you to record your thinking as you model and for students to record their thinking during their initial encounter with the strategy and in subsequent rehearsals in various content text selections.

FIGURE 1.4: Reproducible Organizer for Read-Decide-Explain

Text title: Name:			
Directions: Read each sentence in the text to decide if it answers the "what does the text explicitly say" question asked by your teacher. Explain your answers.			
Chunk	**Read (sentence number)**	**Decide**	**Explain**
Chunk 1			
Read-Decide-Explain+ Directions: Write a one-sentence summary of how the text in this chunk explicitly answers the question.			
Chunk 1—Answer:			
Chunk 2			
Read-Decide-Explain+ Directions: Write a one-sentence summary of how the text in this chunk explicitly answers the question.			
Chunk 2—Answer:			
Chunk 3			
Read-Decide-Explain+ Directions: Write a one-sentence summary of how the text in this chunk explicitly answers the question.			
Chunk 3—Answer:			

Visit **go.solution-tree.com/commoncore** to download and print this figure.

Lesson Plan

The lesson plan for showing your students how to execute the Read-Decide-Explain strategy is found in figure 1.5. Note the optional highlighted Read-Decide-Explain +feature of the lesson that expects students to produce a more rigorous work product—a summary sentence. Using the basic lesson plan with your entire class will enable you to formatively assess how well your students are able to read a text closely to determine what it explicitly says. As they proceed from sentence to sentence in the text and are required to make a decision (yes or no) about whether a given sentence contributes any information that would answer the question and further write a brief explanation about why or why not, there is no room for guessing or elaborating. You will have a very clear picture of just how carefully your students are able to read.

FIGURE 1.5: Lesson Plan for Read-Decide-Explain

Lesson Step	Explanatory Notes for the Teacher
1. Teacher prepares and assembles the necessary materials.	1a Choose content-related and standards-aligned text for teacher modeling and student reading, then: • Chunk text into three parts and number the sentences as shown in the sample text (figure 1.1, page 30) • Write a question using this stem: What does the text explicitly say about . . . ? • Complete the reproducible organizer (figure 1.4) as a key for modeling with your text in preparation for teaching the lesson 1b. Prepare photocopies for students of your selected text, the student-friendly definitions (figure 1.3, page 31), and the strategy's reproducible organizer (figure 1.4). 1c. As appropriate, assemble technology to use in modeling the strategy for students (for example, document camera, PPT slides, SMART Board, overhead transparencies, or posters).
2. Teacher identifies the content standards from state or district standards for students.	Display the content-specific standard you want students to understand and retain as a result of their reading, thinking, and writing. Discuss the standard with students.
3. Teacher shares an advance organizer, reviews the student-friendly definitions, and distributes teacher-prepared materials.	Share the following advance organizer or one of your own choosing: It takes a lot of effort to keep up with the steady stream of information that is accessible to us on a daily basis. In order to be efficient in our efforts and to keep focused on what's most relevant, we can always begin reading with the purpose of answering one important question: What does this text explicitly say about . . . ? Today's strategy will provide us with the opportunity to rehearse reading with that question in mind.

continued →

Lesson Step	Explanatory Notes for the Teacher
4. Teacher models and provides rehearsal opportunities, gradually releasing responsibility to students for doing more of their own thinking and writing.	**Teacher models: Chunk 1** Ask students to silently read the first chunk of text. When they are finished, read your "what does the text explicitly say" question to the class and tell them that, as you read the first text chunk aloud, you will stop after each sentence to decide and explain why it does or does not answer the question. Write your decisions and explanations on the Read-Decide-Explain organizer for chunk 1. **Students work with teacher: Chunk 2** Have students read this chunk silently. Then, as you read it aloud, stop to ask students to decide whether each sentence answers the "what does the text explicitly say" question. Then tell students to write an explanation supporting their answer. Call on students to share their answers and explanations as you discuss, process, and record correct answers on the organizer. **Students work with peers: Chunk 3** Ask students to read the third chunk silently before you read it aloud. Tell students to work independently as they go back to read each sentence, decide whether or not it answers the question, and write an explanation for their answer. When students have independently finished processing the chunk, ask them to work interpedently with a partner to review their answers and explanations—sentence by sentence. Pairs must discuss and agree on each answer and explanation and be prepared to explain and defend them.
5. Teacher formatively assesses student work.	Call on partners to share and explain their answers. Encourage other partners to agree or disagree with answers and explanations. Process and record accurate answers on the organizer. Use the responses and discussions to formatively assess as many students as possible and to determine whether students need more rehearsal with this strategy. NOTE: At this point, you have two options: (1) conclude this lesson by going directly to steps 6 and 7, temporarily skipping the +feature (schedule the +feature for a later class period using the same text and organizers students have completed up to this point), or (2) extend this lesson by incorporating the +feature followed by steps 6 and 7.

Read-Decide-Explain+

Teacher models

Explain to students that they have analyzed whether each sentence in the text answers the "what does the text explicitly say" question. Now, focusing only on those sentences from the text that do answer the question in the first chunk, think aloud to show students how to select the most important information to include in a summary and write a short model summary sentence on the Read-Decide-Explain+ section of your organizer (figure 1.4, page 32). (For more help with writing summaries, see Strategy 7 on page 95).

Students work with teacher

Ask students to decide what important information from sentences in the second chunk would need to be included in a summary. Call on students to share as you process and list accurate information on the organizer. Ask students to write a draft summary sentence using the agreed-upon information. Call on students to share their summary and think aloud to process and record a model on the organizer.

Students work with peers

Tell students to work independently to consider what important information would need to be included in a summary sentence for the third chunk. Ask students to work interdependently with a partner to agree on that information and write a draft summary statement.

Teacher formatively assesses student work

Select several pairs of students to display their summary sentences and facilitate a conversation about the merits of each summary. Help the class select a model summary statement to write on the organizer or facilitate the process as they write a new one to serve as an exemplary model.

6.	Teacher returns to the content standard to identify progress in understanding and retaining new content.	In order to determine what your students have learned from the text, ask them to write an exit ticket in response to this stem: In what ways did the reading, thinking, and writing you did today help you understand the content standard? Explain.
7.	Teacher brings closure to the lesson.	Ask students to reflect on their current level of understanding of the content standard(s) and the literacy skill(s) they worked with today by using "fist to five" hand signals to respond to the following questions: On a scale of fist to five, where making a fist means not at all and holding up all five fingers means you understand it so completely that you could be the teacher, rate your understanding of the following content standard: _____ On a scale of fist to five, where making a fist means not at all and holding up all five fingers means you understand it so completely that you could be the teacher, rate your level of understanding of the following CCSS literacy skill: _____

Visit **go.solution-tree.com/commoncore** to download and print this figure.

Show You Know

The Gist of Show You Know

Students are asked to process a piece of content text by considering two important questions: "What's it about?" and "What about it?" Students practice "telegraphic" highlighting as they identify information in the text that answers the "what about it?" question. In the +feature of the lesson, students work with a partner to ultimately create an infoposter to use as an aid when the teacher asks them to "show you know" what the entire text is explicitly about.

CCR Anchor Standard 1 for Reading: *Read closely to determine what the text says explicitly* and to make logical inferences from it; cite specific textual evidence when writing or speaking to support conclusions drawn from the text.

CCR Anchor Standard 2 for Reading: *Determine central ideas or themes of a text* and analyze their development; *summarize the key supporting details and ideas.*

The Show You Know strategy builds on the Read–Decide–Explain strategy by providing students with additional opportunities to closely read text to determine what it means using a technique called *telegraphic highlighting.*

Telegraphic highlighting is the flip side of a thinking process that most students use daily: sending text messages on their smartphones. Students are highly skilled at choosing a minimum number of "words" to convey the essence or central idea of their message. Telegraphic highlighting requires that students separate out the key words from a text to create a skeletal text message that will be easier to understand and remember.

Show You Know provides another way of scaffolding students' close reading of text so as to hold them accountable for processing every word. Once the words are processed, students then make decisions about which ones are appropriate for use in their "text message" about what the text explicitly means.

Background Knowledge

Perhaps you are discouraged by the amount of time you might have to spend to prepare for showing students how to use a strategy as well as the amount of class time that is necessary to help your students understand the process and apply it to reading content text. We recommend that your team or department work together as a professional learning community, sharing various ways you have used the strategy with your students.

At this moment, both you and your students are at about the same point on the learning continuum. Figure 2.1 summarizes the various levels of transfer (Joyce & Showers, 2002) as you make your way from using a lesson plan for the very first time to becoming a reflective, organized, and strategic teacher who understands the rationale behind each strategy and is able to develop new and improved lessons that target the unique needs of your students. Bruce Joyce and Beverly Showers (2002) call this pinnacle of teaching expertise *executive use*.

FIGURE 2.1: Levels of Transfer Applied to Literacy Strategy Instruction

Levels of Transfer	How the Levels of Transfer Apply to Your Strategy Instruction
Imitative Use	Following the lesson plan exactly as it is written and in some cases using the sample text even though the text may not be relevant to content standards
Mechanical Use	Following the lesson plan using teacher-selected text with no deviation in the lesson plan
Routine Use	Applying the lesson to a new content unit, modifying the activities to meet the needs of two different groups of students
Integrated Use	Planning content lessons and seamlessly integrating a literacy strategy where it will be most effective, for example, to get across the big idea of the unit
Executive Use	Modifying the strategy to use with various types of text as well as to immediately identify the specific strategy that could best accompany a unit or textbook chapter

While you are progressing from the imitative level of instructional effectiveness to becoming a master teacher of literacy strategies, your students will be similarly growing and changing. At the outset of using literacy strategies to support content instruction in your classroom, you are intentionally supporting students. This type of teacher-managed instruction is characterized by activities in which you work directly with students to provide scaffolded opportunities to learn that enable all students, regardless of their categorical labels, demographic characteristics, or learning difficulties, to acquire literacy skills that enable them to achieve at their highest potential (McEwan-Adkins, 2010).

Your goal is to move your students as quickly as possible from teacher-managed literacy activities in the classroom toward independent and self-managed reading and writing activities. These are tasks, assignments, or projects for which students have acquired the necessary skills and strategies, have consolidated and strengthened those skills and strategies through practice and application in familiar settings, and are expert enough in their application of the skills and strategies in new settings to independently manage and complete a wide range of literacy tasks to include reading, writing, presenting, consulting, and teaching (McEwan-Adkins, 2010). As you invest time in your own professional growth, you are simultaneously building a solid foundation for content learning.

Your challenge as a teacher is to use the type of instruction that is most appropriate for the developmental level of your students. This requires the ability to adjust the constantly moving instructional treadmill to keep all students tuned in and turned on to the content of your discipline. The more opportunities for rehearsal of key literacy strategies that you build into your content instruction, the more readily your students will become self-managed, independent learners in your classroom.

Understanding How the Strategy Works

The first step to prepare for modeling and explaining the Show You Know strategy to students is to read and review the sample text in figure 2.2 (Flesch-Kincaid grade level 8.0) and its accompanying organizer. Note that the text has been divided into three chunks. The key to chunking the text you choose is to make sure that each text chunk contains examples that can be processed using the strategy.

FIGURE 2.2: Sample Text for Show You Know

"Caves"
Chunk 1
There are several definitions for the geological formation known as a cave. In general, it is a natural hollow space in the ground or rock, but some experts add that a cave should be large enough for a human to enter. Flowing underground water, wind, ice, ocean waves, or hardened tubes of lava may form caves.

continued →

Chunk 2
Moving water creates limestone caves. When rainwater falls through the air, it absorbs carbon dioxide and becomes slightly acidic. The rainwater seeps into the ground. If the rock layer is made of limestone, the acid in the groundwater slowly dissolves the layers of rock, creating underground openings.
Chunk 3
Once a cave or cavern is formed, groundwater continues to percolate down through the roof. Carrying dissolved minerals, the water may drip from the same spot, undisturbed for hundreds of years. As each drop eventually evaporates, it deposits minerals that dry and harden. Over time, incredible rock formations known as stalactites grow longer. The longest free-hanging stalactite known is almost forty feet in length! Some drops of water reach the cave floor, depositing minerals that become cones, ledges, and stacks called stalagmites. The tallest stalagmite known is nearly as tall as a ten-story building. The world's largest individual cave is in Malaysia. At its highest point it soars up twenty stories. Its widest point could hold seven football fields end to end.

Source: McEwan, Dobberteen, & Pearce, 2008, p. 94.

The sample organizer in figure 2.3 contains a sample infoposter, a student work product from the Show You Know +feature. You have two options when modeling this strategy and assigning it to students: (1) you can record the answers to the "what about it" on the organizer as shown in figure 2.3, or (2) you can highlight the text as shown in figure 2.4.

FIGURE 2.3: Sample Organizer for Show You Know

Text title: "Caves" Name:	
What's it about?	**What about it?**
Directions: Read to get a sense of what the text is about. Write the text topic in the space below.	**Directions:** Either use telegraphic highlighting directly on the text (as shown in figure 2.4) or record in a telegraphic fashion in this area of the organizer the answers to the "what about it" question.
CAVES	• Caves are hollow spaces in ground or rock. • Caves are large enough for humans to enter. • Water, wind, ice, waves, and lava form caves. • Moving water creates limestone caves. • Acid in groundwater dissolves rock and creates underground openings. • Groundwater drips through the roof, evaporates, and deposits minerals—formations are stalactites. • Drops of water deposit minerals on the cave floor—these are called stalagmites. • The world's largest individual cave is in Malaysia.

Show You Know+ Planning Area
Directions: Create an infoposter that you and your partner will use as a guide when you are asked to show you know and understand what the text explicitly says. Your poster may consist of any of the following: chart, outline, diagram, web, summary, acrostic, timeline, or bulleted list. After you use this space to complete the plans, create your finalized infoposter on the back of the handout.

Caves are hollow spaces in the ground or rock.

Acidic rain water helps dissolve rock and create underground openings.

Vast individual caves in Malaysia are the world's largest.

Evaporation of water that drips from the roof deposits minerals.

Stalactites are formed from the roof; stalagmites are formed from water and minerals that reach the cave floor.

FIGURE 2.4: Sample Text With Highlighting

Chunk 1
There are several definitions for the geological formation known as a cave. In general, it is a natural hollow space in the ground or rock, but some experts add that a cave should be large enough for a human to enter. Flowing underground water, wind, ice, ocean waves, or hardened tubes of lava may form caves.

Chunk 2
Moving water creates limestone caves. When rainwater falls through the air, it absorbs carbon dioxide and becomes slightly acidic. The rainwater seeps into the ground. If the rock layer is made of limestone, the acid in the groundwater slowly dissolves the layers of rock, creating underground openings.

Chunk 3
Once a cave or cavern is formed, groundwater continues to percolate down through the roof. Carrying dissolved minerals, the water may drip from the same spot, undisturbed for hundreds of years. As each drop eventually evaporates, it deposits minerals that dry and harden. Overtime, incredible rock formations known as stalactites grow longer. The longest free-hanging stalactite known is almost forty feet in length! Some drops reach the cave floor, depositing minerals that become cones, ledges, and stacks called stalagmites. The tallest stalagmite known is nearly as tall as a ten-story building. The world's largest individual cave is in Malaysia. At its highest point it soars up twenty stories. Its widest point could hold seven football fields end to end.

Source: McEwan, Dobberteen, & Pearce, 2008, p. 94.

Items to Prepare

There are two reproducible figures that support Show You Know. Figure 2.5 is a poster with student-friendly definitions of the terms that you will explain as you show students how to execute this strategy. Some of these terms will be repeated in subsequent strategies. The definitions will always be the same: short, to the point, and using terms that students are likely to know.

FIGURE 2.5: Student-Friendly Definitions for Show You Know

Telegraphic highlighting: Highlighting the key words and phrases in a text

Key words: In telegraphic highlighting, words that tell the reader what the text is explicitly about

Supporting details: Various important facts in the text that help to explain the key idea of the text

Nonessential information: Trivial information in a text that does not answer the question you are asking or support the conclusion you have drawn

Show: Point out or prove something

Know: Be aware of something

Visit **go.solution-tree.com/commoncore** to download and print this figure.

The second reproducible, figure 2.6, is the organizer for you to record your thinking aloud as you model for students and also for students to record their thinking as they become familiar with the strategy. The students can complete the organizer either with a partner or on their own, depending on how quickly the majority of your students become skilled in using this strategy with content text.

FIGURE 2.6: Reproducible Organizer for Show You Know

Text title: Name:	
What's it about?	**What about it?**
Directions: Read to get a sense of what the text is about. Write the text topic in the space below.	**Directions:** Either use telegraphic highlighting directly on the text or record in a telegraphic fashion in this area of the organizer the answers to the "what about it" question.

Show You Know+ Planning Area
Directions: Create an infoposter that you and your partner will use as a guide when you are asked to show you know and understand what the text explicitly says. Your poster may consist of any of the following: chart, outline, diagram, web, summary, acrostic, timeline, or bulleted list. After you use this space to complete the plans, create your finalized infoposter on the back of this handout.

Visit **go.solution-tree.com/commoncore** to download and print this figure.

Lesson Plan

The lesson plan for showing your students how to execute the Show You Know strategy is found in figure 2.7. Show You Know+ is available when you are ready to ramp up the rigor for this strategy.

FIGURE 2.7: Lesson Plan for Show You Know

Lesson Step	Explanatory Notes for the Teacher
1. Teacher prepares and assembles the necessary materials.	1a. Choose content-related and standards-aligned text for teacher modeling and student reading, then: • Chunk text into three parts as shown in the sample text (figure 2.1, page 38). • Complete the reproducible organizer (figure 2.6) as a key for modeling with your text in preparation for teaching the lesson. 1b. Prepare photocopies of the following for students: your selected text, the student-friendly definitions (figure 2.5), and the reproducible Show You Know organizer (figure 2.6). 1c. As appropriate, assemble technology to use in modeling the strategy for students (for example, document camera, PPT slides, SMART Board, overhead transparencies, or posters).
2. Teacher identifies the content standard from state or district standards for students.	Display the content-specific standard you want students to understand and retain as a result of their reading, thinking, and writing. Discuss the standard with students.

continued →

Lesson Step	Explanatory Notes for the Teacher
3. Teacher shares an advance organizer, explains the student-friendly definitions, and distributes teacher-prepared materials.	Share the following advance organizer or one of your own choosing: "I have no special talents. I am only passionately curious." This quote is attributed to Albert Einstein. All teachers want their students to be like Einstein—passionately curious about the content we are teaching. Curiosity is a characteristic of good readers, too. Good readers are passionately curious readers. They attack a text to discover what it is about and then make an effort to decide what about it is important. Today, we are going to work on being curious readers.
4. Teacher models and provides rehearsal opportunities, gradually releasing responsibility to students for doing more of their own thinking and writing.	**Teacher models: Chunk 1** Ask students to read the first chunk silently and then read it aloud, stopping when you can answer the first processing question for this strategy: what's it about? Record your answer on the organizer (figure 2.6, page 42). Next, define telegraphic highlighting using the student-friendly definition and think aloud as you model what you would telegraphically highlight on the text as you answer the "what about it?" question. If students are not permitted to highlight on the actual text, then use the organizer to record the words and phrases that you would have highlighted. Select a student to act as your partner and model as you both verbally show you know and understand the text by only looking at the telegraphed highlights to explain the text to one another. **Students work with teacher: Chunk 2** Students read the second chunk silently, and then you read it aloud. Ask students to telegraphically highlight on the text if they are permitted to or write what they would have highlighted on the organizer if they are not. Call on students to discuss what they have highlighted with you and think aloud as you process their ideas. With their input in mind, think aloud and model accurately highlighting the text. Facilitate the interaction between two students you have selected to complete the "show you know" portion of the strategy. **Students work with peers: Chunk 3** After students have silently read the third chunk of text and you have read it aloud, they will work independently to telegraphically highlight the text (or write on their organizers). Ask students to work interdependently with a partner to agree on their telegraphic highlighting for this chunk. Next, tell students to review all that they have highlighted or recorded on their organizer for the entire text. Students should agree to keep only the most essential "what about it?" information, striking through any words, ideas, or phrases that they agree are not essential. Finally, have students work with their partner as they verbally complete the "show you know" portion of the strategy for the final chunk of text.

5.	Teacher formatively assesses student work.	Ask several pairs to display what they telegraphically highlighted for the third chunk and what they decided to eliminate as not essential from the overall text. Facilitate a discussion of the merits of what is displayed. Record accurate examples on your text or organizer. Call on several pairs to share some of their "show you know" conversations. Formatively assess as many students as possible based on the work displayed and the discussions about the work.
		NOTE: At this point, you have two options: (1) conclude this lesson by going directly to steps 6 and 7, temporarily skipping the +feature (schedule the +feature for a later class period using the same text and organizers students have completed up to this point), or (2) extend this lesson by incorporating the +feature followed by steps 6 and 7.

Show You Know+

Teacher models

Tell students that although they have verbally practiced the Show You Know part of this strategy for each discrete chunk, it is now time to use the Show You Know strategy for the entire text—and this time they get to use an aid. Ask students to follow along as you read the directions from the Show You Know planning area on the organizer (figure 2.6, page 42) and share a model infoposter that you have created. See figure 2.3, page 40, as an example to guide you.

Students work with teacher

Ask students to think back to all of the presentations they have personally done or observed during the course of school that involved a visual aid. Call on students to tell you what makes a presentation with a visual aid good/bad. Record accurate answers on the board. Tell students that you will keep their ideas in mind as you model how you expect them to use the infoposter during their "show you know" presentations by making your own brief presentation.

Students work with peers

Tell students to work interdependently with a partner to create an infoposter. Establish some specific expectations for their "show you know" presentations using the infoposter, reminding them of your own presentation. Tell students to rehearse their presentations with another pair.

Teacher formatively assesses student work

Call on pairs for their "show you know" presentations using their infoposters. Encourage members of the audience to agree with, correct, or extend the information that is presented. Formatively assess as many students as possible based on the work they present and the discussion they have about the work.

6.	Teacher returns to the content standard to identify progress in understanding and retaining new content.	In order to identify student progress with the new content, ask students to write an exit ticket in response to this stem:
		In what ways did the reading, thinking, and writing you did today help you understand the content standard? Explain.

continued →

Lesson Step	Explanatory Notes for the Teacher
7. Closure	Ask students to reflect on their current level of understanding of the content standard(s) and the literacy skill(s) they worked with today by using "fist to five" hand signals to the following questions as you display them, read them aloud, and ask for student responses:
	On a scale of fist to five, where making a fist means not at all and holding up all five fingers means so completely that you could be the teacher, rate your understanding of the following content standard: _____
	On a scale of fist to five, where making a fist means not at all and holding up all five fingers means so completely that you could be the teacher, rate your level of understanding of the following CCSS literacy skill: _____

Visit **go.solution-tree.com/commoncore** to download and print this figure.

Prove It

The Gist of Prove It

Students are given essential statements that draw conclusions about the big ideas of the text. Students read the text, identify specifically where in the text the evidence to support the essential statements is located, and cite the evidence from the text. In the +feature of the lesson, students work to draw their own conclusion about the entire piece of text.

CCR Anchor Standard 1 for Reading: *Read closely to determine what the text says explicitly* and to make logical inferences from it; *cite specific textual evidence when writing or speaking to draw conclusions from the text.*

The ability of students to cite textual evidence to support conclusions they have drawn from their reading of text involves the execution of multiple cognitive processes. First, readers must closely read the text to determine exactly what it says. Next, readers must decide what the central idea of the text actually is and what conclusions can be drawn. Readers must then pull out various statements in the text that support their conclusions. Finally, if a written or spoken product is required, readers must pull these various components together and produce a clear and coherent oral or written statement.

We recommend that instead of expecting your students to read, draw conclusions, and cite evidence in one giant leap, you scaffold the task for them by writing an essential statement, a statement that contains your conclusion about the explicit meaning of a short segment of content text. At this point, your essential statement should deal strictly with the facts of the text. This strategy gives you the opportunity to zero in on a critical content standard and see how your students respond. If you are in the habit of writing essential questions on the board, turn your questions into essential statements and expect your students to find evidence in the text to support the statements.

Background Knowledge

There are two bodies of knowledge underlying the Prove It strategy: (1) the importance of avoiding assumptive teaching in which you give assignments to students based on the belief that they have previously been taught the skills needed to accomplish the task, and (2) the importance of using writing in the service of reading comprehension.

Avoid Assumptive Teaching Through the Provision of Temporary Scaffolds

The practice of presenting students with essential statements to scaffold the acquisition of a new strategy or process has two major benefits: (1) struggling readers will have immediate access to more challenging content, and (2) all students will be able to discuss the big ideas of a text and write about material at a far more abstract level. Harold L. Herber and Joan Nelson Herber (1993) summarize the learning principle on which this strategy is based: "It is easier to recognize the relationship between an idea and the relevant information than it is to create an expression of the idea that can be induced from that information" (p. 145). Essential statements, declarative statements (Herber & Herber, 1993), or text previews (Graves, Cooke, & LaBerge, 1983; Tierney & Readence, 2000) serve as temporary life preservers to keep struggling students afloat in the deep waters of content text. Your goal is to help students experience the delight of moving through the deep water absent the anxiety of drowning that pervades the thought life of struggling students.

Use Writing in the Service of Reading Comprehension

Reading and writing are inseparable in the content classroom. That is why the strategies in this book are accompanied by one or more customized organizers to help students keep track of their thinking as they read (Englert, 1995; Raphael, Kirschner, & Englert, 1986). These organizers, or thinksheets as they are called by some, are designed to serve as instructional scaffolds that enable students to complete a cognitive task that would be frustrating or even impossible without the scaffold (Applebee, 1986; Applebee & Langer, 1983; Herber & Nelson, 1975; Vygotsky, 1962, 1978). Writing in the service of reading comprehension and content acquisition has been shown to be an effective intervention for older learners at risk as well as a key aspect of raising the achievement bar for all students, with special emphasis on closing the achievement gap (Collins, Lee, Fox, & Madigan, 2008; Collins, Madigan, & Lee, 2008).

Understanding How the Strategy Works

The optimal way to prepare for showing your students how to execute the various component processes of Prove It is to first read the sample text in figure 3.1 (Flesch-Kincaid grade level 10.0) and then work through the accompanying graphic organizer, figure 3.2 (page 50). Recall that this text is meant to be illustrative of how the strategy works. Choose the text you will use based on your content and the needs of your students.

FIGURE 3.1: Sample Text for Prove It

"The History of the Internet"

Chunk 1

In 1945 Vannevar Bush wrote an article for the Atlantic Monthly magazine. In it he described a future that included a workspace with a keyboard and glowing screen. He envisioned a machine that was a file and a library that could be accessed from anywhere.

Bush was the Director of the Office of Scientific Research and Development of the United States. He organized a research partnership between the military and universities. Funding from the partnership later helped MIT [Massachusetts Institute of Technology] to create the famed Lincoln Laboratory. The people in this partnership wanted computers to share information on research and development in scientific and military fields. They planted the seed of the Internet.

Research heated up when the Soviet Union launched the first artificial earth satellite Sputnik I, in 1957. Worried that the USSR [Union of Soviet Socialist Republics] would take the lead in science and technology, the United States created the Advanced Research Projects Agency, or ARPA. The agency operated as part of the Department of Defense. The concept was to provide a communications network that would keep working even if a nuclear attack destroyed some of its sites.

Chunk 2

ARPA selected J. C. R. Licklider of MIT to head their Information Processing Techniques Office. He had already been promoting the idea of a global network of computers that allowed users to access data from anywhere in the world. In 1963 Larry Roberts of Lincoln Laboratory and others joined his group. Licklider made agreements with MIT, the University of California at Los Angeles (UCLA), and the research firm BBN to start work on his plan.

In 1965 Larry Roberts was ready to conduct a test. He connected a computer in Massachusetts with a computer in California. He did it over dial-up telephone lines. From this researchers learned that telephone lines could work but they were inefficient and expensive. The scientists decided to use a new idea called packet switching to send information. First the information was broken into small units. Next it was labeled with where it came from and where it was going. The information could then be passed from computer to computer.

Within two years ARPA researchers met at a conference in Michigan. Roberts explained his plan for the ARPANET. They decided that a special computer called an interface Message Processor, or IMP, should connect the network. It worked like the routers of today. Researchers first sent information between UCLA, Stanford Research Institute, University of California at Santa Barbara, and University of Utah in 1969.

continued →

Chunk 3

In those days there were no personal computers in homes or offices. Then Intel released the first microprocessor chip. Computers could be smaller, cheaper, and faster. The concept of email soon followed, and the @ symbol was chosen to link usernames and addresses. Scientists Vinton Cerf and Bob Khan developed a new protocol called TCP/IP. The changes made working with the computers easier. In 1977 Steve Wozniak and Steve Jobs announced the Apple II computer. At last, computers were available and affordable for the public. As the commands became standardized, it was simpler for people to learn to use the nets that were being developed.

By 1982, the computer was honored on a Time magazine cover as its "Man of the Year!" The ARPANET was retired and transferred to the National Science Foundation system in 1990. Before long, universities and research facilities in Europe and the United States were linked. The government of the United States soon turned management over to independent online services such as Delphi, AOL, and Prodigy. Although portable computers were still a thing of the future, desktop units were common in offices and even homes. The University of Wisconsin produced a Domain Name System that made it easy to access other servers.

Today, Internet users enjoy Web pages, chat rooms, message boards, and online sales. The trend is toward high-speed and wireless connections and Internet access through smart phones and pocket PCs. The dream of scientists has become a reality and an important part of global culture.

Source: McEwan, Dobberteen, & Pearce, 2008.

FIGURE 3.2: Sample Organizer for Prove It

Text title: **"The History of the Internet"**
Name:
Directions: Read the text closely to find proof for the essential statements. Write the sentence(s) from the text that proves the essential statement in the "prove it" box for each chunk.
Chunk 1
Teacher-Generated Essential Statement 1
The United States felt threatened by what the USSR had already accomplished and might one day be capable of accomplishing.
Prove it:<ul><li>Research heated up when the Soviet Union launched the first artificial earth satellite, Sputnik I, in 1957.</li><li>Worried that the USSR would take the lead in science and technology, the United States created ARPA.</li><li>The concept was to create a communication network that would keep working, even if a nuclear attack destroyed some of its sites.</li></ul>
Chunk 2
Teacher-Generated Essential Statement 2
The Internet exists as we know it today, in part because scientists were willing to test, review, and refine ideas along the way.

Prove it:	
• Researchers learned that telephone lines could work, but they were inefficient and expensive.	
• The scientists decided to use a new idea called packet switching to send information.	
Chunk 3	
Teacher-Generated Essential Statement 3	
Because of developments that increased accessibility, the computer was ultimately recognized by *Time* magazine as its "Man of the Year."	
Prove it:	
• Then Intel released the first microprocessor chip.	
• The concept of email soon followed, and the @ symbol was chosen to link usernames and addresses.	
• Scientists Vinton Cerf and Bob Khan developed a new protocol called TCP/IP.	
• In 1977 Steve Wozniak and Steve Jobs announced the Apple II computer.	
• As the commands became standardized, it was simpler for people to learn to use the nets that were being developed.	

Prove It+ Planning Area	
Record the three teacher-generated essential statements in the boxes below.	**Apply the steps from figure P1.2 (page 23) and practice drawing a conclusion based on the essential statements.**
The United States felt threatened by what the USSR had already accomplished and might one day be capable of accomplishing.	All the information is about what caused the computer to evolve to what it is today. Without all of these things happening when they did, we may not have the computer as we know it today.
The Internet exists as we know it today, in part, because scientists were willing to test, review, and refine ideas along the way.	
Because of developments that increased accessibility, the computer was ultimately recognized by *Time* magazine as its "Man of the Year!"	

What's your conclusion?	
Without political pressures and the decisions and visions of innovators, it may have taken quite a bit longer for computers to become a reality in our homes and workplaces.	
What's the "winning" conclusion?	

After a close reading of the sample organizer, you might have concluded that this strategy is nothing more than an exercise in copying text. In one sense, you are right. But in the most important sense, you are wrong. Although students initially copy your essential statements and statements from the text they have identified as evidence into their organizers, Carl Bereiter and Marlene

Scardamalia (1987) call this exercise "knowledge telling." They describe it as an important transition—from identifying important information and writing it down to knowledge transformation in which students condense the information and write a summary and conclusion using their own thoughts and words.

Note that although you are giving a writing assignment, you are not directly teaching writing skills. Your students are using writing as a tool for learning content (Boscolo & Mason, 2001).

Items to Prepare

There are two reproducible figures to support your instruction. Figure 3.3 is a poster with student-friendly definitions of the terms that are specific to this strategy.

FIGURE 3.3: Student-Friendly Definitions

Textual evidence: Phrases or sentences in the text that prove a statement or conclusion
Conclusion: A decision you make about what the evidence in the text means, sometimes referred to as "drawing a conclusion"
Prove: Show the truth of a statement
Cite: Write down the evidence you found in the text

Visit **go.solution-tree.com/commoncore** to download and print this figure.

The second reproducible, figure 3.4, is an organizer for you and your students to complete as you process the content text you have selected for your first Prove It lesson.

FIGURE 3.4: Reproducible Organizer for Prove It

Text title:
Name:
Directions: Read the text closely to find proof for the essential statements. Write the sentence(s) from the text that proves the essential statement in the "prove it" box for each chunk.
Chunk 1   **Teacher-Generated Essential Statement 1**
Prove it:

Chunk 2
Teacher-Generated Essential Statement 2
Prove it:
Chunk 3
Teacher-Generated Essential Statement 3
Prove it:

Prove It+ Planning Area	
Record the three teacher-generated essential statements in the boxes below.	Apply the steps from figure P1.2 (page 23) and practice drawing a conclusion based on the essential statements.
What's your conclusion?	
What's the "winning" conclusion?	

Visit **go.solution-tree.com/commoncore** to download and print this figure.

Lesson Plan

Figure 3.5 (page 54) contains the lesson plan for the Prove It strategy. Use this lesson plan with various types of content text until you feel that your students are ready to move up to the Prove It+ component of the lesson, in which they will choose what they believe to be the best or strongest evidence and write a "this proves that" statement based on their evidence.

FIGURE 3.5: Lesson Plan for Prove It

Lesson Step	Explanatory Notes for the Teacher
1. Teacher prepares and assembles the necessary materials.	1a. Choose content-related and standards-aligned text for teacher modeling and student reading, then: • Chunk text into three parts as shown in the sample text (figure 3.1, page 49). • Write an essential statement (a conclusion) based on the central idea and supporting evidence of each chunk of your text. Use the steps in figure P1.2 (page 23) as a guide when you draw your conclusions and write your essential statements. • Complete the reproducible organizer (figure 3.4, page 52) as a key for modeling with your text in preparation for teaching the lesson. 1b. Prepare photocopies for students of your selected text, the student-friendly definitions (figure 3.3, page 52), the strategy's reproducible organizer (figure 3.4), and the mini-lesson for how to draw conclusions (figure P1.2, page 23). 1c. As appropriate, assemble technology to use in modeling the strategy for students (for example, document camera, PPT slides, SMART Board, overhead transparencies, or posters). 1d. Prepare butcher paper or an area on the board along with markers for students to write their conclusions as part of Prove It+.
2. Teacher identifies the content standard from state or district standards for students.	Display the content-specific standard you want students to understand and retain as a result of their reading, thinking, and writing. Discuss the standard with students.
3. Teacher shares an advance organizer, reviews the student-friendly definitions, and distributes teacher-prepared materials.	Share the following advance organizer or one of your own choosing: People may be entitled to their opinions, but all opinions are not necessarily equal. Debate team members know the importance and power of identifying and utilizing evidence to support their positions during a debate. The team that is best able to support its argument with credible and substantial evidence is most likely the team that will win. Today, we will work on the skill of reading and identifying relevant evidence from a piece of text.

| 4. | Teacher models and provides rehearsal opportunities, gradually releasing responsibility to students for doing more of their own thinking and writing. | **Teacher models: Chunk 1**

Ask students to read the first chunk silently. Read the essential statement for chunk 1 to the class. Tell them that, as you read this text chunk aloud, you will model identifying evidence that helps "prove it" (the essential statement). If necessary, model a processing technique as a scaffold for students: _____ _____ (insert the potential evidence) proves _____ (insert the essential statement). Read and stop after each sentence, explaining why it is or is not evidence that proves the essential statement. Write statements that can be used as evidence on the Prove It organizer.

Students work with teacher: Chunk 2

Read the chunk aloud after students have read it silently. Ask students to read the chunk again in order to locate and underline evidence on their text. Call on students to share the evidence they underlined and ask them to explain and support their answers. Process answers and record correct evidence on the Prove It organizer.

Students work with peers: Chunk 3

Read the third chunk aloud after students have read the chunk silently. Then, have student work with a partner and discuss, agree on, and underline the sentences that provide evidence that proves the essential statement. Partners should be prepared to explain and support their answers. |
| 5. | Teacher formatively assesses student work. | Call on partners to share and explain their underlined Prove It statements. Encourage other students to agree or disagree. Process and record accurate evidence on the organizer. Begin to discuss the idea of whether or not each essential statement has sufficient evidence to prove it. If students are able to identify evidence and articulate whether or not the amount of evidence is sufficient, they are demonstrating a strong understanding of this strategy. Formatively assess as many of the students as possible.

NOTE: At this point, you have two options: (1) conclude this lesson by going directly to steps 6 and 7, temporarily skipping the +feature (schedule the +feature for a later class period using the same text and organizers students have completed up to this point), or (2) extend this lesson by incorporating the +feature followed by steps 6 and 7. |

Prove It+

Teacher models

Tell students that up to this point, they have searched for evidence to prove your essential statements. Reveal to students that the essential statements are really conclusions that you have drawn about the text. Now it is time for them to learn how to draw their own conclusion—and you will show them how in a mini-lesson. Introduce and explain figure P1.2, how to draw a conclusion. Next, ask students to focus on your completed organizer for chunk 1. Explain to students that they can see an example of the relationship between evidence and a conclusion by looking at the "prove it" statements (evidence) and the essential statement (conclusion). Explain the process that you followed as you created the essential statement for this chunk.

continued →

Students work with teacher

Continue to explain the relationship between the evidence and conclusions with the two remaining chunks.

Students work with peers

Tell students to copy and paste the essential statements from the organizer to the Prove It+ planning area. They will use the information from the three essential statements in order to draw a conclusion about the entire text. Ask students to work with a partner to apply the steps from figure P1.2 (page 23) in order to practice drawing a conclusion about the entire text in the second column of the planning area. When both partners feel confident in the quality of their conclusion, ask them to record it in the "What's your conclusion?" box of the organizer. When nearly all partners are finished with their work, tell them to go to the board (or a piece of butcher paper), write their conclusion, and sign their initials.

Teacher formatively assesses student work

When all conclusions are posted, ask partners to read and discuss the conclusions. Partners vote by putting a hash mark beside what they consider to be the best conclusions. Each partnership may vote three times (and not for their own conclusion). When voting is complete, go to the board and facilitate a discussion of the merits of top three or four "winning" conclusions. With student input, select the best conclusion to record on your organizer. Ask students to write the winning conclusion on their organizers as well. Formatively assess as many students as possible based on their work and discussion.

Lesson Step	Explanatory Notes for the Teacher
6. Teacher returns to the content standard to identify progress in understanding and retaining new content.	In order to identify student progress with the new content, ask students to write an exit ticket in response to this stem: In what ways did the reading, thinking, and writing you did today help you understand the content standard? Explain.
7. Closure	Ask students to reflect on their current level of understanding of the content standard(s) and the literacy skill(s) they worked with today by using "fist to five" hand signals to the following questions as you display them, read them aloud, and ask for student responses: On a scale of fist to five, where making a fist means not at all and holding up all five fingers means so completely that you could be the teacher, rate your understanding of the following content standard: _____ On a scale of fist to five, where making a fist means not at all and holding up all five fingers means so completely that you could be the teacher, rate your level of understanding of the following CCSS literacy skill: _____

Visit **go.solution-tree.com/commoncore** to download and print this figure.

Read Like a Detective

The Gist of Read Like a Detective

Students play the role of a detective and are asked to locate evidence within the text to support a teacher-generated inference. In the +feature, students are asked to determine if there is sufficient evidence to support the inference and are expected to use the evidence they have gathered to respond to a constructed response.

CCR Anchor Standard 1 for Reading: *Read closely to determine what the text says explicitly and to make logical inferences from it; cite specific textual evidence when writing or speaking to draw conclusions from the text.*

The question that has probably popped into your mind as you prepare to dig into this strategy is this: What are the similarities between what detectives in a police department do on a daily basis and the reading habits I am trying to instill in my students? There are two. In order to "read like a detective," students must be able to do the following: (1) make logical inferences, and (2) support their conclusions by citing specific evidence.

For students who are not quite prepared to make the leap from reading the text independently to making logical inferences and citing textual evidence, we propose that you ease them into this heavy-duty assignment through the back door. Rather than approaching the process head-on by expecting students to make logical inferences independently, do some of the heavy lifting for them by presenting them with an inference you have made from the text. Once students begin to understand the inferring process, you will be able to remove the scaffold (the teacher-generated inference) and expect them to make their own inferences.

Background Knowledge

Making logical inferences is a thinking process that figures largely in the job description of police detectives. Detectives are featured in thousands of police procedural mysteries and dozens of movies and television shows as these fictional sleuths figure out who did it, how they did it, and why by making logical inferences. In the course of figuring out what actually happened, a detective will often have a pretty good idea of who did it but will have to fill in the missing pieces of the puzzle by asking questions and locating evidence to make a solid case.

Robert Mislevy (1995) states, "Inference is reasoning from what one knows [background knowledge and experience] and what one observes [the factual] to explanations, conclusions, or predictions" (p. 2). It is a cognitive process that requires moving back and forth between three different levels of comprehension. William Gray (1960) described these levels very simply: (1) *reading the lines*—reading closely to determine what the text explicitly says, (2) *reading between the lines*—reading closely to determine what the text implicitly says, that is, what is not directly stated but can be inferred, and (3) *reading beyond the lines*—using one's prior knowledge to analyze and synthesize what is read in such a way as to make higher level and more elaborative inferences.

For example, in Strategy 1, Read-Decide-Explain, students were instructed in a strategy to help them "read the lines." They were asked to commit to their understanding of a sentence by voting yes or no about whether the text explicitly answered a question posed by the teacher. The answer was either right there in the text or it wasn't. Students couldn't make wild guesses because they were expected to explain the reason for their decision. Reading the lines is the most basic kind of comprehension, and if readers don't grasp the basics of reading the lines, making logical inferences from text will be almost impossible.

Inferring is viewed as a somewhat mysterious process in William Gray's description of reading between the lines. One might conclude that there are invisible lines of print running beneath the text that hold the key to its meaning, and only the application of a secret potion or a hot iron will magically lift the missing words to the surface of the paper and help the reader understand what the text actually means. Skilled readers have learned that inferring involves not just reading between the lines to determine the author's intent, but also reading beyond the lines to draw on their own background knowledge and experiences to make sense of the text.

When confronted with inferential questions (in class discussions, informal silent reading assessments, or standardized tests), the default strategy for many readers is *imagining* rather than inferring. Dewitz and Dewitz (2003) speculate, "It may be a coping strategy, or it may be learned, as teachers have overstressed what students know without directing them back to the text to justify their understandings and their interpretations" (p. 428). When confronted with large numbers of students who seem powerless to make the logical inferences demanded by the standards, you might readily conclude that the ability to infer is something that students are born with. As one teacher is said to have asserted at a parent-teacher conference, "Kids either know how to infer or they don't, and there's nothing I can do to teach them how." We submit that when you and your students tease apart the various layers of inferences that skilled readers make, you will understand the importance of scaffolding the inferential process to give students multiple opportunities to make logical inferences.

Understanding How the Strategy Works

The most efficient way to get up to speed is to first read the sample text in figure 4.1 (Flesch-Kincaid grade level 6.5). It is divided into three chunks to align with the sample organizer in figure 4.2, page 60. Once you have read through these two figures, you will be able to assimilate the lesson plan in preparation for showing your students how this strategy works.

FIGURE 4.1: Sample Text for Read Like a Detective

"The Lost Dutchman's Mine"
Chunk 1
Over two centuries ago, the king of Spain granted land in Arizona to a local family. Apache Indians killed those who came to claim it. A survivor drew a map that he declared led to a rich mine. In 1870, another man came and befriended his Apache neighbors. They led him to a canyon where he saw nuggets of gold. They let him take what he could carry, which turned out to be worth over six thousand dollars. When he tried to return to the mine, he was killed.
Chunk 2
Later, two German prospectors purchased the rights to the land from the owners. First they worked peacefully, and records show that they brought out nuggets worth thousands of dollars. When one of the miners was killed under mysterious circumstances, his partner fled for his life without revealing the location of the gold. Some Apaches filled in the mine and toppled rock landmarks. Only one landmark remained, a sharp pinnacle of rock. Mistaking the German accents of the miners for Dutch, the locals called the place the Lost Dutchman's Mine, and most people believed it was cursed.
Chunk 3
Later, two soldiers rode into a town with their saddlebags filled with gold nuggets. They mentioned a landmark, a pinnacle of rock, before riding out to gather more treasure. When the soldiers failed to return, a search party discovered their bodies. The last known victim of the mine's curse set out in 1931. He said he had the original map. His headless body was recovered a short time later. Does wealth still wait in the mountains, or does something else wait for those unlucky enough to find it?

Source: McEwan, Dobberteen, & Pearce, 2008, p. 71.

FIGURE 4.2: Sample Organizer for Read Like a Detective

Text title: "The Lost Dutchman's Mine" Name:		
Inference: From the text, we can infer that the author wants us to believe that the mine is cursed.		
Detective's Questions		
Chunk	**Column A** **What sentences in the text relate to the inference?**	**Column B** **Do the sentences provide evidence to support the inference? Explain.**
1	Apache Indians killed those people who came to claim the land. A neighbor who befriended the Apaches was killed when he returned to the mine.	So far it only seems as if the author is sharing details that support the fact that the Apaches are protecting their land from greedy prospectors.
2	German prospectors worked peacefully until one miner was killed under mysterious circumstances. The Apaches toppled almost all of the landmarks. The locals called it the Lost Dutchman's Mine, and most believed it was cursed.	The author uses the word *mysterious* to describe the death of a prospector and directly states that most people believed the mine was cursed.
3	Two soldiers who mentioned where they had mined were killed. The last known victim's headless body was recovered shortly after he stated he had the original map.	The author continues to share a cause-and-effect pattern between those who visit the mine and death. The author ends with an ominous rhetorical question about what might wait in the mountains—"wealth" or "something else" for those "unlucky enough to find it."
Read Like a Detective+		
+Prompt: Remember that an inference is a type of conclusion based on explicit evidence from the text and the reader's own reasoning and background knowledge. Using your extensive detecting skills, write a constructed response to explain whether there is enough explicit evidence to support the inference. Provide textual evidence to support your response.		
Constructed Response There is enough evidence for this detective to conclude that the author wants us to believe in a curse. The number of deaths, the "mysterious circumstances" surrounding at least one death, and the fact that "most people believed it [the mine] was cursed" make a strong case to support the inference.		

Items to Prepare

There are three reproducible figures to support the Read Like a Detective strategy. Figure 4.3 contains a set of inference stems. These stems can be used to inform the inference statements you provide to students and, later in Strategy 6, will guide students in making inferences independently. There are four categories of stems: (1) stems that refer to the author's assumptions or beliefs, (2) stems that refer to the author's purpose in writing the text, (3) stems that refer to the author's sources for information found in the text, and (4) stems that refer to the author's assumptions about the world. In this strategy, figure 4.3 is intended to scaffold your inference making as you model for students. In Strategy 6, this same figure will scaffold your students' independent inference making.

FIGURE 4.3: Inference Stems for Read Like a Detective

Stems That Refer to the Author's Assumptions or Beliefs
1. I infer that the author believes . . .
2. I infer that the author would support the idea that . . .
3. I infer that the author would be opposed to . . .
4. I infer that the author feels strongly about . . .
Stems That Refer to the Author's Purpose(s) in Writing
5. I infer that the author wants readers to believe . . .
6. I infer that the author wants readers to support the idea that . . .
7. I infer that the author wants readers to take some action.
Stems That Refer to the Author's Sources for Information Found in the Text
8. I infer that the author consulted a wide variety of information sources.
9. I infer that the author relied mostly on personal experiences.
10. I infer that the author relied mostly on personal background knowledge.
Stems That Refer to the Author's Assumptions About the World
11. I infer that the author has an optimistic and positive worldview.
12. I infer that the author has a fairly pessimistic worldview.

Visit **go.solution-tree.com/commoncore** to download and print this figure.

Figure 4.4 (page 62) is a poster with student-friendly definitions of the terms that you will be using to explain various aspects of this strategy. Your goal as you use the various strategies is to keep spiraling back to important terms until their definitions are automatic for both you and your students.

FIGURE 4.4: Student-Friendly Definitions

Inference: A type of conclusion based on explicit evidence from the text and the reader's own reasoning and background knowledge

Evidence: Textual proof that supports your conclusion or inference

Decide: Make up your mind; figure something out

Believe: Think that something is true

Support: Agree with something

Oppose: Disagree with something

Feel strongly about: Agree with something and be willing to argue or debate about it with others

Read: Get meaning from the text

Reasoning: Thinking, understanding, making an inference, or drawing a conclusion

Visit **go.solution-tree.com/commoncore** to download and print this figure.

The third reproducible, figure 4.5, is the organizer that your students will use as they learn to read like detectives.

FIGURE 4.5: Reproducible Organizer for Read Like a Detective

Text title: Name:		
Inference:		
Detective's Questions		
Chunk	Column A **What sentences in the text relate to the inference?**	Column B **Do the sentences provide evidence to support the inference? Explain.**
1		
2		
3		

Read Like a Detective+
+Prompt: Remember that an inference is a type of conclusion based on explicit evidence from the text and the reader's own reasoning and background knowledge. Using your extensive detecting skills, write a constructed response to explain whether there is enough explicit evidence to support the inference. Provide textual evidence to support your response.
Constructed Response

Visit **go.solution-tree.com/commoncore** to download and print this figure.

Lesson Plan

Figure 4.6 is a lesson plan for showing your students how to read like a detective. The highlighted feature of the lesson, Read Like a Detective+, motivates you and your students to take the next step after they have made a logical inference and cited their evidence—writing a one- or two-sentence summary of the evidence.

FIGURE 4.6: Lesson Plan for Read Like a Detective

Lesson Step	Explanatory Notes for the Teacher
1. Teacher prepares and assembles the necessary materials.	1a. Choose content-related and standards-aligned text for teacher modeling and student reading, then: • Chunk your text into three parts as shown in the sample text (figure 4.1, page 59). • Write an inferential statement about the text you have selected as shown in the sample organizer in figure 4.4. (See sample inference stems in figure 4.3, page 61.) • Complete the reproducible organizer (figure 4.5) as a key for modeling with your text in preparation for teaching the lesson. 1b. Prepare photocopies for students of your selected text, the student-friendly vocabulary definitions (figure 4.4), and the strategy's reproducible organizer (figure 4.5). 1c. As appropriate, assemble technology to use in modeling the strategy for students (or example, document camera, PPT slides, SMART Board, overhead transparencies, or an enlarged poster version).

continued →

Lesson Step	Explanatory Notes for the Teacher
2. Teacher identifies the content standard from state or district standards for students.	Display the content-specific standard you want students to understand and retain as a result of their reading, thinking, and writing. Discuss the standard with students.
3. Teacher shares an advance organizer, reviews the student-friendly definitions, and distributes teacher-prepared materials.	Share the following advance organizer or one of your own choosing: Police detectives, whether in books, movies, or TV series, have an uncanny ability to sift through piles of documents and reports to make the connections that solve the crime. Today, we are going to work on our ability to read like detectives by sorting through evidence left behind by the author in a piece of text.
4. Teacher models and provides rehearsal opportunities, gradually releasing responsibility to students for doing more of their own thinking and writing.	**Teacher models: Chunk 1** Read the inferential statement that you generated for this piece of text aloud to your students. Remind students that an inference is based on evidence (in the text) as well as reasoning (in the brain). Tell them they are about to read with the purpose of investigating only whether evidence in the text sufficiently supports the statement. Ask students to silently read the first text chunk, and then read it aloud to them. Think aloud as you consider the first question you will investigate and respond to in column A on the organizer: What sentences in the text relate to the inference? Show students how to read sentence by sentence to determine which statements from the text relate or seem connected to the inference. Record them on the organizer. Read the second question aloud from column B: Do the sentences provide evidence to support the inference? Think aloud about how you made the decision as to whether the related statements provided evidence to support the inference. Record your answer and explanation in column B of the organizer. **Students work with teacher: Chunk 2** Ask students to read the second chunk silently, then read it aloud to them. Ask students to underline the statements from the text that they believe answer the first question: What sentences in the text relate to the inference? Call on students to share and explain their answers—sentence by sentence—as you think aloud regarding whether you agree. Record accurate answers on the organizer. Call on students to discuss the second question with you: Do the sentences provide evidence to support the inference? After ideas have been shared, formulate and record an answer and explanation on the organizer that is accurate and reflects the best thinking generated.

4.	Teacher models and provides rehearsal opportunities, gradually releasing responsibility to students for doing more of their own thinking and writing. *(continued)*	**Students work with peers: Chunk 3** After students silently read the third text chunk and you read it aloud to them, ask them to underline the statements from the text that they believe answer the first question (column A). Have students work interdependently with a partner to agree on the statements and record them on their organizers. Next, ask partners to discuss the second question (column B) and agree on and record their answers and explanations on their organizers.
5.	Teacher formatively assesses student work.	Have several pairs display their answers to the two questions for chunk 3, and facilitate a discussion of the merits of the answers. Record accurate and exemplary answers on the organizer. Formatively assess as many students as possible from the work displayed and the discussion. NOTE: At this point, you have two options: (1) conclude this lesson by going directly to steps 6 and 7, temporarily skipping the +feature (schedule the +feature for a later class period using the same text and organizers students have completed up to this point), or (2) extend this lesson by incorporating the +feature followed by steps 6 and 7.

Read Like a Detective+

Teacher models

Read the +prompt aloud (figure 4.5, page 62) as students follow along. Tell students that in order to respond to the +prompt, they will have to consider the quantity (column A) and quality (column B) of evidence that the author provides and that they have identified while reading and processing the entire text. Model this process with the information from chunk 1. If there is strong evidence in chunk 1, highlight it on the organizer and tell students that they may choose to use this highlighted evidence as textual support when they answer the +prompt.

Students work with teacher

Ask students to consider the quantity and quality of evidence in chunk 2 and the cumulative effect it has in relation to chunk 1. Have students share their answers as you process them for accuracy. If there is strong evidence in chunk 2, ask students to discuss what it is as you consider their thinking and highlight the correct answer(s) on the organizer. Tell students that they may choose to use this highlighted evidence as textual support when they answer the +prompt.

Students work with peers

Ask students to work independently to consider the quantity and quality of evidence in chunk 3 and the cumulative effect it has in relation to chunks 1 and 2. Have partners work interdependently to reach consensus on their answers and highlight any strong evidence from this chunk of the text on their organizer. Call on pairs to process answers, and guide students to make an accurate decision regarding whether the cumulative evidence from all three chunks is sufficient. Using that answer and the evidence that has already been highlighted, ask peers to complete the +prompt.

Teacher formatively assesses student work

Call on several pairs to display their answers to the +prompt. Ask students to compare posted answers and facilitate a discussion about the merits of each. Students can either identify one answer as being exemplary or can write an entirely new exemplary answer as a class with your guidance.

continued →

Lesson Step	Explanatory Notes for the Teacher
6. Teacher returns to the content standard to identify progress in understanding and retaining new content.	In order to identify student progress with the new content, ask students to write an exit ticket in response to this stem: In what ways did the reading, thinking, and writing you did today help you understand the content standard? Explain.
7. Closure	Ask students to reflect on their current level of understanding of the content standard(s) and the literacy skill(s) they worked with today by using "fist to five" hand signals to the following questions as you display them, read them aloud, and ask for student responses: On a scale of fist to five, where making a fist means not at all and holding up all five fingers means so completely that you could be the teacher, rate your understanding of the following content standard: _____ On a scale of fist to five, where making a fist means not at all and holding up all five fingers means so completely that you could be the teacher, rate your level of understanding of the following CCSS literacy skill: _____

Visit **go.solution-tree.com/commoncore** to download and print this figure.

Question Like an Investigative Reporter

The Gist of Question Like an Investigative Reporter

Students assume the role of investigative reporter and are asked to frame their "reporter's questions" as they read the text and make inferences. In the +feature of the lesson, students are asked to write a headline and explain why it is appropriate to the text.

CCR Anchor Standard 1 for Reading: *Read closely to determine what the text says explicitly and to make logical inferences from it;* cite specific textual evidence when writing or speaking to draw conclusions from the text.

CCR Anchor Standard 2 for Reading: *Determine central ideas or themes of a text* and analyze their development; *summarize the key supporting details and ideas.*

In this strategy, you show your students how to step into the role of an investigative reporter—an individual who specializes in finding answers to specific questions in a wide range of printed texts. In order to ask direct questions like an investigative reporter, students must be able to do the following: read closely to extract meaning from text, ask direct and relevant questions while they are reading the text, make logical inferences, and cite evidence from the text to support their inferences. You can scaffold this process for students in one of two ways: (1) provide a set of question stems such as investigative reporters might pose from which students will choose their own questions as they read or (2) select one or two question stems that are most appropriate for the text you have selected.

Background Knowledge

Questioning is as common in schools as homework and tests, and often it is just as ineffective in promoting meaningful learning. That's because the wrong individuals, in our opinion, are asking the questions: the teachers. Students are supposed to come up with correct answers as evidence of their comprehension, but more often than not, teachers end up answering their own questions. Isabel L. Beck, Margaret G. McKeown, Rebecca L. Hamilton, and Linda Kucan (1997) suggest that the typical Initiate, Respond, and Evaluate (IRE) questioning model (Dillon, 1988; Mehan, 1979) leaves much to be desired when it comes to uncovering students' comprehension breakdowns or showing them how to become more adept at asking and answering their own questions. It is the generation and answering of higher-level questions by students that "encourage deeper processing and more thorough organization" (Just & Carpenter, 1987, p. 422).

This strategy is about making logical inferences from text by tackling the text as an investigative reporter might—by asking and answering higher level questions of the authors of texts during the reading process. Even seemingly dry and dusty textbooks have real people as authors, and engaging students in reading the minds and examining the motives of authors will pay surprising dividends in their engagement with text.

Investigative reporters, particularly those working on complex and difficult topics, must sift and sort through legal documents, databases of public records, documents from state and federal agencies, tax records, regulatory reports, policies and procedures, correspondence between individuals, and historical documents, searching for answers to various questions that are whirling around in their minds. For each kind of text reporters read, they are engaged in a dialogue with the author of the text, asking questions of this individual to better grapple with difficult ideas in the text or make sense of badly written text.

Beck and her colleagues (1997) call this process *questioning the author* (QtA) and suggest that one way to make reading more meaningful is to humanize the individuals behind the texts:

> The starting point in QtA is to let students know that the book's [text's] content is simply someone's ideas written down, and that this person may not have always expressed things in the clearest or easiest way for readers to understand. Armed with this view of an author, as a human being who is potentially fallible, students can view texts as less impersonal, authoritative, and incomprehensible. (p. 18)

For the investigative reporter, the human beings may be lawyers, Supreme Court justices, company CEOs, trade union officials, government workers, or elected officials. However, wherever there is text, there is an author or a team of authors sitting at a computer or slouched in a chair with a yellow pad and pen writing down ideas, telling stories, or making arguments. Investigative reporters often work in solitude, and while they are reading, they are posing questions for the various authors of all of the texts they peruse in an attempt to understand just exactly what is going on. However, the secret to excellent investigative reporting is not being intimidated by a host of important and powerful people. They are fallible authors who need to be questioned about their writing, the actions and thoughts that lie behind the writing.

In the background knowledge discussion in Strategy 4, we suggested three levels of comprehension: reading the lines, reading between the lines, and reading beyond the lines. In this strategy, students are primarily focused on *reading between the lines* to determine the precise meanings that the author of the text intended to convey. Just ahead in Strategy 6, we will tackle reading beyond the lines as we ask students to make more elaborative inferences that require bringing their own knowledge and experience to bear on the bigger questions of a text.

Understanding How the Strategy Works

The most efficient way to understand this strategy is to first read the sample text in figure 5.1 (Flesch–Kincaid grade level 7.2). It is divided into three chunks to align with the sample organizer.

FIGURE 5.1: Sample Text for Question Like an Investigative Reporter

"Vietnam Revisited: I Was a Refugee Long Before Katrina"
Chunk 1
Recently, I've found myself struggling to describe where I come from. I have lived in Houston for just over a month, since the day my husband and I left New Orleans with our son and dog, two days before Hurricane Katrina struck the Gulf Coast.
As New Orleans was destroyed before our eyes, I wept for all those who lost their homes, and their lives. As sympathetic friends and family called me, begging to help, however, I found it difficult to feel too sorry for myself. Losing my home is not the most momentous thing to ever happen to me. I don't consider myself a victim of Katrina. I lost my home long before the winds and high waters swept over New Orleans.
I am a refugee from Vietnam, not from New Orleans. Thirty years ago, my mother left Vietnam with her six children, carrying little else but a valise packed with sepia-toned photographs and a heart full of courage and faith. My father was in prison, and my mother had to make the decision to leave without him in order to save her children from concentration camps or death. She was headed for America, where she didn't speak the language, didn't know anything about the culture and knew no one.

continued →

Chunk 2

In 1975, when we came to the States, we were called refugees. We huddled together at Camp Pendleton in California, until we were sent to Alexandria, Va., where a Roman Catholic church had offered us sponsorship.

Shortly after we arrived in America, we learned of my father's miraculous escape from Vietnam, just hours before the fall of Saigon. With incredible fortune guiding him, my father made the perilous journey from the South China Sea, and eventually to a camp in Pennsylvania, where a U.S. soldier gave him the bus fare to meet his family.

We were very fortunate. Yet, we started with nothing. The church found us housing, but my parents did not have jobs; we had no clothing and no toys. We learned English from scratch, and tried to create a home for ourselves in our new country. We folded paper to make toys, and taught ourselves to read. We wore whatever the church parishioners donated to us, and had no idea what was fashionable, which in a way gave us some freedom. We were different, but we didn't try too hard to fit in. And most importantly, we didn't try to re-create our old lives, the lives we had known back in Vietnam.

After their narrow escapes from Vietnam, my parents managed to confront the most daunting task of all—to raise their children in a foreign land. My parents held full-time jobs, worked over-time and modeled for all of us that perseverance borne out of extreme hardship. What amazes me most about my parents is that they accepted right away that their stay in America was not temporary. They would never return home.

I, on the other hand, could not help but find my way back to the place where I was born, some 25 years after I had left Saigon. When I arrived, however, I found myself very much a foreigner. I dressed, walked and talked differently.

Some locals spoke to me doubtfully in Vietnamese, but I could see on their faces that they didn't expect me to understand them. I sought out my parents' former home in Saigon, and snapped some pictures. Later, I found out that I had never actually lived there. In my search for home, I only found myself to be a stranger.

Chunk 3

When I hear from others affected by Hurricane Katrina that they are mourning the loss of their childhood home, or the home that belonged to their family for generations, I feel great sympathy for them. In a strange way, I also feel envious that they have such a clear image of what was their home. After all of these evacuations, and refugee experiences, the only thing I'm sure of is that I can't call any place home. My home no longer exists as a picture in my mind, or as a warm memory embedded in my soul. I don't have a home.

Yet, I didn't lose my home to Katrina. In fact, I have lost nothing. I have only gained. I have gained perspective. I have gained a deep sense of gratitude for all those who have reached out to me and my family, 30 years ago and today. I have gained a powerful resiliency and, most importantly, an appreciation for the grace that I have experienced in my life.

My one-year-old son talks a lot, but up until last week, had never completed a coherent full sentence. All of a sudden, a few days ago, he said, "I love you." I don't know how my journey has led me to this place—America, Houston, in a grocery store parking lot with my son and hearing his first full sentence. But I do know that feeling the comfort of home is not what's most important.

I suppose I will always be searching for my home, but I am also certain that I will never find it. And I hope I never do. The journey, as difficult and tiring as it can be, is worth it.

Figure 5.2 is a sample organizer for Question Like an Investigative Reporter. Once you have read through the sample text and seen how the strategy works on the organizer, you will be able to assimilate the lesson plan in preparation for showing your students how this strategy works.

FIGURE 5.2: Sample Organizer for Question Like an Investigative Reporter

Text title: "Vietnam Revisited" Name:			
Directions: As you ask investigative questions, choose from the following reporter's question stems. (For additional question stems, see figure 5.3, page 73.) **Reporter's Question Stems:** • What's a possible explanation? • What future challenges might be faced? • What caused _____? • What might be the future benefits?			
Column A **Excerpt of text about which you have a question**	**Column B** **Reporter's question**	**Column C** **My "right now" answer (likely to be an inference)**	**Column D** **My "now that I have read more of the text" answer and explanation**
Chunk 1			
"Losing my home was not the most momentous thing to ever happen to me."	What's a possible explanation?	The author has had something even more "momentous" than losing her home already happen to her.	Leaving Vietnam and coming to America without her father was the most momentous thing that ever happened to her.
"She [my mother] headed for America, where she didn't speak the language…and knew no one."	What future challenges might the family face?	The family won't have anywhere to live, and the mother will struggle to earn money to support her family if she can't speak the language.	A Roman Catholic church sponsored the family so they had housing; the father was reunited with the family, but neither parent initially had a job.
Chunk 2			
"A U.S. soldier gave him [the father] bus fare to meet his family."	What caused the soldier to give the author's father money?	He wanted to help a father reunite with his family.	We don't know for sure, but the soldier helps the family, and the church helps the family, and the author has a "sense of gratitude" for those who reached out.

continued →

Column A **Excerpt of text about which you have a question**	Column B **Reporter's question**	Column C **My "right now" answer (likely to be an inference)**	Column D **My "now that I have read more of the text" answer and explanation**
Chunk 2			
"What amazed me most about my parents is that they accepted right away that their stay in America was not temporary. They would never return home."	What's a possible explanation?	They didn't feel safe returning to Vietnam—a place they had to leave in order to avoid having their children put in a concentration camp.	It can't be the safety issue because the author travels to Vietnam. It could be that the parents had already "gained perspective," something the author doesn't gain until after Katrina.
Chunk 3			
"I don't have a home."	What's a possible explanation?	The author doesn't have a feeling of permanence from having safely lived in the same place for a long time.	She will always be searching for a home and is certain and hopeful she won't find it. Not having a home is giving her a "journey."
"I have gained a powerful resiliency and, most importantly, an appreciation for the grace that I have experienced in my life."	What might be the future benefits?	She is strong enough to withstand most any challenge.	She doesn't think that having the "comfort of home" is what's most important and is glad that she has faced difficulties.
Question Like an Investigative Reporter+			
+Prompt: A title or headline has the purpose of making a first impression with the reader and establishing a short and quick context for the text that will follow. You will notice that your teacher removed the headline/title from this text. As an investigative reporter, it is your job to write an appropriate headline or title for this text and explain why it is appropriate.			
Headline/Title: Home Is Where the Heart Is			
Explanation: This is an often-used cliché, and it applies to this story. The author doesn't seem to believe she will ever have a permanent home, and that is OK because her heart is with her family.			

Items to Prepare

There are three reproducible figures to support the Question Like an Investigative Reporter strategy. Figure 5.3 contains a set of question stems. These stems can be used to scaffold questioning, giving students multiple ways to access the information "between the lines."

FIGURE 5.3: Question Stems for Question Like an Investigative Reporter

1.	Based on the title, pictures, and/or introduction, what predictions (inferences) can I make about the text?
2.	What does the author tell us might be an explanation for _____?
3.	Who does the author think is most responsible for _____?
4.	According to the author, does this (_____) have any connection to that (_____)? What does the author suggest the connection is?
5.	What does the author tell us caused _____ to happen?
6.	What does the author believe is the biggest problem?
7.	What does the author suggest might be the solution?
8.	What does the author suggest might be the future consequences/benefits/challenges related to _____?
9.	What will happen next?
10.	How long might _____ take?
11.	What resources/changes/discoveries does the author suggest will be necessary for _____ to happen?
12.	What legal issues may need to be resolved about _____?
13.	Who is opposed to / in favor of _____?
14.	What does the author suggest are some other theories about _____?
15.	What might be the next step in this process?
16.	What might/would have happened if _____?
17.	What does the author mean here?
18.	Is the author explaining things clearly, or will I have to reorganize the text?

Visit **go.solution-tree.com/commoncore** to download and print this figure.

Figure 5.4 is a poster with student-friendly definitions of the terms that you will be using to explain various aspects of the strategy. Your goal as you use the various strategies is to keep spiraling back to important terms until their definitions are automatic for both you and your students.

FIGURE 5.4: Student-Friendly Definitions for Question Like an Investigative Reporter

Inference: A type of conclusion based on explicit evidence from the text and the reader's own reasoning and background knowledge
Evidence: Textual proof that supports an inference
Decide: Make up your mind; figure something out
Believe: Think that something is true
Support: Agree with something
Oppose: Disagree with something
Feel strongly about: Agree with something and be willing to argue or debate about it with others
Question: Ask someone for information or raise a doubt about the truth of something

Visit **go.solution-tree.com/commoncore** to download and print this figure.

The third reproducible, figure 5.5, is the organizer that you and your students will use as they learn to read like detectives.

FIGURE 5.5: Reproducible Organizer for Question Like an Investigative Reporter

Text title:
Name:

Directions: As you ask investigative questions, choose from the following reporter's question stems. (For additional question stems, see figure 5.3, page 73.)

Reporter's Question Stems:

- What's a possible explanation?
- What future challenges might be faced?
- What caused _____?
- What might be the future benefits?

Column A Excerpt of text about which you have a question	Column B Reporter's question	Column C My "right now" answer (likely to be an inference)	Column D My "now that I have read more of the text" answer and explanation
Chunk 1			
Chunk 2			

Chunk 3			

Question Like an Investigative Reporter+
+Prompt: A title or headline has the purpose of making a first impression with the reader and establishing a short and quick context for the text that will follow. You will notice that your teacher removed the headline/title from this text. As an investigative reporter, it is your job to write an appropriate headline or title for this text and then explain why it is appropriate.
Headline/Title: **Explanation:**

Visit **go.solution-tree.com/commoncore** to download and print this figure.

Lesson Plan

Figure 5.6 is a lesson plan for showing your students how to question what they are reading with the mindset of an investigative reporter. The highlighted feature of the lesson, Question Like an Investigative Reporter+, motivates you and your students to take the next step after they have made logical inferences and cited their evidence—writing a headline for the article or a title for the book that resulted from their investigative process.

FIGURE 5.6: Lesson Plan for Question Like an Investigative Reporter

Lesson Step	Explanatory Notes for the Teacher
1. Teacher prepares and assembles the necessary materials.	1a. Choose content-related and standards-aligned text for teacher modeling and student reading, then: • Chunk text into three parts as shown in the sample text (figure 5.1, page 69), but don't distribute the text until students are ready to work on the third chunk. • Provide scrap paper for students to cover their text. • Remove the title or headline from the text.

continued →

Lesson Step	Explanatory Notes for the Teacher
1. Teacher prepares and assembles the necessary materials. *(continued)*	• Select four to six examples from the list of the investigative reporter's question stems (figure 5.3, page 73) that students can use as they question the author or the information in the text. • Complete the reproducible organizer (figure 5.5, page 74) as a key for modeling with your text in preparation for teaching the lesson. 1b. Prepare photocopies for students of your selected text, the student-friendly vocabulary definitions (figure 5.4, page 73), and the strategy's reproducible organizer (figure 5.5). 1c. As appropriate, assemble technology to use in modeling the strategy for students (for example, document camera, PPT slides, SMART Board, overhead transparency, or posters).
2. Teacher identifies the content standard from state or district standards for students.	Display the content-specific standard you want students to understand and retain as a result of their reading, thinking, and writing. Discuss the standards with students.
3. Teacher shares an advance organizer, reviews the student-friendly definitions, and distributes teacher-prepared materials.	Share the following advance organizer or one of your own choosing: Superman cleverly disguised himself as a mild-mannered reporter named Clark Kent, who, with the help of his hidden super powers, had a real "nose for the news"—an expression used to describe the sixth sense top-notch reporters seem to have. Today, we are going to work on our investigative reporting skills—our ability to read a text and ask reporter's questions, make inferences, and closely read the text to see if we can support our inferences.
4. Teacher models and provides rehearsal opportunities, gradually releasing responsibility to students for doing more of their own thinking and writing.	**Teacher models: Chunk 1** Tell students that they will not get a copy of the text until they are ready to read chunk 3 and, for now, they will follow along by looking at the text that you are displaying. Keep the text chunk covered and reveal each line only as you read it. Start reading the first chunk aloud and stop when you find an idea or statement in the text that makes you, as an investigative reporter, curious—something that you wonder about or is worth exploring more deeply. Write the statement in the "excerpt of text" box on the organizer (column A). Next, select a reporter's question stem from the top of the organizer (or see figure 5.3 for additional stems) that will help you to frame your question and record it in the "reporter's question" box (column B). Now, model making an inference or a decision in order to provide an answer to the reporter's question and record it in the "right now" box (column C).

4. Teacher models and provides rehearsal opportunities, gradually releasing responsibility to students for doing more of their own thinking and writing. *(continued)*	Tell students that as you read the rest of the text, you will look for further information that will help you to verify the accuracy of your answer. If/when you find it, you will record it in the "now that I have read more of the text" box on the organizer (column D). Tell students that you may have to read the entire text before deciding if you have enough information to verify your "right now" answer. Continue reading aloud to search for the next places in this chunk that require your investigative questioning skills or places that provide more information about any of the "right now" inferences. **Students work with teacher: Chunk 2** As you read this chunk, you will only reveal each sentence as you read it aloud. Students follow along silently by looking at the text you are displaying and listening to you read. Tell students to ask you to stop if they see/hear anything in the text that makes them curious or that might be worthy of more investigation or deeper thinking. When students stop you, process what students have identified and selected. If it is appropriate, record it in the "excerpt of text" box on the organizer. Ask students to look at the reporter's question stems and try to frame a question. Call on students to share their questions, and record the best example on the organizer. Give students some think time to create a "right now" answer. Process student examples and record a model example on the organizer. Continue this pattern of reading aloud and having students stop you at appropriate places in the text. Repeat the earlier pattern for filling out the organizer as you model for students. Finally, ask students to determine if this chunk has any additional information that will help verify any of the "right now" answers from chunk 1 or this chunk. If so, go back and record responses in the appropriate boxes. **Students work with peers: Chunk 3** Give students a copy of the text at this time along with a sheet of paper to cover the third chunk. Ask students to read each sentence silently before taking turns to read it aloud with their partner. Students will use the sheet of paper to cover the rest of the chunk and reveal only the line that they are currently reading. Students should stop after each sentence to decide if it seems worthy of investigation. If it does, they should select a stem to frame and record their question on the organizer. Partners should agree on and record their "right now" answers on their organizers for the text excerpt and continue reading to find more text to investigate and question. Finally, ask students to determine if this chunk has any additional information that will help verify any of the "right now" answers from chunk 1, 2, or 3. If so, they should go back and record responses in the appropriate boxes.

continued →

Lesson Step	Explanatory Notes for the Teacher
5. Teacher formatively assesses student work.	Call on pairs to display their text excerpts, "right now" answers, and any "now that I have read more of the text" responses. Process responses for accuracy as well as quality and record models on the organizer. Formatively assess as many students as possible while they are displaying and discussing the work.
	NOTE: At this point, you have two options: (1) conclude this lesson by going directly to steps 6 and 7, temporarily skipping the +feature (schedule the +feature for a later class period using the same text and organizers students have completed up to this point), or (2) extend this lesson by incorporating the +feature followed by steps 6 and 7.

Question Like an Investigative Reporter+

Teacher models

Ask students to notice, if they haven't already, that you have removed the headline or title from this piece of text. That's because it is their job as the reporter to write the headline or title. Remind students of two important things to remember when writing headlines:

1. Keep it short—no more than fifteen words
2. The headline is a contract you are making with the reader to share what the article is mainly about. See figure 14.5 (page 188) for additional rules about headlines.

Students work with teacher

Keeping what we know about headlines in mind, ask students to brainstorm what "important ideas" a great headline for this text would need to include. Record accurate ideas in a list on the board.

Students work with peers

Ask student to work interdependently with a peer to create a headline that would work well for this text. When they have agreed on one, they should record it in the Question Like a Reporter+ section of the organizer and complete their explanation of why it is a good headline for the story.

Teacher formatively assesses student work

Have several students display their headlines and explanations and facilitate a conversation with the class about the merits of each. Students may select an exemplary headline/explanation from those that are displayed, or the students may write a new headline together as a class with your guidance. Record the selected model on the organizer. Be sure to share the "original" headline/title to see which students like best—theirs or the author's! Formatively assess as many students as possible from the work they display and their discussion.

6. Teacher returns to the content standard to identify progress in understanding and retaining new content.	In order to identify student progress with the new content, ask students to write an exit ticket in response to this stem:
	In what ways did the reading, thinking, and writing you did today help you understand the content standard? Explain.

7. Closure	Ask students to reflect on their current level of understanding of the content standard(s) and the literacy skill(s) they worked with today by using "fist to five" hand signals to the following questions as you display them, read them aloud, and ask for student responses:
	On a scale of fist to five, where making a fist means not at all and holding up all five fingers means so completely that you could be the teacher, rate your understanding of the following content standard: _____
	On a scale of fist to five, where making a fist means not at all and holding up all five fingers means so completely that you could be the teacher, rate your level of understanding of the following CCSS literacy skill: _____

Visit **go.solution-tree.com/commoncore** to download and print this figure.

Think Like a Private Investigator

The Gist of Think Like a Private Investigator

Students assume the role of private investigator as they read the text to find clues to make inferences about the author's beliefs and assumptions. In the +feature of the lesson, students practice summarizing not only their understanding of the author's beliefs and assumptions, but their own beliefs as well.

CCR Anchor Standard 1 for Reading: Read closely to determine what the text says explicitly and to make logical inferences from it; cite specific textual evidence when writing or speaking to draw conclusions from the text.

CCR Anchor Standard 2 for Reading: Determine central ideas or themes of a text and analyze their development; *summarize the key supporting details and ideas.*

Think Like a Private Investigator (PI) is the third strategy in part I to focus on making logical inferences from text and then citing specific evidence from the text to support those inferences. In Strategy 4 we suggested that your students read like detectives, looking for clues in the text about inferences made by the teacher. The inference you provided to your students based on your own reading of the text served as a scaffold to whet their reading appetites for becoming skilled reading detectives. In Strategy 5, you gradually released more responsibility for making inferences to your students but continued to provide scaffolding with a set of inferential question stems.

Now in Strategy 6, students are expected to think like private investiga-tors. PIs generally work independently and are therefore forced to do a lot of independent thinking, often carrying on internal conversations with them-selves about what the collected evidence means. PIs may have an assistant, but they do not have an entire police force to help them search for information and suspects as do police detectives. Nor do PIs have the support network of newspaper, magazine, television network, or book publisher resources that often supplement the efforts of investigative reporters. PIs are on their own, in much the same way that your students are on their own when they are faced with making inferences from text found on standardized tests, state assess-ments, the ACT, or the SAT.

PIs are always thinking about their cases, and although they may work on the clock, charging clients by the hour when they are doing surveillances or writing reports, they do not stop thinking about difficult cases when the clock stops. This kind of ongoing cognitive processing is essential when students are reading more challenging texts and drawing major conclusions about what they have read.

Background Knowledge

Students and even teachers often have difficulty nailing down precisely what ought to be happening in their brains during the process of inferring. We suggest sharing the following synonyms for the verb *infer* to help students understand that whenever they make a statement using one of the following verbs, they have likely made an inference about something: *surmise, construe, deduce, think, judge, believe, conclude, understand, gather, figure, sense,* and *assume.* The word that jumps out in this list is *think.* Whenever students use the words "I think" at the beginning of a statement, they have likely made an infer-ence or drawn a conclusion about something that is germane to their own life experiences. They know how to infer when the topics are familiar ones. They only need to transfer that thinking ability to more unfamiliar topics in your content.

There are three categories of inferences: (1) anaphoric resolutions (McKoon & Ratcliff, 1992), (2) knowledge-based inferences (Johnson & von hoff Johnson, 1986), and (3) elaborative, higher-level inferences (Pressley & Afflerbach, 1995).

Anaphoric Resolutions

Anaphora are words or phrases in a text that stand for other words, and anaphoric relationships describe how pronouns and phrases in the text relate to their referents in the text. Text would be very boring if every time the author wanted to refer to Grandma in his story, he was limited to using the word *Grandma*. Instead, the author can use pronouns like *she, her,* and *hers*. If Grandma is speaking, the author can use *I, my,* and *mine*. Or, the author can draw upon an almost unlimited supply of words or phrases that can also stand for *Grandma* in the text: *an old lady, my father's mother, a geriatric genius, a senior citizen, an old gal,* and *a role model*. When asked to select a main idea or write a short sentence about what the story is mainly about, students may not even recognize that Grandma is the star of the show unless they understand the role of anaphoric relationships. Anaphora can be found in expository as well as narrative text. Note the number of pronouns in the sample texts shown in figure 6.1.

FIGURE 6.1: Mini-Text Examples of Various Types of Inferences

Text Sample A: "The Coyote" (Merlin, 2000)
I often wander around in the desert by myself and have been very fortunate in seeing lots of wildlife and in observing many of the miracles that happen every day in nature.
One of my favorite memories is of an encounter with Coyote.
I was walking up a lushly vegetated wash at dawn one summer morning. A coyote started ambling across the wash, then suddenly realized I was there. He began to trot away, so I sat down on the sand. That immediately aroused his interest since it's not a typical reaction from people, and it's also a very non-threatening gesture. So the coyote stopped and sat down, watching me. I simply sat, waiting for him to make the next move. He did. He lay down and put his head on his paws, still watching and assessing me. I lay down resting my head on my hands staring into those intelligent brown eyes. After a minute he rolled on his side, so of course I did too. We spent several wonderful minutes changing positions and rolling around.
Suddenly Coyote sat up cocking his ears around. He glanced at me one last time as if to say goodbye, then moved off into the brush, just before a horseback rider came into view down the wash. It was an incredible, magical feeling staring into the soul of Coyote and finding myself judged worthy of a few private moments of play.

Text Sample B: "Powering Down" (Lazaroff, 2000)
Being a hummingbird is like driving a car with a one-gallon gas tank: there is an almost constant need to refuel. Hummingbirds are often perilously close to the limits of their energy reserves. On cold nights, when the costs of keeping warm are especially high, it may be too risky for a hummingbird even to keep its engine idling.
At such times, a hummingbird bristles its feathers to let its body heat escape, and its temperature quickly approaches that of its surroundings. Its heart rate drops dramatically and it may stop breathing for minutes at a time. It appears lifeless, clinging motionlessly to its branch with its head drawn close to its body and its bill pointing sharply upward. At daybreak it revs its metabolic engines and warms itself again. This sort of temporary hibernation is called torpor. Hummingbirds become torpid not only to deal with fuel crises, but also to save energy for migration. And since birds lose moisture with every breath, becoming torpid also helps desert hummingbirds conserve water.

Sources: Merlin, "The Coyote," © 2000. Courtesy of the Arizona-Sonora Desert Museum, from A Natural History of the Sonoran Desert.

Lazaroff, "Powering Down," © 2000. Courtesy of the Arizona-Sonora Desert Museum, from A Natural History of the Sonoran Desert.

Knowledge-Based Inferences

Knowledge-based inferences are those in which a reader's ability to make an inference is highly dependent on having specific kinds of background knowledge stored in long-term memory. For example, in Text Sample A, readers need to know answers to the following questions to fully comprehend the text:

- What is the feeling being described in this text? (wonderment and awe)

- What is the time of day? (sunup)

- What is the exact location being described? (a desert wash)

In Text Sample B, readers need a fair bit of background knowledge about energy conservation, both in automobiles and in living creatures, to make the inferences needed to understand this text. Note the highlighted portions in the text that develop the concept of energy conservation and its importance to the survival of hummingbirds.

Elaborative Inferences

Elaborative inferences are based on those in which a reader's ability to make an inference is dependent on specialized knowledge from various disciplines. For example, in a study by Cynthia Shanahan, Timothy Shanahan, and Cynthia Misischia (2011), verbal protocols were collected from experts in the fields of history, chemistry, and mathematics. The expert participants were members of three groups: (1) college professors teaching those disciplines, (2) teacher educators at the university level training high school teachers in those disciplines, and (3) high school teachers teaching the disciplines to students. Analysis of the protocols revealed that expert readers in these three fields generally read text in their discipline using the following criteria:

- Sourcing—The experts in this study always considered the source of the text as well as the perspective of the text's author.

- Contextualization—The experts considered when the text was written and what influences might have shaped the writing of the text.

- Corroboration—The experts considered whether there were agreements or similarities and disagreements or differences between the text and others.

- Text structure—The experts considered how the information in the text was organized.

- Rereading—Close reading was reported to be important, and rereading was focused on information identified to be important.

- Interest—The experts separated new and known information.

As you seek to model and directly teach your students how to make inferences as they read content text from your specific discipline, keep these various types of elaborative inferences in mind. As you become more skilled in modeling for students, point out for them how these various criteria have informed your thinking about a content text.

Understanding How the Strategy Works

Figure 6.2 contains sample text (Flesch-Kincaid grade level 7.2) for you to read before you walk your way through a completed organizer based on that text.

FIGURE 6.2: Sample Text For Think Like a PI

"Vietnam Revisited: I Was a Refugee Long Before Katrina"
Chunk 1
Recently, I've found myself struggling to describe where I come from. I have lived in Houston for just over a month, since the day my husband and I left New Orleans with our son and dog, two days before Hurricane Katrina struck the Gulf Coast.
As New Orleans was destroyed before our eyes, I wept for all those who lost their homes, and their lives. As sympathetic friends and family called me, begging to help, however, I found it difficult to feel too sorry for myself. Losing my home is not the most momentous thing to ever happen to me. I don't consider myself a victim of Katrina. I lost my home long before the winds and high waters swept over New Orleans.
I am a refugee from Vietnam, not from New Orleans. Thirty years ago, my mother left Vietnam with her six children, carrying little else but a valise packed with sepia-toned photographs and a heart full of courage and faith. My father was in prison, and my mother had to make the decision to leave without him in order to save her children from concentration camps or death. She was headed for America, where she didn't speak the language, didn't know anything about the culture and knew no one.
Chunk 2
In 1975, when we came to the States, we were called refugees. We huddled together at Camp Pendleton in California, until we were sent to Alexandria, Va., where a Roman Catholic church had offered us sponsorship.
Shortly after we arrived in America, we learned of my father's miraculous escape from Vietnam, just hours before the fall of Saigon. With incredible fortune guiding him, my father made the perilous journey from the South China Sea, and eventually to a camp in Pennsylvania, where a U.S. soldier gave him the bus fare to meet his family.
We were very fortunate. Yet, we started with nothing. The church found us housing, but my parents did not have jobs; we had no clothing and no toys. We learned English from scratch, and tried to create a home for ourselves in our new country. We folded paper to make toys, and taught ourselves to read. We wore whatever the church parishioners donated to us, and had no idea what was fashionable, which in a way gave us some freedom. We were different, but we didn't try too hard to fit in. And most importantly, we didn't try to re-create our old lives, the lives we had known back in Vietnam.
After their narrow escapes from Vietnam, my parents managed to confront the most daunting task of all—to raise their children in a foreign land. My parents held full-time jobs, worked over-time and modeled for all of us that perseverance borne out of extreme hardship. What amazes me most about my parents is that they accepted right away that their stay in America was not temporary. They would never return home.

continued →

I, on the other hand, could not help but find my way back to the place where I was born, some 25 years after I had left Saigon. When I arrived, however, I found myself very much a foreigner. I dressed, walked and talked differently.

Some locals spoke to me doubtfully in Vietnamese, but I could see on their faces that they didn't expect me to understand them. I sought out my parents' former home in Saigon, and snapped some pictures. Later, I found out that I had never actually lived there. In my search for home, I only found myself to be a stranger.

Chunk 3

When I hear from others affected by Hurricane Katrina that they are mourning the loss of their childhood home, or the home that belonged to their family for generations, I feel great sympathy for them. In a strange way, I also feel envious that they have such a clear image of what was their home. After all of these evacuations, and refugee experiences, the only thing I'm sure of is that I can't call any place home. My home no longer exists as a picture in my mind, or as a warm memory embedded in my soul. I don't have a home.

Yet, I didn't lose my home to Katrina. In fact, I have lost nothing. I have only gained. I have gained perspective. I have gained a deep sense of gratitude for all those who have reached out to me and my family, 30 years ago and today. I have gained a powerful resiliency and, most importantly, an appreciation for the grace that I have experienced in my life.

My one-year-old son talks a lot, but up until last week, had never completed a coherent full sentence. All of a sudden, a few days ago, he said, "I love you." I don't know how my journey has led me to this place—America, Houston, in a grocery store parking lot with my son and hearing his first full sentence. But I do know that feeling the comfort of home is not what's most important.

I suppose I will always be searching for my home, but I am also certain that I will never find it. And I hope I never do. The journey, as difficult and tiring as it can be, is worth it.

Source: Katherine Dinh. Copyright 2005 Houston Chronicle Publishing Company. Reprinted with permission. All rights reserved.

Use figure 6.3 to experience the steps of the organizer so you will feel confident about teaching them to your students.

FIGURE 6.3: Sample Organizer for Think Like a PI

Text title: "Vietnam Revisited" Name:		
Column 1 Locate and record a text excerpt that seems to reveal the author's beliefs or assumption about the world.	**Column 2** Infer what the excerpt reveals about the author's beliefs or assumptions regarding the world.	**Column 3** How do the author's assumptions about the world relate to your beliefs or assumptions about the world?
Chunk 1		
"I found it difficult to feel too sorry for myself. Losing my home is not the most momentous thing to ever happen to me."	Life is filled with difficulties and challenges. When you have been through something really horrible, other lesser challenges will never seem as bad.	When I am faced with a challenge, I do sometimes reflect back on other bigger challenges I have faced in the past—but that may not stop me from feeling sorry for myself.

"I am a refugee from Vietnam, not from New Orleans."	Although the people forced to leave New Orleans were called refugees, fleeing because of Hurricane Katrina was not the same "refugee" experience as leaving Vietnam had been thirty years before.	I agree that not all tragedies are created equal. Something that I think is trivial, someone else may think is devastating.
Chunk 2		
"We were different, but we didn't try too hard to fit in."	She believes that it is OK to be different.	I used to like the Apple company's motto: "Think Different." Although now I would add "but not too different."
Chunk 3		
"I have gained a deep sense of gratitude . . . a powerful resiliency and most importantly, an appreciation for the grace that I have experienced in my life."	She knows the importance of being thankful and seems to focus on the cup being half full. She has learned to survive and thrive through life's challenges. She welcomes the challenges.	I believe I am resilient but not grateful—although I have much to be thankful for.
"I will always be searching for my home, but I am also certain that I will never find it. And I hope I never do. The journey, as difficult and tiring as it can be, is worth it."	The author has learned a lot from her challenges and knows that she is who she is because of the journey. She doesn't want an easier road.	I understand the importance of the journey, but I am quite content to have a "home."
Think Like a PI+		
+Prompt 1: Summarize your major beliefs/assumptions about the world based on your response to this text.		
Although I am resilient, I feel sorry for myself when I am facing challenges rather than welcoming them. I don't really appreciate the things for which I should be thankful.		
+Prompt 2: Summarize the author's major beliefs/assumptions about the world based on this text.		
Some experiences in life provide us with harder lessons—and more to be grateful for. We should learn to welcome life's harder "journeys" because those are the ones from which we learn the most.		

Items to Prepare

There are three reproducible figures to support the Think Like a PI strategy. Figure 6.4 (page 88) contains a set of elaborative inference stems to guide your students' thinking. The stems scaffold the process of making elaborative inferences by giving students a variety of ways to get into the minds of the authors who have written the texts they are reading.

FIGURE 6.4: Elaborative Inference Stems for Think Like a PI

Stems That Refer to the Author's Assumptions or Beliefs
1.   I infer that the author believes . . .
2.   I infer that the author would support the idea that . . .
3.   I infer that the author would be opposed to . . .
4.   I infer that the author feels strongly about . . .
Stems That Refer to the Author's Purpose(s) in Writing
5.   I infer that the author wants readers to believe . . .
6.   I infer that the author wants readers to support the idea that . . .
7.   I infer that the author wants readers to take some action.
Stems That Refer to the Author's Sources for Information Found in the Text
8.   I infer that the author consulted a wide variety of information sources.
9.   I infer that the author relied mostly on personal experiences.
10. I infer that the author relied mostly on personal background knowledge.
Stems That Refer to the Author's Assumptions About the World
11. I infer that the author has an optimistic and positive worldview.
12. I infer that the author has a fairly pessimistic worldview.

Visit **go.solution-tree.com/commoncore** to download and print this figure.

Figure 6.5 is a poster with student–friendly definitions of the terms that you will be using to explain various aspects of the strategy. Note that some terms are recycled from prior strategies. English learners (ELs) and struggling students will need frequent reminding and reteaching about important terms before they can automatically follow directions or read test items containing the terms.

FIGURE 6.5: Student-Friendly Definitions for Think Like a PI

Inference: A type of conclusion based on explicit evidence from the text and the reader's own reasoning and background knowledge
Evidence: Textual proof that supports your conclusion or inference
Decide: Make up your mind; figure something out
Believe: Think that something is true
Support: Agree with something
Oppose: Disagree with something
Feel strongly about: Agree with something and be willing to state your case for others
Summarize: To write or tell the meaning of what you have read in your own words

Visit **go.solution-tree.com/commoncore** to download and print this figure.

The third reproducible, figure 6.6, is the organizer you will use as you model from the text and your students will use as they learn to think like PIs.

FIGURE 6.6: Reproducible Organizer for Think Like a PI

Text Title: Name:		
Column 1 Locate and record a text excerpt that seems to reveal the author's beliefs or assumption about the world.	**Column 2** Infer what the excerpt reveals about the author's beliefs or assumptions regarding the world.	**Column 3** How do the author's assumptions about the world relate to your beliefs or assumptions about the world?
Chunk 1		
Chunk 2		
Chunk 3		
Think Like a PI+		
+Prompt 1: Summarize your major beliefs/assumptions about the world based on your response to this text.		

continued →

+**Prompt 2:** Summarize the author's major beliefs/assumptions about the world based on this text.

Visit **go.solution-tree.com/commoncore** to download and print this figure.

Lesson Plan

Figure 6.7 is a lesson plan for showing your students how to make elaborative inferences during their reading of content text. The highlighted feature of the lesson, Think Like a PI+, motivates you and your students to take the next step after they have made a logical inference and cited their evidence—writing a one- or two-sentence summary of the evidence.

FIGURE 6.7: Lesson Plan for Think Like a PI

Lesson Step	Explanatory Notes for the Teacher
1. Teacher prepares and assembles the necessary materials.	1a. Choose content-related and standards-aligned text for teacher modeling and student reading, then: • Chunk the text into three parts as shown in the sample text (figure 6.2, page 85). • Refer to figure 6.4 (elaborative inference stems) on page 88 to select stems appropriate for your text—adding to or replacing the stem that is in column 2 on the reproducible organizer. • Complete the reproducible organizer (figure 6.6, page 89) as a key for modeling with your text in preparation for teaching the lesson. 1b. Prepare photocopies for students of your selected text, the student-friendly vocabulary definitions (figure 6.5, page 88), and the strategy's reproducible organizer (figure 6.6). 1c. As appropriate, assemble technology to use in modeling the strategy for students (for example, document camera, PPT slides, SMART Board, overhead transparencies, or posters).
2. Teacher identifies the content standard from state or district standards for students.	Display the content-specific standard you want students to understand and retain as a result of their reading, thinking, and writing. Discuss the standards with students.

3.	Teacher shares an advance organizer, reviews the student-friendly definitions, and distributes teacher-prepared materials.	Share the following advance organizer or one of your own choosing: Actor Robert Downey Jr. in the Sherlock Holmes movies gives us some clues about how to be a successful private investigator. A successful PI is always curious and has the ability to use logical reasoning to solve even the most difficult case. When we work to think like a private investigator today, we will need to be both curious and logical. The text will be our evidence as we look for clues to make inferences about the author's beliefs and assumptions about the world.
4.	Teacher models and provides rehearsal opportunities, gradually releasing responsibility to students for doing more of their own thinking and writing.	**Teacher models: Chunk 1** Ask students to read the first chunk silently, then tell students that as you read the text aloud, you will model your private investigator skills by searching for an idea or statement in the text (a clue) that seems to reveal the author's assumptions about the world. As you locate an example, record it in column 1. Think aloud as you consider what this text (your evidence) reveals about the author's assumptions. Record your ideas in column 2. Finally, think aloud as you make a connection between what you believe to be the author's assumptions about the world and how those assumptions relate to your assumptions about the world. Be sure to write your own personal response in column 3—you will use your column 3 response in the +feature of the lesson plan. Continue to read aloud through this chunk and repeat this process for each additional text excerpt. **Students work with teacher: Chunk 2** Ask students to read the chunk silently before you read it aloud to them. Ask students to look for clues in the text that reveal the author's assumptions about the world and underline them. Call on students to share what they have underlined and select a text excerpt that is accurate and record it on the organizer. Ask students to make an inference about what the excerpt means and have them share their ideas. Process their ideas and write a model response in column 2 of the organizer. Tell students to reflect on how the author's beliefs/assumptions relate to their own. Call on students to share their answers and process them, but be certain to complete column 3 of the organizer with your own personal response. Repeat this process for every text excerpt that serves as a clue to the author's assumptions about the world. **Students work with peers: Chunk 3** Ask students to read the chunk silently before you read it aloud. Have students work independently to underline clues in the text that reveal the author's beliefs/assumptions about the world. Have students make an inference about what each excerpt reveals before they pair with a peer.

continued →

Lesson Step	Explanatory Notes for the Teacher
4. Teacher models and provides rehearsal opportunities, gradually releasing responsibility to students for doing more of their own thinking and writing. *(continued)*	Now, working interdependently, partners agree on the text excerpts (clues) they have identified (column 1) and the meaning of them (column 2). Working independently, students will think about and relate their own beliefs/assumptions about the world to the author's and record their answers on the organizer. You should complete column 3 with your own personal response.
5. Teacher formatively assesses student work.	Call on pairs to display their work from chunk 3 as you facilitate a discussion on the merits of the work. Record accurate responses as models for columns 1 and 2. Call on individual students to share their responses to how their assumptions about the world relate to the author's, then share and record your own model response on the organizer. Formatively assess as many students as possible based on their displayed work and discussion. NOTE: At this point, you have two options: (1) conclude this lesson by going directly to steps 6 and 7, temporarily skipping the +feature (schedule the +feature for a later class period using the same text and organizers students have completed up to this point), or (2) extend this lesson by incorporating the +feature followed by steps 6 and 7.

Think Like a PI+

Teacher models

Ask students to focus on column 3 as you display your completed organizer. This is where you have identified how the author's assumptions about the world relate to your beliefs or assumptions. Make a bulleted list from the information in this column of your organizer and record it on the board. Show students how to summarize the bulleted list and record the summary on the Think Like a PI+ portion of the organizer for +prompt 1. (For additional support on writing summaries, see Strategy 7 [page 95] and figure P1.2 [page 23], How to Write a Summary.)

Students work with teacher

Ask students to look at column 3 of their own organizers and make a bulleted list from the information there. Ask students to follow the process that you modeled by turning their list into a summary and recording it on their organizer for +prompt 1. Call on students to share their statements as you offer feedback.

Students work with peers

Ask students to look at +prompt 2 and follow along as you read it aloud. Ask students to work in pairs to look at column 2 of the organizer where they have made decisions about the author's beliefs or assumptions. Ask students to work together to turn this information into a bulleted list. Have students follow the process you just modeled (and they just rehearsed) by writing a summary of the author's beliefs or assumptions about the world. Ask students to record responses on their organizers for this prompt.

Teacher formatively assesses student work

Have several partners display their summary statements as you facilitate a discussion of the merits of each. Have students reach consensus on which response should be used as the model, or have students work together to write an entirely new response. Record the model response on the organizer.

6.	Teacher returns to the content standard to identify progress in understanding and retaining new content.	In order to identify student progress with the new content, ask students to write an exit ticket in response to this stem: In what ways did the reading, thinking, and writing you did today help you understand the content standard? Explain.
7.	Closure	Ask students to reflect on their current level of understanding of the content standard(s) and the literacy skill(s) they worked with today by using "fist to five" hand signals to the following questions as you display them, read them aloud, and ask for student responses: On a scale of fist to five, where making a fist means not at all and holding up all five fingers means so completely that you could be the teacher, rate your understanding of the following content standard: _____ On a scale of fist to five, where making a fist means not at all and holding up all five fingers means so completely that you could be the teacher, rate your level of understanding of the following CCSS literacy skill: _____

Visit **go.solution-tree.com/commoncore** to download and print this figure.

Snapshot Summary

The Gist of Snapshot Summary

Using the metaphor of taking a snapshot to summarize and preserve a memory, students are asked to read a text and create a "snapshot summary" of what each chunk of text is most importantly about. In the +feature of the lesson, students work to write a sentence summary for the entire text.

CCR Anchor Standard 1 for Reading: *Read closely to determine what the text says explicitly and to make logical inferences from it;* cite specific textual evidence when writing or speaking to draw conclusions from the text.

CCR Anchor Standard 2 for Reading: *Determine central ideas or themes of a text* and analyze their development; *summarize the key supporting details and ideas.*

The Snapshot Summary strategy consists of a several-step process to scaffold the following literacy tasks: read a chunk of content text carefully to see what it explicitly says, write a snapshot summary that describes the central idea of each text chunk, and use the snapshot summaries to write a one-sentence summary of the text.

Background Knowledge

Ann L. Brown and Jeanne D. Day (1983) define summarizing as "the ability to work recursively on information to render it as succinctly as possible" (p. 1). The adverb *recursively* is an interesting one that is seldom used outside of scholarly research. It means to keep coming back to a learning objective or a work product over and over again until it's mastered or completed to one's satisfaction. Notice the verb in their definition: *work.* Summarizing requires diligent mental work. Brown and Day further state that summarizing "requires judgment and effort, knowledge and strategies" (p. 1).

Literacy strategies such as Snapshot Summary in which a model is demonstrated for students and they are then provided with an organizer to scaffold their processing have the power to improve students' recall of what they have read compared to simply being given a reading assignment with a list of questions to answer (Pressley, Burkell, et al., 1995).

David Pearson and Linda Fielding (1991) point out:

> Any sort of systematic attention to clues that reveal how authors attempt to relate ideas to one another or any sort of systematic attempt to impose structure upon a text, especially in some sort of visual representation of the relationships among key ideas, facilitates comprehension as well as both short-term and long-term memory for the text. (p. 832)

Summarizing can be defined in various ways, but the definition we prefer is to succinctly state the meaning of what you have read in your own words. The ultimate goal of summarizing in content classrooms is that students will be able to write a summary (as short as a sentence or as long as a paragraph) about what they have read.

Summaries generally have the following characteristics: they are short; they do not contain unimportant details or irrelevant sidebar comments; they tell only what is most important about the text. If time permits, develop a file of good summaries from the real world: a summary of a particularly exciting basketball or football game; a one-sentence book review such as might be found in the *New York Times* best-seller list, or an obituary that summarizes the life of a famous person in one paragraph. You can no doubt find many nonexamples of summaries in your collection of student work products: a complete retelling of the plot of a book with all of the details you don't need to know to get the central idea, any statement that is copied word for word from the Internet or the blurb and back cover copy of a book, and any statement that purports to be a summary but does not state the central idea.

Understanding How the Strategy Works

To become skilled at employing the Snapshot Summary so that you can show your students how to use it, first look at the sample text in figure 7.1 (Flesch-Kincaid grade level 10.0). The text is divided into three chunks in order to make the summarizing steps more manageable.

FIGURE 7.1: Sample Text for Snapshot Summary

"Vultures"
Chunk 1
In cartoon fiction, vultures are ghastly portents of death, circling ominously overhead when explorers are lost in the desert. In reality, vultures play a much more wholesome role. By cleaning up the carcasses of dead animals, they act as the sanitation department of the natural world.
Chunk 2
Vultures are perfectly designed for living on carrion. They may have to wait a few days in between meals, so in searching for food they burn up very little energy, soaring for hours with scarcely a flap of their broad wings. Their search is aided by keen eyesight and, in the case of the Turkey Vulture, a well-developed sense of smell, unusual among birds. And although their naked wrinkled heads may be unattractive to human eyes, the lack of feathers on their heads is a decided advantage when the birds are involved in the messy business of tearing open dead animals.
Chunk 3
The vultures found in the warmer parts of Europe, Asia, and Africa are in the same family as are hawks and eagles. The vultures of the Americas come from a totally different background; they are now known to be more closely related to storks. It seems remarkable that these two completely unrelated groups of vultures should be so similar in structure and appearance. The similarities are probably adaptations to the same feeding behavior, an example of what is called convergent evolution.

Source: Kaufman, K. © 2000. Courtesy of the Arizona-Sonora Desert Museum, from A Natural History of the Sonoran Desert, *p. 377.*

Figure 7.2 is a completed organizer based on the text. You may wish to come back to this sample again to review the process immediately before you teach the lesson.

FIGURE 7.2: Sample Organizer for Snapshot Summary

Text title: "Vultures" **Name:**
Directions: Write a short phrase or sentence (a snapshot summary) to describe what each text chunk is most importantly about.
Chunk 1
Like a sanitation department cleans a city, vultures help nature by eating the remains of dead animals.
Chunk 2
Everything about vultures, from their eyesight to their naked wrinkled heads, is designed to help them survive by eating dead animals.
Chunk 3
Although completely unrelated, vultures from different parts of the world look similar, possibly due to convergent evolution.

continued →

Snapshot Summary+
+Prompt: Succinctly combine or blend the snapshot summary statements to create a one-sentence text summary in the space below.
In spite of being completely unrelated, and as a possible example of convergent evolution, vultures from different parts of the world are similarly designed to survive by eating the remains of dead animals.

Items to Prepare

There are two reproducible figures available for use with your students as you show them how to use this strategy. Figure 7.3 contains student-friendly definitions for the terms that are used with this strategy.

FIGURE 7.3: Reproducible Student-Friendly Definitions

Summarize: Write or tell the meaning of what you have read in your own words
Summary: A short statement that tells what the text is most importantly about
Central idea: What the text is mainly about
Supporting details: Various important facts in the text that help to explain the key idea of the text
Snapshot summary: A sentence or phrase you write that states the central idea of one chunk of text you have read
Text summary: A sentence that combines or blends several snapshot summary statements to create a summary of the entire text
Succinct: Very short and clear

Visit **go.solution-tree.com/commoncore** to download and print this figure.

The second reproducible, figure 7.4, is an organizer for you to use as you process the content text you select for modeling and for your students to record their thinking.

FIGURE 7.4: Reproducible Organizer for Snapshot Summary

Text title: **Name:**
Directions: Write a short phrase or sentence (a snapshot summary) to describe what each text chunk is most importantly about.
Chunk 1

Chunk 2
Chunk 3
Snapshot Summary+
+Prompt: Succinctly combine or blend the snapshot summary statements to create a one-sentence text summary in the space below.

Visit **go.solution-tree.com/commoncore** to download and print this figure.

Lesson Plan

The lesson plan for Snapshot Summary is shown in figure 7.5. When your students are ready for the challenge of summarizing your selected text using Snapshot Summary+, use figure 7.6 (page 102), a checklist for evaluating summary sentences.

FIGURE 7.5: Lesson Plan for Snapshot Summary

Lesson Step	Explanatory Notes for the Teacher
1. Teacher prepares and assembles the necessary materials.	1a. Choose content-related and standards-aligned text for teacher modeling and student reading, then: • Chunk the text into three parts as shown in the sample text (figure 7.1, page 97). • Complete the reproducible organizer (figure 7.4) as a key for modeling with your text in preparation for teaching the lesson. 1b. Prepare photocopies for students of your selected text, the student-friendly definitions (figure 7.3), the strategy's reproducible graphic organizer (figure 7.4), and the summary checklist (figure 7.6, page 102). 1c. As appropriate, assemble technology to use in modeling the strategy for students (for example, document camera, PPT slides, SMART Board, overhead transparencies, or posters).

continued →

Lesson Step	Explanatory Notes for the Teacher
2. Teacher identifies the content standard from state or district standards for students.	Display the content-specific standard you want students to understand and retain as a result of their reading, thinking, and writing. Discuss the standard with students.
3. Teacher shares an advance organizer, reviews the student-friendly definitions, and distributes teacher-prepared materials.	Share the following advance organizer or one of your own choosing: We no doubt all have taken a quick snapshot of places, people, or events to capture an image that will summarize and preserve a memory. Today, we are going to create a snapshot summary of a piece of text—a summary that will help us remember the text.
4. Teacher models and provides rehearsal opportunities, gradually releasing responsibility to students for doing more of their own thinking and writing.	**Teacher models: Chunk 1** Have students read the first chunk silently and then read it aloud. Think aloud as you follow the steps in figure P1.2, page 23 (How to Write a Summary) to create a summary that captures a snapshot of what this chunk is most importantly about. Make it clear to students that you constructed your summary in your own words. Write your snapshot summary on the organizer. Ask students to help you check your summary for accuracy by looking back in the text. If necessary, make adjustments to the summary on the organizer. **Students work with teacher: Chunk 2** After students read the chunk silently and you read it aloud, ask students to follow the steps and jot down a summary that captures a snapshot of what this chunk is most importantly about. Students should go back into the text to check their summary for accuracy. Call on students to share their snapshot summary. Process student examples and select a summary to write on the organizer (figure 7.4, page 98) as a model. **Students work with peers: Chunk 3** After students read the third chunk silently and you read it aloud, they will start working interdependently with a partner to write a summary that shows their understanding of what this chunk is most importantly about. Partners should go back in the text to check for accuracy.
5. Teacher formatively assesses student work.	Call on partners to display their snapshot summary. Process student examples and select a quality summary to write on the organizer as a model. Formatively assess as many students as possible from the displayed work and discussion. NOTE: At this point, you have two options: (1) conclude this lesson by going directly to steps 6 and 7, temporarily skipping the +feature (schedule the +feature for a later class period using the same text and organizers students have completed up to this point), or (2) extend this lesson by incorporating the +feature followed by steps 6 and 7.

Snapshot Summary+

Teacher models

Read the +prompt aloud (figure 7.4, page 98) as students follow along. Share the summary checklist (figure 7.6, page 102) with students and review the quality criteria column. Tell students that you expect them to use the checklist to guide them before they write and help them review the +summaries after they are written.

Students work with teacher

With the checklist in mind, ask students to brainstorm and identify the information from the snapshot summaries that absolutely must be included in the text summary. Process student answers and make a bulleted list of accurate ideas on the board for students to use as a type of word bank if needed.

Students work with peers

Students will work interdependently with peers to produce and record a one-sentence text summary.

Teacher formatively assesses student work

Call on several pairs to display their text summary sentences. Ask students to use the checklist and their understanding of what makes a good summary to discuss the merits of the summaries as you facilitate the conversation. The class will either select an exemplar summary from those displayed or write an entirely new summary together as a class. Formatively assess as many students as possible based on their work and discussion.

6.	Teacher returns to the content standard to identify progress in understanding and retaining new content.	In order to identify student progress with the new content, ask students to write an exit ticket in response to this stem: In what ways did the reading, thinking, and writing you did today help you understand the content standard? Explain.
7.	Closure	Ask students to reflect on their current level of understanding of the content standard(s) and the literacy skill(s) they worked with today by using "fist to five" hand signals to the following questions as you display them, read them aloud, and ask for student responses:
		On a scale of fist to five, where making a fist means not at all and holding up all five fingers means so completely that you could be the teacher, rate your understanding of the following content standard: _____
		On a scale of fist to five, where making a fist means not at all and holding up all five fingers means so completely that you could be the teacher, rate your level of understanding of the following CCSS literacy skill: _____

Visit **go.solution-tree.com/commoncore** to download and print this figure.

FIGURE 7.6: Checklist for Evaluating Summary Sentences

Directions: As you prepare to write a text summary or as you review a summary that has already been written, use the following checklist to help determine the quality of the summary.

Quality Criteria	Yes, explain . . .	No, explain . . .
If you had not read the text yourself, would you have been able to get a good sense of what it was most importantly about from the text summary sentence?		
Was there anything critically important to understanding this text that was left out of the summary?		
Was there anything unimportant that was included that could be left out?		

Visit **go.solution-tree.com/commoncore** to download and print this figure.

Identify-Analyze-Summarize

The Gist of Identify-Analyze-Summarize

Students are asked to identify the central idea of a text and then analyze the text to identify the key supporting details and ideas in each chunk. In the +feature of the lesson, students complete a short constructed response that summarizes the key supporting details and ideas of each chunk.

CCR Anchor Standard 1 for Reading: *Read closely to determine what the text says explicitly* and to make logical inferences from it; cite specific textual evidence when writing or speaking to draw conclusions from the text.

CCR Anchor Standard 2 for Reading: *Determine central ideas or themes of a text and analyze their development; summarize the key supporting details and ideas.*

The Identify-Analyze-Summarize strategy will become one of your favorites for the possibilities it affords your students to rehearse two of the most challenging academic tasks they face: (1) figuring out what the central idea of a text actually is, and (2) then writing a one-sentence summary setting forth that idea. The strategy is designed to hold students accountable for a number of tasks: reading the text closely to determine what it explicitly says, determining the central or main idea of the text, analyzing the development of those ideas in the text, and then summarizing the key supporting details and ideas.

Background Knowledge

A number of years ago, eminent historians Doris Kearns Goodwin (1987) and Stephen Ambrose (1994) were taken to task by their literary peers for failing to summarize the ideas of others in their own words and then forgetting to cite the sources from which they inadvertently "borrowed" the information (Goldstein, 2002; Kirkpatrick, 2002). We thought of many of our former students. Despite our seemingly clear instructions and warnings, they persistently copied paragraphs from the World Book Encyclopedia onto their note cards and then diligently copied the same paragraphs into their final research reports. Even more disheartening was our inability to show them how to do it differently. Today's students are still cutting and pasting, only it's now from the Internet.

Restating the meaning of what one reads in one's own words—different words from those used in the original text—is a challenging assignment for all readers and writers. Whether we're famous historians, educational authors, teachers, or a class of eighth graders preparing for a high-stakes assessment, we share a common problem: shortcutting the comprehension step in the summarizing process. We don't want to invest the time and cognitive effort that is essential, no matter how smart we are, to struggle with extracting and constructing meaning from text. The University of Washington Psychology Writing Center (2005) gives this advice to its students regarding the summarizing of text: "If you can't put the information into your own words, you aren't ready to write about it [or talk about it]. To learn how to paraphrase what you want to write, try to explain it to someone else without referring to your source" (p. 2).

Summarizing has its roots in a time-honored tradition of reading comprehension instruction: finding the main idea. In days gone by, main idea instruction consisted of little more than reading short selections and circling the best title for the selection. That was then. This is now. Identify-Analyze-Summarize scaffolds the steps of summarizing and provides another way to rehearse this important reading-thinking-writing process.

Understanding How the Strategy Works

Figure 8.1 is a sample text (Flesch-Kincaid grade level 10.1) for you to read and process as you walk through the sample organizer in figure 8.2 (page 106). Note the highlighted Identify-Analyze-Summarize +feature found in the sample organizer. This component of the lesson ramps up the rigor of the strategy by expecting students to write three summaries, one for each of the three chunks of text.

FIGURE 8.1: Sample Text for Identify-Analyze-Summarize

"Stories of an Attack 70 Years Ago Will Live Forever"
Chunk 1
I was attending a Sunday afternoon youth meeting at church in Baltimore when someone came in with the news. The Japanese had bombed the U.S. Navy base at Pearl Harbor.

The next day at school, the principal called the entire student body into the auditorium and we sat there and listened as President Roosevelt delivered his famous "day that will live in infamy" speech to the nation. I am forever grateful to our school principal for his foresight and leadership in having us all hear that most memorable address by the president. That same day, Dec. 8, Congress, with only one member dissenting, voted to declare war on Japan and a few days later on Germany and other Axis nations.

A lot has unfolded in my life since that fateful day, Dec. 7, 1941. I was 14 and enjoying my first year of high school when the lives of Americans, including mine, were about to change forever. The Selective Service Act had been passed in 1940 and now American males, 18 to 45, were being drafted into the armed services. A teacher whom I liked and admired was the first person I knew to be drafted, and that somehow brought the war closer to home. My brother, Bill, was 18 and subject to the draft while attending Western Maryland College. Initially, college students were given deferments to complete their degrees, but soon the needs of the military brought that exemption to an end, and my brother was drafted a year before graduation.

As we continued our high school studies we all wondered when our turns would come, and we began to prepare for the inevitable call by the military. I explored a Navy program called radar technician training. I was gaining the educational requirements in high school and began thinking of enlistment in the Navy RT program—a better choice than to be drafted into the Army infantry, I thought.

Chunk 2

With dad at my side I did enlist in January 1945, a few weeks before graduating from high school. Dad was again with me as I waited for my train at Baltimore's Mount Royal station to go to Chicago and the Great Lakes Naval Training Station for boot camp. I was sad to leave my dad, anxious about the future, but excited to board the B&O Railroad's Capitol Limited, a famous train that I had dreamed of someday riding. Sleep in my coach seat did not come easy during that long night.

Many weeks later, I learned that Dad had represented me at my graduation ceremony and had gone up on the stage to receive an honor I had been awarded. I can only guess at his feelings. Looking back, it is hard to imagine what my parents were going through with both of their sons away preparing for or fighting in a war. Just a few weeks later, while I was finishing boot camp, my brother Bill was killed in action in Europe following the Battle of the Bulge. I will never forget that Sunday morning when I opened the letter from home that Dad had painfully written to advise me of my brother's death. It had been impossible for him to reach me by phone.

Chunk 3

But my family's story of sadness was only one of probably millions who were affected by tragedies during the Second World War, the war that started for the United States with Pearl Harbor 70 years ago today.

Yes, there still are many of us who will relive events that began with Pearl Harbor. And many more who will know through family members the stories that have been passed down about the war. The day will come when there are no more firsthand accounts, just as has happened with World War I, but the stories will live forever.

For all of us, Pearl Harbor day will be a time to give thanks. Thanks to those who gave their lives and suffered as a result of the war and thanks that our great nation was preserved as a democracy and a land of opportunity.

FIGURE 8.2: Sample Organizer for Identify-Analyze-Summarize

Text title: "Stories of an Attack" Name:	
Directions: As you determine the central idea for each chunk, record your answers in column 1. Analyze and list the key supporting details and ideas used to develop the central idea in column 2.	
Column 1 **Central Idea**	**Column 2** **Key Supporting Details and Ideas**
Chunk 1	
What is this chunk mainly about? The author feels the impact of the war's beginning.	The Japanese bomb Pearl Harbor. Students hear the president's speech. A teacher and the author's brother are drafted. The author considers enlisting.
Chunk 2	
What is this chunk mainly about? The author's family faces hardships because of the war.	Before graduating, the author enlists. The author's father represents him at graduation. The author's brother was killed in action. The author learns of his brother's death in a letter from their father.
Chunk 3	
What is this chunk mainly about? It is important to give thanks to those who sacrificed.	It is the 70th anniversary of the bombing of Pearl Harbor. Pearl Harbor is a day to give thanks to those who suffered. The war resulted in the preservation of democracy.
Identify-Analyze-Summarize+	
+Prompt: Write a constructed response that summarizes the key supporting details and ideas of the central idea of each chunk.	
Chunk 1	
Chunk 1 summary The author feels the impact of the war as both a favorite teacher and his brother are drafted, and he considers enlisting.	
Chunk 2	
Chunk 2 summary The family faces hardships as the author enlists before graduating and learns, while at boot camp, that his brother was killed in action.	
Chunk 3	
Chunk 3 summary On the 70th anniversary of Pearl Harbor, the author gives thanks to those who sacrificed in order to preserve democracy.	

Items to Prepare

There are two reproducible figures to support Identify-Analyze–Summarize. The first reproducible, figure 8.3, contains a set of student-friendly definitions you will explain as you model and think aloud for your students regarding how to execute this strategy. Keep the definitions handy to remind yourself of two important rules: (1) remain consistent regarding the definitions that you use during strategy instruction so as not to confuse students, and (2) teach the student-friendly definitions recursively by coming back to the definitions repeatedly during instruction.

FIGURE 8.3: Student-Friendly Definitions for Identify-Analyze-Summarize

---

Central idea: What the text is mainly about

Process: Read, write, think, or talk about something

Consensus: An agreement you reach with someone by talking about something

Read: Get meaning from text

Summarize: Write or explain the meaning of what you have read in your own words

Analyze: Trace the development of an idea or theme

Key supporting details: Important information and ideas that tell about the central idea of the text

Development: The way an author gradually tells more and more about content so the reader can have a better understanding

---

Visit **go.solution-tree.com/commoncore** to download and print this figure.

The second reproducible, figure 8.4, is the organizer you will use in modeling the strategy and students will subsequently use to demonstrate their reading and thinking processes.

FIGURE 8.4: Reproducible Organizer for Identify-Analyze-Summarize

Text title:	
Name:	
Directions: As you determine the central idea for each chunk, record your answers in column 1. Analyze and list the key supporting details and ideas used to develop the central idea in column 2.	
Column 1 **Central Idea**	**Column 2** **Key Supporting Details and Ideas**
Chunk 1	
What is this chunk mainly about?	

continued →

Column 1 Central Idea	Column 2 Key Supporting Details and Ideas
Chunk 2	
What is this chunk mainly about?	
Chunk 3	
What is this chunk mainly about?	
Identify-Analyze-Summarize+	
+Prompt: Write a constructed response that summarizes the key supporting details and ideas of the central idea of each chunk.	
Chunk 1	
Chunk 1 summary	
Chunk 2	
Chunk 2 summary	
Chunk 3	
Chunk 3 summary	

Visit **go.solution-tree.com/commoncore** to download and print this figure.

Lesson Plan

The lesson plan for showing your students how to execute this strategy for the acquisition of content knowledge is found in figure 8.5.

FIGURE 8.5: Lesson Plan for Identify-Analyze-Summarize

Lesson Step	Explanatory Notes for the Teacher
1. Teacher prepares and assembles the necessary materials.	1a. Choose content-related and standards-aligned text for teacher modeling and student reading, then: • Chunk text into three parts as shown in the sample text (figure 8.1, page 104). • Complete the reproducible organizer (figure 8.4, page 107) as a key for modeling with your text in preparation for teaching the lesson. 1b. Prepare photocopies for students of your selected text, the reproducible student-friendly definitions (figure 8.3), and the reproducible organizer (figure 8.4). In anticipation of teaching Identify-Analyze-Summarize+, prepare photocopies of figure P1.2 (How to Write a Summary, page 23), and figure 7.6 (Summary Checklist, page 102).

1. Teacher prepares and assembles the necessary materials. *(continued)*	1c. As appropriate, assemble technology to use in modeling the strategy for students (for example, document camera, PPT slides, SMART Boards, overhead transparencies, or enlarged posters).
2. Teacher identifies the content standard from state or district standards for students.	Display the content-specific standard you want students to understand and retain as a result of their reading, thinking, and writing. Discuss the standard with students.
3. Teacher shares an advance organizer, reviews the student-friendly definitions, and distributes teacher-prepared materials.	Share the following advance organizer or one of your own choosing: Have you ever worked to put together a puzzle? Usually you start by looking at the picture of the completed puzzle from the lid. After that, you begin to spread the puzzle pieces out on a table to see if you can figure out where each piece goes and how it contributes to the picture. In some ways, reading a text is like putting together a puzzle. As proficient readers, we make an effort to identify the central ideas and then analyze how the "pieces" of the text—the supporting details and ideas—fit together to contribute to its development. Today, we are going to practice putting together the puzzle pieces of a text.
4. Teacher models and provides rehearsal opportunities, gradually releasing responsibility to students for doing more of their own thinking and writing.	**Teacher models: Chunk 1** Ask students to silently read the first chunk of text, and then read it aloud to them. Tell students that you will think aloud as you identify the central idea by answering this question: What is the information in this chunk mainly about? (See figure P1.2, page 23, for more information.) Record the central idea in column 1 of the organizer (figure 8.4, page 107). Now, refer back to the text in order to analyze the text, and make a list of the key supporting details and ideas used to develop the central idea. Read each sentence aloud to model analyzing the text in order to identify the key supporting details and ideas that are used to develop the central idea. Record your answers in column 2. **Students work with teacher: Chunk 2** Ask students to silently read the second chunk of text, and then read it aloud to them. Ask students to answer this question: What is the information in this chunk mainly about? Call on students to share their central idea answer, and select a model to record on the organizer. Next, ask students to analyze the chunk and underline what they identify as key supporting details and ideas. Call on students to share. Discuss and record accurate answers on the organizer.

continued →

Lesson Step	Explanatory Notes for the Teacher
4. Teacher models and provides rehearsal opportunities, gradually releasing responsibility to students for doing more of their own thinking and writing. *(continued)*	**Students work with peers: Chunk 3** Ask students to silently read the third chunk of text, and then read it aloud to them. Ask students to work independently to answer this question: What is the information in this chunk mainly about? Tell students to work with a partner in order to reach consensus on their answers. After reaching consensus, tell partners to work together to analyze, agree on, and underline key supporting details and ideas.
5. Teacher formatively assesses student work.	Have several pairs share what they identified as being the central idea in chunk 3 as you record an accurate answer on the organizer. Have several pairs display their key supporting details and ideas, and facilitate a discussion. Record accurate answers on the organizer. Formatively assess as many students as possible while they are presenting, sharing, and processing answers. NOTE: At this point, you have two options: (1) conclude this lesson by going directly to steps 6 and 7, temporarily skipping the +feature (schedule the +feature for a later class period using the same text and organizers students have completed up to this point), or (2) extend this lesson by incorporating the +feature followed by steps 6 and 7.

Identify-Analyze-Summarize+

Teacher models

Read the +prompt aloud to students as they follow along (figure 8.4, page 107). Tell students that in order to respond to the prompt, they will need to write a summary. Call on students to share their understanding of the critical attributes of a summary as you record accurate answers on the board. (See figure 7.6, Summary Checklist, page 102, and figure P1.2, How to Write a Summary, page 23, for additional information about summaries.)

Students work with teacher

Using the list of attributes recorded on the board along with information from figure P1.2, model the process of writing a summary for chunk 1 in the "model summary" section of the organizer.

Students work with peers

Ask students to work interdependently to use the list of attributes along with your model to complete a summary for chunk 2. Ask partners to display their summaries and facilitate a discussion regarding the merits. Select a model to record on the organizer.

Ask students to work independently to write a summary for chunk 3.

Teacher formatively assesses students

Call on several students to display their summaries. Facilitate a discussion of the merits. Ask the class to select a model summary or ask them to create an entirely new summary as a model for the class. Record the model on the organizer.

6.	Teacher returns to the content standard to identify progress in understanding and retaining new content.	In order to identify student progress with the new content, ask students to write an exit ticket in response to this stem: In what ways did the reading, thinking, and writing you did today help you understand the content standard? Explain.
7.	Closure	Ask students to reflect on their current level of understanding of the content standard(s) and the literacy skill(s) they worked with today by using "fist to five" hand signals to the following questions as you display them, read them aloud, and ask for student responses: On a scale of fist to five, where making a fist means not at all and holding up all five fingers means so completely that you could be the teacher, rate your understanding of the following content standard: _____ On a scale of fist to five, where making a fist means not at all and holding up all five fingers means so completely that you could be the teacher, rate your level of understanding of the following CCSS literacy skill: _____

Visit **go.solution-tree.com/commoncore** to download and print this figure.

What-How-Why (Individuals)

The Gist of What-How-Why (Individuals)

Students read a piece of content-related text written about an individual or individuals and decide how and why the ideas in that text are primarily developed. In the +feature of the lesson, students are challenged to write a constructed response that analyzes the development.

CCR Anchor Standard 3 for Reading: *Analyze how and why individuals, events, or ideas develop and interact over the course of the text.*

The final standard in the Key Ideas and Details section of the CCR Anchor Standards for Reading in Grades 6–12 states this expectation for students: "Analyze how and why individuals, events, or ideas develop and interact over the course of a text." The standard raises the reading and thinking bar to a new and much higher level of thinking: *analysis*. One dictionary definition states that to analyze is to "examine methodically and in detail the constitution or structure of information, typically for purposes of explanation and interpretation" (Apple Dictionary, 2009). We define *analysis* in the student-friendly definitions as "a close, careful, and thoughtful reading of the text to figure out how the author develops (writes about) individuals, events, or ideas." The term *develop* in this context reminds us of the nearly nonexistent process of developing film in a darkroom. As the film develops, all of the details of the photo slowly emerge. Similarly, as authors write about (develop) individuals, events, and ideas over the course of a text, readers can gradually understand and gain a more complete picture of the content, whether it be content about individuals, events, or ideas.

To scaffold this standard for you and your students, we have created three strategies, one for each of the topics: individuals, events, or idea. Strategy 10 focuses on events, and Strategy 11 works with ideas (concepts).

Background Knowledge

Reread the anchor standard to which this strategy is aligned. It calls for an *analysis* of how individuals, events, or ideas *develop* in the text. This standard seems to imply that individuals, events, or ideas have a life of their own in the text. However, make no mistake, unless an author takes a pen in hand or puts fingers to a keyboard, text does not magically appear. Behind the development of individuals, events, or ideas on the printed page is an author.

The author chooses *what* to write about. The author chooses *how* to develop or write about an individual, event, or idea by providing descriptions, using details, giving examples, making comparisons, providing definitions, sharing anecdotes, asking rhetorical questions, or using illustrations. Finally, the author chooses one or more purposes to be achieved by the printed text—the *why* of the text. Students will be unable to master What-How-Why unless they can get into the minds of the authors who have written the texts they read. Remember that the reader's ultimate goal in achieving this standard is to analyze text in order to determine how and why the author developed an individual, event, or idea over the course of a text.

Identify the "What"

The first step of the What-How-Why strategy asks you and your students to figure out the "what" of the text you are reading, extracting meaning as quickly as you can. We recommend that you and your students read the text closely to identify the "what." Is the text about individuals, events, or ideas? People, events, and simple ideas or concepts are easier to identify. But the task grows a bit more challenging when readers must identify a big idea like democracy or global warming, or a complicated process like mitosis or photosynthesis.

Identify the "How"

Once you (and your students) have determined the "what" of your selected text, you must then select one of several possibilities to answer the "how" question. There are multiple ways in which authors might choose to present the ideas and information they want to share with their readers: details, descriptions, comparisons, examples, explanations, causes, illustrations, anecdotes, and so forth. In Strategies 14 and 15 in the upcoming Craft and Structure section, we will dig more deeply into the ways authors organize and present their ideas and information and formally label them as text structures. For the time being, however, you will rely on the What-How-Why prompts to help your students become more skilled at analyzing text.

Identify the "Why"

The "why" step of this strategy relates to the author's purpose in writing the text. The challenge is to understand texts in which authors use several different ways to share ideas and information because they have multiple purposes underlying their writing.

Understanding How the Strategy Works

There are two resources to help you understand how What-How-Why (Individuals) works. The first, figure 9.1, is a sample text (Flesch-Kincaid grade level 10.6) in which the "what" is an individual, who also happens to be one of the authors of the text. The second resource, figure 9.2 (page 116), is a sample organizer that analyzes the text in figure 9.1. Walking through the text with the help of this organizer will prepare you for showing your students how to employ Strategy 9.

FIGURE 9.1: Sample Text for What-How-Why (Individuals)

Excerpt From *Chickahominy Indians-Eastern Division: An Ethnohistory*
Chunk 1
I am a member of the Chickahominy Indians-Eastern Division (CIED). My ancestors hunted, fished, and lived in the tidewater area of Virginia long before the English arrived in 1607. And that was where I was born and had my beginnings. When I was seventeen years old, however, my family moved to New York City. Several family members had already settled there, and although Manhattan was a drastic change from rural Virginia, we quickly became New Yorkers—learning to navigate the public transportation system instead of country roads and living amidst multistory apartment buildings instead of tall pines.
Chunk 2
To that point in my life, there had been little conversation in our home about "being Indian." The social climate in Virginia during the first half of the 20th century was not sympathetic to our people, and we learned to work hard, say little, and blend in.
I do not remember any chapters in our history books about Virginia Indians, and frankly, my background knowledge about the tribe was sketchy.
Chunk 3
After graduating from Wheaton College in Illinois, I settled in the Chicago area. My career was in business, finance, and real estate sales and management.
In later years, whenever one of my grandchildren was assigned a report about Indians and called to get my opinion, I had a stock answer: "When the English settlers landed in Jamestown in 1607, my forefathers were there." One of my granddaughters was quite baffled by this statement. She later told her mother, "Grandpa says he had four fathers."

Source: Reprinted by permission of Adkins & Adkins, 2006. From the Preface of Chickahominy Indians-Eastern Division: An Ethnohistory. *Xlibris Press.*

FIGURE 9.2: Sample Organizer for What-How-Why (Individuals)

Text title: Excerpt from preface of *Chickahominy Indians-Eastern Division: An Ethnohistory* **Name:**	

What individual(s) develop and interact: A member of the Chickahominy Indian tribe

Column A How the individuals develop and interact	Column B Why the individuals develop and interact
Authors develop individuals by: • Providing descriptions • Using details • Giving examples • Making comparisons • Providing definitions • Sharing anecdotes • Asking rhetorical questions • Using illustrations	Authors develop individuals in order to: • Show us "why" • Provide a sense of or about something • Show outcomes or results • Explain their decisions or actions • Lead us to draw conclusions • Encourage us to interpret situations or events • Show us the importance of • Help us recognize evidence for • Help make the case for or about

Directions: Use the information from column A and column B to select possible responses to the prompts for each chunk.

Chunk 1

How the individuals develop and interact:

The author uses details, descriptions, and comparisons.

Why the individuals develop and interact:

The author wants to give a sense of his ancestry and help us understand the drastic change that occurred in his life when he moved from rural Virginia to New York.

Chunk 2

How the individuals develop and interact:

The author uses details, examples, explanations, and causes.

Why the individuals develop and interact:

The author wants to give a sense of how he learned to "work hard, say little, and blend in" and to help us understand why he didn't have much background knowledge about the tribe.

Chunk 3

How the individuals develop and interact:

The author uses details, illustrations, and anecdotes.

Why the individuals develop and interact:

The author wants to help us understand why his stock answer is confusing to his granddaughter and really insufficient.

What-How-Why+
+Prompt: Write a brief constructed response that analyzes the text and shows your understanding about how and why individuals develop and interact over the course of the text. Embed textual evidence to strengthen your response.
Constructed Response Planning Area
Use the information you have analyzed and written about on the organizer to complete the sentence stem.
Sentence Stem: The author develops the individuals in the text primarily by using . . . in order to . . .
Write your completed stem: The author develops the individual in the text primarily by using details in order to explain why he knows so little about the tribe.
Constructed Response
The author develops the individual in the text (himself) primarily with details about the lessons he learned during his childhood in Virginia—to "work hard, say little, and blend in." The author realizes that because of the "social climate in Virginia," he has a "sketchy" background about the tribe and only "stock answers" for his grandchildren whenever they ask his opinion about Indians.

Items to Prepare

There are three reproducible figures that support your instruction of What-How-Why (Individuals). The first, figure 9.3, provides a mini-lesson for students in how to embed textual evidence in their written responses. This skill will be utilized in the +feature of the lesson plan in this strategy as well as in Strategies 10 and 11.

FIGURE 9.3: How to Embed Textual Evidence

One of the skills you need to master as you analyze and write about text is how to select and use quotations from the text to cite as evidence. This kind of evidence is called textual evidence.
Here is an example of a student-generated sentence. It makes a statement about the text without providing any evidence to support the statement.
• The author develops the text primarily with details about the lessons he learned during his childhood in Virginia.
This second sentence uses embedded quotations that provide evidence.
• The author develops the text primarily with details about lessons he learned to "work hard, say little, and blend in," during his childhood in Virginia to explain why he has a "sketchy" background about his tribe and only "stock answers" for his grandchildren whenever they ask his opinion about Indians.
The words and phrases with quotation marks around them in the second example are called embedded quotations. These words and phrases are directly copied from the original text. You can copy selected words and phrases from an author's work if you put quotation marks around them. These embedded quotations are called evidence because they illustrate or prove a statement you make about the author's writing.

continued →

Blending words and phrases from someone else's text into your own writing requires some clever sentence writing. Sometimes you will need to write and rewrite your sentence to make it flow.

Here are the steps to writing a complete sentence with embedded textual evidence:

1.	Pick out some words and phrases that illustrate or provide evidence of the point you are trying to make in your statement. You might be trying to support a conclusion you have drawn from the text or evaluate an argument and specific claims the author has made in the text. Write them down in your own words and phrases so you can study and reread them.
2.	Now, think about and jot down some possible ways you might write a sentence about the central idea of the text, a conclusion you have drawn about what the text means, or how you want to evaluate an argument or claims the author has made. These ideas are the beginning of the rough draft of your sentence.
3.	Now experiment with placing the words and phrases you selected from the text in step 1 into the ideas you want to have in the sentence you wrote down in step 2. Choose the order so that the words flow smoothly. Sometimes the only way to determine if the sentence "feels" right is to read it aloud to see how it sounds.

Visit **go.solution-tree.com/commoncore** to download and print this figure.

Figure 9.4 is a reproducible handout of the student-friendly definitions for this strategy. These definitions are specific to analyzing text in which an individual or a group of individuals who share common characteristics are the "what" of the What–How–Why strategy.

FIGURE 9.4: Student Friendly Definitions for What-How-Why (Individuals)

Individual(s): A single person or a group of people with similar characteristics

Analysis: A close, careful, and thoughtful reading of the text to figure out how the author develops (writes about) an individual or group of similar individuals

Develop: The way an author reveals more and more information about an individual(s) throughout the text in order to help the reader understand that individual more completely

Textual evidence: Phrases or sentences in the text that prove a statement or conclusion

Embed: Put quotation marks around words or phrases from the text that you are inserting into your own writing

What: The topic or content of the text

How: In what way

Why: The reason or purpose for something

Figure 9.5 is the reproducible organizer for What–How–Why (Individuals). This organizer serves two purposes: (1) you will use it to record your thinking in anticipation of modeling the strategy for your students, and (2) your students will use it as they work with you to learn how to execute the strategy on their own.

FIGURE 9.5: Reproducible Organizer for What-How-Why (Individuals)

Text title:
Name:

What individual(s) develop and interact:

Column A How the individuals develop and interact	Column B Why the individuals develop and interact
Authors develop individuals by: • Providing descriptions • Using details • Giving examples • Making comparisons • Providing definitions • Sharing anecdotes • Asking rhetorical questions • Using illustrations	Authors develop individuals in order to: • Show us "why" • Provide a sense of or about something • Show outcomes or results • Explain their decisions or actions • Lead us to draw conclusions • Encourage us to interpret situations or events • Show us the importance of • Help us recognize evidence for • Help make the case for or about

Directions: Use the information from column A and column B to select possible responses to the prompts for each chunk.

Chunk 1

How the individuals develop and interact:

Why the individuals develop and interact:

Chunk 2

How the individuals develop and interact:

Why the individuals develop and interact:

Chunk 3

How the individuals develop and interact:

Why the individuals develop and interact:

What-How-Why+

+Prompt: Write a brief constructed response that analyzes the text and shows your understanding about how and why individuals develop and interact over the course of the text. Embed textual evidence to strengthen your response.

continued →

Constructed Response Planning Area
Use the information you have analyzed and written about on the organizer to complete the sentence stem.
Sentence Stem: The author develops individuals in the text primarily by using . . . in order to . . . **Write your completed stem:**
Constructed Response

Visit **go.solution-tree.com/commoncore** to download and print this figure.

Lesson Plan

The lesson plan for showing your students how to execute the What–How–Why strategy in text where individuals (a person or a particular group of individuals that share common characteristics) are the "what" of the text is found in figure 9.6. As in earlier strategies, the +feature of the lesson demands a more rigorous work product from your students. If your students have not had prior experiences with citing textual evidence, you may wish to teach a mini–lesson about how to embed textual evidence before you begin the actual lesson (see figure 9.3).

FIGURE 9.6: Lesson Plan for What-How-Why (Individuals)

Lesson Step	Explanatory Notes for the Teacher
1. Teacher prepares and assembles the necessary materials.	1a. Choose content-related and standards-aligned text for teacher modeling and student reading (note that your chosen text must feature an individual), and then: • Chunk the text into three parts as shown in the sample text (figure 9.1, page 115). • Complete the reproducible organizer (figure 9.5, page 119) as a key for modeling with your text in preparation for teaching the lesson. 1b. Prepare photocopies for students of your selected text, a mini-lesson for teaching students how to embed textual evidence (figure 9.3, page 117), the student-friendly definitions (figure 9.4, page 118), and the What-How-Why reproducible organizer for individuals (figure 9.5).

1.	Teacher prepares and assembles the necessary materials. *(continued)*	1c.	As appropriate, assemble technology to use in modeling the strategy for students (for example, document camera, PPT slides, SMART Board, overhead transparencies, or an enlarged poster version)
2.	Teacher identifies the content standard from state or district standards for students.		Display the content-specific standard you want students to understand and retain as a result of their reading, thinking, and writing. Discuss the standard with the students.
3.	Teacher shares an advance organizer, reviews the student-friendly definitions, and distributes teacher-prepared materials.		Share the following advance organizer or one of your own choosing: Authors write about individuals for many reasons. Perhaps they are respected, memorable, or influential. Maybe they are well loved, like Mother Theresa, or loathed, like Hitler. Or, an author may write about individuals at a time in their lives when they are becoming self-aware or facing a particular challenge about which readers might be interested. Authors may even write about themselves! Our challenge as a reader is first to understand what the text is about and then to discover how and why the individuals are developed and interact over the course of the text. This strategy will provide practice in tackling these challenges.
4.	Teacher models and provides rehearsal opportunities, gradually releasing responsibility to students for doing more of their own thinking and writing.		**Teacher models: Chunk 1** Ask students to read the first text chunk silently. You will then read it aloud, stopping as soon as you can identify the individuals the author has chosen to write about. Record the answer on the "What individuals develop and interact" row of the organizer (figure 9.5, page 119). Ask students to look at column A on the organizer as you discuss the items on the list and explain how this list will serve as a reference and resource for how ideas are developed— what you will now model identifying. Armed with these examples, start reading aloud from the beginning of the chunk again, this time to identify examples in the text to answer how the author is developing the individual(s). Record the answers on the organizer and continue to think aloud as you process and record answers for the rest of this chunk. Next, tell students it is time to analyze why the author is developing these individuals—what is the author's purpose? Ask students to refer to column B on the organizer and explain the items from the list. Armed with this information, start reading the chunk aloud again from the beginning and think aloud as you process and write reasons that relate to the author's purpose on the organizer. **Students work with teacher: Chunk 2** After students read the second chunk silently and you read it aloud to them, tell students you want them to see if they can identify and underline examples in the text related to how the author is developing individuals (column A). Call on students to share their ideas. Think aloud, process, and record accurate examples on the organizer.

continued →

Lesson Step	Explanatory Notes for the Teacher
4. Teacher models and provides rehearsal opportunities, gradually releasing responsibility to students for doing more of their own thinking and writing. *(continued)*	Next, ask students to focus on answering the "why?" question. Give them time to underline sections of the text that might relate to or be important clues regarding the author's purpose or why the author is developing these individuals (column B). Call on students to share their answers. Facilitate a conversation as they discuss and defend their answers. Capture accurate student answers on the organizer. **Students work with peers: Chunk 3** After students read the third chunk silently and you read it aloud to them, tell students you want them to work independently to identify how and why the author is developing individuals in this chunk of text. Have students work interdependently with a peer to agree on their answers for "how?" in this chunk. Next, have partners discuss, agree on, and record possible answers for the "why?" question.
5. Teacher formatively assesses student work.	Call on partners to display their answers to "how?" and "why?" for chunk 3. Facilitate a conversation as students discuss the merits of the work that is displayed. Record accurate models on the organizer. Formatively assess as many students as possible from the work that is displayed and the discussion. NOTE: At this point, you have two options: (1) conclude this lesson by going directly to steps 6 and 7, temporarily skipping the +feature (schedule the +feature for a later class period using the same text and organizers students have completed up to this point), or (2) extend this lesson by incorporating the +feature followed by steps 6 and 7.

What-How-Why (Individuals)+

Teacher models

Ask students to follow along as you read the +prompt aloud (figure 9.5, page 119). Tell students that in order to provide a well-written response to the prompt, they will need to embed words and phrases (evidence) from the text into their answers. Use figure 9.3 (page 117) as a guide for showing them how to effectively embed textual evidence into their writing. Next, tell students they will need to go to the planning area on their organizers where they will work to complete the sentence stem.

Students work with teacher

Tell students that the stem requires them to do some synthesizing and narrowing of information from the text. Ask students to think about what criteria they can use to narrow their choices in order to answer the stem. Write accurate examples on the board. Working independently, ask students to apply the criteria to narrow their "how" and "why" choices and be prepared to defend them.

Students work with peers

Next, as students work interdependently with a peer, ask them to reach consensus on their answers and complete the sentence stem that will guide them as they write the constructed response. Finally, ask students to move from the simple completion of the sentence stem to writing a more developed and elaborate response to the +prompt—one that will include embedded textual evidence. Give partners work time. As students work, circulate to answer questions and give feedback.

	Teacher formatively assesses students	
	Call on several pairs of students to display their answers to the prompt. Ask students to compare displayed answers and facilitate a discussion about the merits of each. Students can either identify one answer as exemplary or can write an entirely new exemplary answer as a class with your guidance.	
6.	Teacher returns to the content standard to identify progress in understanding and retaining new content.	In order to identify student progress with the new content, ask students to write an exit ticket in response to this stem: In what ways did the reading, thinking, and writing you did today help you understand the content standard? Explain.
7.	Closure	Ask students to reflect on their current level of understanding of the content standard(s) and the literacy skill(s) they worked with today by using "fist to five" hand signals to the following questions as you display them, read them aloud, and ask for student responses: On a scale of fist to five, where making a fist means not at all and holding up all five fingers means so completely that you could be the teacher, rate your understanding of the following content standard: _____ On a scale of fist to five, where making a fist means not at all and holding up all five fingers means so completely that you could be the teacher, rate your level of understanding of the following CCSS literacy skill: _____

Visit **go.solution-tree.com/commoncore** to download and print this figure.

What-How-Why (Events)

The Gist of What-How-Why (Events)

Students read a piece of content-related text about a recurring, current, or historical event and decide how and why the ideas in that text are primarily developed. In the +feature of the lesson, students are challenged to write a constructed response that analyzes the development.

CCR Anchor Standard 3 for Reading: *Analyze how and why* individuals, events, or ideas *develop and interact over the course of the text.*

In Strategy 9, you worked with your students to show them how to analyze the development of individuals in informational text. Here in Strategy 10 our focus turns to how authors write about events. An analysis of how events develop over the course of a text would likely take place during the reading of a history text showing how a conflict, war, or a period in history, such as the Great Depression or civil rights movement, unfolded over time. Texts describing more short-term or ongoing personal events, are also amenable to this type of analysis.

Background Knowledge

If you have used Strategy 9, you are familiar with the background knowledge discussion found on pages 114–115. If not, you may wish to take a few moments to read that short section to prepare you for modeling this strategy and supporting students as they write their own analyses of the text you select for them to read.

Understanding How the Strategy Works

Figure 10.1 contains the sample text (Flesch–Kincaid grade level 7.7) for this strategy. It describes a recurring event, the gathering of students and teachers in a school courtyard before the first bell. This short text is packed with details, descriptions, and comparisons.

FIGURE 10.1: Sample Text for What-How-Why (Events)

"In the Courtyard"
Chunk 1
The first buses begin dropping off students in the morning at about 6:30 a.m. By 7:00 a.m., all of the buses have dumped their weary occupants into the bus drive. Students arrive half asleep, carrying books and backpacks. Some are listening to music, with ear buds in their ears. Others are talking to friends on their cell phones. But everyone is headed toward the courtyard, which is in the center of the school.
Chunk 2
Once most students have gone to their lockers, they begin to form into groups in the courtyard. Some students sit at the picnic tables that are permanently bolted in place to eat their breakfast. You can usually find the same people eating at the same tables day after day. The boys' soccer team and their girlfriends dominate two tables. The cheerleaders sit at another table. Students wearing gang colors have laid claim to another table. On the small, grassy hill at the courtyard's north end, skateboarders, along with sprinklings of students who have spiked hair, rule. In front of this small hill, kids are playing a form of hacky sack, but they usually end up turning the game into dodge ball. On the various benches placed throughout the courtyard, groups of friends sit in clumps of threes and fours, talking, laughing, sharing secrets, and gossiping. Not all students are with someone—some are standing alone along one of the walls, usually listening to something on their MP3 players, looking bored or completely lost in the music.
Chunk 3
Teachers and administrators patrol the courtyard, stopping now and then to talk to students and constantly reminding those who get too loud to settle down. When the first bell rings for first-period class, the students are slow to react and then begin to move reluctantly to their classrooms. By the third and final bell, all that remains in the courtyard are the wrappers from some students' snacks and the echo of administrators and hall monitors calling out to a few straggling students who, although they know they have nowhere else to go, still do not want to go to class.

Source: McEwan, Burnett, & Lowery, 2008.

Visit **go.solution-tree.com/commoncore** to download and print this figure.

Figure 10.2 is a sample organizer demonstrating how this text was analyzed to show how this event developed over just a short period of time.

FIGURE 10.2: Sample Organizer for What-How-Why (Events)

Text title: "In the Courtyard" Name:
What event(s) develop and interact: Students arriving at school and gathering in the courtyard

Column A **How the events develop and interact**	Column B **Why the events develop and interact**
Authors develop ideas by: • Providing descriptions • Using details • Giving examples • Making comparisons • Providing definitions • Sharing anecdotes • Asking rhetorical questions • Using illustrations • Providing a sequence or order	Authors develop ideas in order to: • Show us "why" • Provide a sense of or about something • Show outcomes or results • Explain their decisions or actions • Lead us to draw conclusions or make inferences • Encourage us to interpret situations or events • Show us the importance of • Help us recognize evidence for • Help make the case for or about • Point out the importance of • Help us visualize

Use the information from column A and column B to select possible responses to the prompts for each chunk.

Chunk 1

How the events develop and interact:

The author uses details and descriptions, and refers to a sequence of events.

Why the events develop and interact:

The author wants us to visualize the image of sleepy students headed toward the courtyard.

Chunk 2

How the events develop and interact:

The author uses descriptions, comparisons, and details.

Why the events develop and interact:

The author wants us to visualize the self-segregated groups around the courtyard and make note of the details that imply the courtyard is not safe.

Chunk 3

How the events develop and interact:

The author uses details and descriptions, and refers to a sequence of events.

Why the events develop and interact:

The author wants us to notice the interaction among the teachers, administrators, and students; note the students' reluctance to go to class; wonder about why students leave trash behind; and wonder about why students do not want to go to class.

What-How-Why+

+Prompt: Write a brief constructed response that analyzes the text and shows your understanding of how and why events develop and interact over the course of the text. Embed textual evidence to strengthen your response.

continued →

Constructed Response Planning Area
Use the information you have analyzed and written about on the organizer to complete the sentence stem.
Sentence Stem: The author develops the events in the text primarily by using . . . in order to . . .
Write your completed stem: The author develops the events in the text primarily with details in order to help us make the inference that the courtyard may not be safe.
Constructed Response In what appears to be a description of the mundane daily event of students arriving at school, the author uses subtle details (picnic tables that are "permanently bolted in place" and teachers and administrators who "patrol the courtyard") along with the descriptions of the various cliques of segregated students to provide the reader with enough evidence to infer that the courtyard may not be safe.

Items to Prepare

There are three reproducible figures that support this strategy. The first figure was introduced in Strategy 9: figure 9.3 (page 117), How to Embed Textual Evidence. The second reproducible, figure 10.3, contains a set of student-friendly definitions that specifically relate to this strategy as well as some of repeated definitions from the student-friendly definitions from Strategy 9.

FIGURE 10.3: Student-Friendly Definitions

Event: A single event in time, a recurring event in time, or a historical event that extends over years or in some cases decades
Analysis: A close, careful, and thoughtful reading of the text to figure out how the author develops (writes about) an event
Develop: The way an author tells more and more about an event or period in history throughout the text in order to help the reader understand the event more clearly
Textual evidence: Phrases or sentences in the text that prove a statement or conclusion
Embed: Put quotation marks around words or phrases from the text that you are inserting into your own writing
What: The topic or content of the text
How: In what way
Why: The reason or purpose for something

Visit **go.solution-tree.com/commoncore** to download and print this figure.

The third reproducible, figure 10.4, is an organizer on which to record the analysis of text dealing with events. You can use it to record your thinking in preparation for modeling the strategy for your students. They, in turn, will use figure 10.4 for recording their thinking as they work with you through the strategy.

FIGURE 10.4: Reproducible Organizer for What-How-Why (Events)

Text title: Name:	
What event(s) develop and interact:	
Column A **How the events develop and interact**	**Column B** **Why the events develop and interact**
Authors develop events by: • Providing descriptions • Using details • Giving examples • Making comparisons • Providing definitions • Sharing anecdotes • Asking rhetorical questions • Using illustrations • Providing a sequence or order	Authors develop events order to: • Show us "why" • Provide a sense of or about something • Show outcomes or results • Explain their decisions or actions • Lead us to draw conclusions or make inferences • Encourage us to interpret situations or events • Show us the importance of • Help us recognize evidence for • Help make the case for or about • Point out the importance of • Help us visualize

Use the information from column A and column B to select possible responses to the prompts for each chunk.

Chunk 1

How the events develop and interact:

Why the events develop and interact:

Chunk 2

How the events develop and interact:

Why the events develop and interact:

Chunk 3

How the events develop and interact:

Why the events develop and interact:

What-How-Why+
+Prompt: Write a brief constructed response that analyzes the text and shows your understanding about how and why events develop and interact over the course of the text. Embed textual evidence to strengthen your response.

continued →

Constructed Response Planning Area
Use the information you have analyzed and written about on the organizer to complete the sentence stem.
Sentence Stem: The author develops the events in the text primarily by using . . . in order to . . .   **Write your completed stem:**
Constructed Response

Visit **go.solution-tree.com/commoncore** to download and print this figure.

Lesson Plan

The lesson plan for helping your students ease into text analysis when the topic of the text is an event—either a recurring event such as the one found in the text sample, a sustained event such as a war or conflict, or a one-time event with a long-lasting impact such as 9/11—is found in figure 10.5. Similarly to Strategy 9, the +feature of this lesson contains an opportunity for students to respond to a prompt by effectively embedding textual evidence into a single sentence.

FIGURE 10.5: Lesson Plan for What-How-Why (Events)

Lesson Step	Explanatory Notes for the Teacher
1. Teacher prepares and assembles the necessary materials.	1a. Choose content-related and standards-aligned text for teacher modeling and student reading (Note that your chosen text must feature an event), then: • Chunk the text into three parts as show in in the sample text (figure 10.1, page 126). • Complete the reproducible organizer (figure 10.4, page 129) as a key for modeling with your text in preparation for teaching the lesson. 1b. Prepare photocopies for students of your selected text, a mini-lesson for teaching students how to embed textual evidence (figure 9.3, page 117), the student-friendly definitions (figure 10.3, page 128), and the What-How-Why reproducible organizer for events (figure 10.4). 1c. As appropriate, assemble technology to use in modeling the strategy for students (for example, document camera, PPT slides, SMART Board, overhead transparencies, or an enlarged poster version).

2.	Teacher identifies the content standard from state or district standards for students.	Display the content-specific standard you want students to understand and retain as a result of their reading, thinking, and writing. Discuss the standard with the students.
3.	Teacher shares an advance organizer, reviews the student-friendly definitions, and distributes teacher-prepared materials.	Share the following advance organizer or one of your own choosing: Authors write about events for many reasons. They may be explaining the chronology of the event; they may be showcasing the importance of the event; or they may be discussing the event in order to draw some conclusions about it. Our challenge as a reader is first to understand what the text is about and then to discover how and why the events are developed and interact over the course of the text. This strategy will provide practice in tackling these challenges.
4.	Teacher models and provides rehearsal opportunities, gradually releasing responsibility to students for doing more of their own thinking and writing.	**Teacher models: Chunk 1** Ask students to read the first text chunk silently. You will then read it aloud, stopping as soon as you can identify the event(s) the author has chosen to write about. Record the answer on the "What event(s) develop and interact" row of the organizer (figure 10.4, page 129). Ask students to look at column A on the organizer as you discuss the items on the list and explain how this list will serve as a reference and resource for how ideas are developed—what you will now model identifying. Armed with these examples, start reading aloud from the beginning of the chunk again, this time to identify examples in the text to answer "how" the author is developing the event(s). Record the answers on the organizer and continue to think aloud as you process and record answers for the rest of this chunk. Next, tell students it is time to analyze why the author is developing these events—what is the author's purpose? Ask students to refer to column B on the organizer and explain the items from the list. Armed with this information, start reading the chunk aloud again from the beginning and think aloud as you process and write reasons that relate to the author's purpose on the organizer. **Students work with teacher: Chunk 2** After students read the second chunk silently and you read it aloud to them, tell students you want them to see if they can identify and underline examples in the text related to how the author is developing events (column A). Call on students to share their ideas. Think aloud, process, and record accurate examples on the organizer. Next, ask students to focus on answering the "why?" question. Give them time to underline sections of the text that might relate to or be important clues regarding the author's purpose or why the author is developing these events (column B). Call on students to share their answers. Facilitate a conversation as they discuss and defend their answers. Capture accurate student answers on the organizer.

continued →

Lesson Step	Explanatory Notes for the Teacher
4. Teacher models and provides rehearsal opportunities, gradually releasing responsibility to students for doing more of their own thinking and writing. *(continued)*	**Students work with peers: Chunk 3** After students read the third chunk silently and you read it aloud to them, tell students you want them to work independently to identify how and why the author is developing events in this chunk of text. Have students work interdependently with a peer to agree on their answers for "how?" in this chunk. Next, have partners discuss, agree on, and record possible answers for the "why?" question.
5. Teacher formatively assesses student work.	Call on partners to display their answers to "how?" and "why?" for chunk 3. Facilitate a conversation as students discuss the merits of the work that is displayed. Record accurate models on the organizer. Formatively assess as many students as possible from the work that is displayed and discussed. NOTE: At this point, you have two options: (1) conclude this lesson by going directly to steps 6 and 7, temporarily skipping the +feature (schedule the +feature for a later class period using the same text and organizers students have completed up to this point), or (2) extend this lesson by incorporating the +feature followed by steps 6 and 7.

What-How-Why (Events)+

Teacher models

Ask students to follow along as you read the +prompt (figure 10.4, page 129) aloud. Tell students that in order to provide a well-written response to the prompt, they will need to embed words and phrases (evidence) from the text into their answers. Use figure 9.3, page 117, as a guide for showing them how to effectively embed textual evidence into their writing. Next, tell students they will need to go to the planning area on their organizers where they will work to complete the sentence stem.

Students work with teacher

Tell students that the stem requires them to do some synthesizing and narrowing of information from the text. Ask students to think about what criteria they can use to narrow their choices in order to answer the stem. Write accurate examples on the board. Working independently, ask students to apply the criteria to narrow their "how" and "why" choices and be prepared to defend them.

Students work with peers

Next, as students work interdependently with a peer, ask them to reach consensus on their answers and complete the sentence stem that will guide them as they write the constructed response. Finally, ask students to move from the simple completion of the sentence stem to writing a more developed and elaborate response to the +prompt—one that will include embedded textual evidence. Give partners work time. As students work, circulate to answer questions and give feedback.

Teacher formatively assesses students

Call on several pairs of students to display their answers to the prompt. Ask students to compare displayed answers and facilitate a discussion about the merits of each. Students can either identify one answer as exemplary or can write an entirely new exemplary answer as a class with your guidance.

6.	Teacher returns to the content standard to identify progress in understanding and retaining new content.	In order to identify student progress with the new content, ask students to write an exit ticket in response to this stem: In what ways did the reading, thinking, and writing you did today help you understand the content standard? Explain.
7.	Closure	Ask students to reflect on their current level of understanding of the content standard(s) and the literacy skill(s) they worked with today by using "fist to five" hand signals to the following questions as you display them, read them aloud, and ask for student responses: On a scale of fist to five, where making a fist means not at all and holding up all five fingers means so completely that you could be the teacher, rate your understanding of the following content standard: _____ On a scale of fist to five, where making a fist means not at all and holding up all five fingers means so completely that you could be the teacher, rate your level of understanding of the following CCSS literacy skill: _____

Visit **go.solution-tree.com/commoncore** to download and print this figure.

What-How-Why (Ideas)

The Gist of What-How-Why (Ideas)

Students read a piece of content-related text about ideas (concepts or themes) and decide how and why the ideas in that text are primarily developed. In the +feature of the lesson, students are challenged to write a constructed response that analyzes the development.

CCR Anchor Standard 3 for Reading: *Analyze how and why* individuals, events, or *ideas develop and interact over the course of the text.*

In Strategy 9, you worked with students to analyze how authors develop (write about) individuals over the course of a text. This type of analysis applies primarily during the reading of biographies, memoirs (autobiographies), journals, speeches, and historical accounts. Then in Strategy 10, we explored how historians or journalists trace the development of events over the course of a text. Now, in Strategy 11 our focus turns to how authors develop ideas, concepts, or themes within their writing. Ideas are often more difficult to identify in a given text unless the author clearly lays out definitions and descriptions to set the stage.

Background Knowledge

If you have used Strategy 9, you are familiar with the background knowledge discussion found on pages 114–115. If not, you may wish to take a few moments to read that short section to prepare you for modeling this strategy and supporting students as they write their own analyses of a text.

Understanding How the Strategy Works

Figure 11.1 is a sample text (Flesch–Kincaid grade level 11.0) in which the "what" that is developed is an overall theme—the ironies of war. The author of the text traces this theme through the major conflicts in which American men and women have given their lives on battlefields.

FIGURE 11.1: Sample Text for What-How-Why (Ideas)

"Remembering the Origins of Veterans Day"
Chunk 1
How many Americans know why we observe what we now call Veterans Day on November 11th? How many know what this national holiday originally commemorated? How many read the presidential proclamations issued yearly to guide our remembrance?
World War II veteran Paul Fussell wrote in his award-winning 1975 study of the human significance of World War I, The Great War and Modern Memory, "Every war is ironic because every war is worse than expected." The supreme irony is how easy it is for those of us who are not veterans or do not know veterans to hold onto unrealistic expectations about war.
On Oct. 8, 1954, President Dwight D. Eisenhower signed Proclamation 3071. It informs us that on June 4, 1926, Congress passed a resolution that Americans should observe the anniversary of the end of World War I, Nov. 11, 1918, with appropriate ceremonies. In 1938, Congress made Nov. 11 a legal holiday called Armistice Day. Eisenhower changed Armistice Day into Veterans Day because of "two other great military conflicts in the intervening years," World War II and the Korean War. Eisenhower declared these wars necessary "to preserve our heritage of freedom." He called upon us as American citizens "to reconsecrate ourselves to the task of promoting an enduring peace so that [the] efforts [of veterans] shall not have been in vain."
Chunk 2
Ironically, two years later we began promoting enduring peace with 58,178 official American military casualty deaths in the Vietnam War between June 8, 1956, and May 15, 1975. The start is ironically hard to pinpoint because there was no formal declaration of war. The last casualties occurred two weeks after the war ended with the fall of Saigon on April 30, 1975.
As our troops pull out of Iraq, there will be ironic deaths like these and like British soldier-poet Wilfred Owen's. Owen voluntarily returned to the fighting in France in July 1918 so that he could write about the realities of trench warfare. He was killed on Nov. 4, a week before the armistice. In the preface to his poems, Owen wrote, "My subject is War, and the pity of War. The Poetry is in the pity." Their realism strips away the lofty sentiments about noble sacrifices in most presidential Veterans Day proclamations. His poems and his death remind us instead how long it takes and how much it costs to stop wars once we start them.
The very word "armistice" offers a strong warning. It means "a temporary cessation of the use of weapons by mutual agreement." It reminds us that no war will end all wars.
Chunk 3
Indeed, Kurt Vonnegut, who as an American POW survived the firebombing of Dresden, Germany, grasped the irony of doing away with Armistice Day. Born Nov. 11, 1922, he recalled that, when he was a boy, "all the people of all the nations which had fought in the First World War were silent during the 11th minute of the 11th hour of Armistice Day," the moment when "millions upon millions of human beings stopped butchering one another."

Veterans told him that on the battlefield, "the sudden silence was the Voice of God." So it must have seemed.

Obscenely ironic was that, after the armistice had been generally announced at 5 a.m., generals still ordered soldiers into battle. The 11,000 casualties suffered in the war's final six hours exceeded those on D-Day. Henry Gunther, a U.S. Army private from Baltimore, was killed at 10:59 a.m.

These stories don't tell us everything about what makes war so traumatic for veterans. But they continue a long tradition of soldiers trying to tell us. At the start of this tradition, Homer and the Greek tragedians distilled the essence of what veterans have to say: Owen's pity, Fussell's irony, Vonnegut's deep feelings of senseless absurdity and Eisenhower's sincere longing for an enduring peace.

Make Veterans Day meaningful wherever you are.

Source: Thanks to Tony Palaima for permission to publish his opinion piece. Originally published in the Austin American-Statesman *on November 8, 2011.*

Figure 11.2 is a sample organizer that will lead you through the process of reading the sample text and understanding the steps of the strategy.

FIGURE 11.2: Sample Organizer for What-How-Why (Ideas)

Text title: "Remembering the Origins of Veterans Day" Name:	
What ideas develop and interact: The ironies of war	
Column A **How the ideas develop and interact**	**Column B** **Why the ideas develop and interact**
Authors develop ideas by:<ul><li>Providing descriptions</li><li>Using details</li><li>Giving examples</li><li>Making comparisons</li><li>Using statistics</li><li>Providing definitions</li><li>Sharing anecdotes</li><li>Asking rhetorical questions</li><li>Using illustrations</li><li>Sharing quotations</li></ul>	Authors develop ideas in order to:<ul><li>Show us "why"</li><li>Provide a sense of or about something</li><li>Show outcomes or results</li><li>Explain decisions or actions</li><li>Lead us to draw conclusions or make inferences</li><li>Encourage us to interpret situations or events</li><li>Show us the importance of</li><li>Help us recognize evidence for</li><li>Help make the case for or about</li><li>Make us feel something</li><li>Help us understand something</li></ul>
Use the information from column A and column B to select possible responses to the prompts for each chunk.	

continued →

Chunk 1

How the ideas develop and interact:

The author uses rhetorical questions, examples, and quotations.

Why the ideas develop and interact:

The author wants us to feel a sense of guilt if we can't answer the rhetorical questions, read examples of what people think about war, and understand the ironies of war.

Chunk 2

How the ideas develop and interact:

The author uses statistics, examples, and quotations.

Why the ideas develop and interact:

The author wants us to understand the devastation caused by war, see the irony of war, and read examples of what people think about war.

Chunk 3

How the ideas develop and interact:

The author uses examples, statistics, and quotations.

Why the ideas develop and interact:

The author wants us to read examples of what people think about war and understand the ironies of war.

What-How-Why+

+Prompt: Write a brief constructed response that analyzes the text and shows your understanding about how and why ideas develop and interact over the course of the text. Embed textual evidence to strengthen your response.

Constructed Response Planning Area

Use the information you have analyzed and written about on the organizer to complete the sentence stem.

Sentence Stem: The author develops ideas in the text primarily by using . . . in order to . . .

Write your completed stem: The author develops ideas in the text primarily with examples in order to show evidence for the ironies of war.

Constructed Response

The author develops the text primarily with examples of the ideas that individuals, like war veteran and author Kurt Vonnegut and President Dwight D. Eisenhower, convey as they wrote about war in order to show evidence for the "senseless absurdity" and many ironies of war.

Items to Prepare

There are three reproducible figures that support this strategy. The first one can be found in Strategy 9, figure 9.3 (page 117), How to Embed Textual Evidence. Your students may already have a copy of this in their notebooks. A set of student-friendly definitions that specifically relate to this strategy is found in figure 11.3.

FIGURE 11.3: Student-Friendly Definitions

Idea: An opinion or belief, a concept, or a theme

Concept: A concrete idea of what something is

Theme: An abstract idea of what something is (for example, loyalty, family)

Opinion: A judgment about something that may or may not be based on fact

Belief: An acceptance that a statement is true

Analysis: A close, careful, and thoughtful reading of the text to figure out how the author develops (writes about) an idea, concept, or theme

Develop: The way an author tells more and more about an idea, concept, or theme throughout the text in order to help the reader understand that idea, concept, or theme more clearly

Textual evidence: Phrases or sentences in the text that prove a statement or conclusion

Embed: Put quotation marks around words or phrases from the text that you are inserting into your own writing

What: The topic or content of the text

How: In what way

Why: The reason or purpose for something

Visit **go.solution-tree.com/commoncore** to download and print this figure.

The third reproducible is the organizer you will use in modeling the strategy and students will subsequently use to demonstrate their reading and thinking processes.

FIGURE 11.4: Reproducible Organizer for What-How-Why (Ideas)

Text title:
Name:

What ideas develop and interact:	
Column A **How the ideas develop and interact**	**Column B** **Why the ideas develop and interact**
Authors develop ideas by: • Providing descriptions • Using details • Giving examples • Making comparisons • Using statistics • Providing definitions	Authors develop ideas in order to: • Show us "why" • Provide a sense of or about something • Show outcomes or results • Explain their decisions or actions • Lead us to draw conclusions or make inferences

continued →

Column A How the ideas develop and interact	Column B Why the ideas develop and interact
• Sharing anecdotes • Asking rhetorical questions • Using illustrations • Sharing quotations	• Encourage us to interpret situations or events • Show us the importance of • Help us recognize evidence for • Help make the case for or about • Make us feel something • Help us understand something

Use the information from column A and column B to select possible responses to the prompts for each chunk.

Chunk 1 **How the ideas develop and interact:** **Why the ideas develop and interact:**

Chunk 2 **How the ideas develop and interact:** **Why the ideas develop and interact:**

Chunk 3 **How the ideas develop and interact:** **Why the ideas develop and interact:**

What-How-Why+
+Prompt: Write a brief constructed response that analyzes the text and shows your understanding about how and why ideas develop and interact over the course of the text. Embed textual evidence to strengthen your response.
Constructed Response Planning Area
Use the information you have analyzed and written about on the organizer to complete the sentence stem.
Sentence Stem: The author develops the text primarily by using . . . in order to . . . **Write your completed stem:**
Constructed Response

Visit **go.solution-tree.com/commoncore** to download and print this figure.

Lesson Plan

The lesson plan for helping your students ease into text analysis when the topic of the text is an idea (or a concept or theme) is found in figure 11.5. As in Strategies 9 and 10, the +feature of the lesson expects students to embed textual evidence into their response. Recall that a resource for this skill can be found in figure 9.3 on page 117.

FIGURE 11.5: Lesson Plan for What-How-Why (Ideas)

Lesson Step	Explanatory Notes for the Teacher
1. Teacher prepares and assembles the necessary materials.	1a. Choose content-related and standards-aligned text for teacher modeling and student reading (the text chosen for this strategy needs to be about an idea or a theme), then: • Chunk the text into three parts as shown in in the sample text (figure 11.1, page 136). • Complete the reproducible organizer (figure 11.4, page 139) as a key for modeling with text in preparation for teaching the lesson. • Determine if you will use the optional resource (figure 9.3, How to Embed Textual Evidence, page 117). 1b. Prepare photocopies for students of your selected text, the student-friendly definitions (figure 11.3, page 139), the reproducible organizer for ideas (figure 11.4, page 139), and figure 9.3, page 117, if students do not already have copies of this resource. 1c. As appropriate, assemble technology to use in modeling the strategy for students (for example, document camera, PPT slides, SMART Board, overhead transparencies, or an enlarged poster version).
2. Teacher identifies the content standard from state or district standards for students.	Display the content-specific standard you want students to understand and retain as a result of their reading, thinking, and writing. Discuss the standard with the students.
3. Teacher shares an advance organizer, reviews the student-friendly definitions, and distributes teacher-prepared materials.	Share the following advance organizer or one of your own choosing: Authors write about ideas, concepts, or themes for many reasons. An author may be particularly interested in or knowledgeable about certain ideas (how to improve student achievement, for example) or may be focused on ideas that are timely (how political campaigns should be funded, for example). Our challenge as a reader is first to understand what the text is about and then to discover how and why the ideas, themes, or concepts are developed and interact over the course of the text. This strategy will provide practice in tackling these challenges.

continued →

Lesson Step	Explanatory Notes for the Teacher
4. Teacher models and provides rehearsal opportunities, gradually releasing responsibility to students for doing more of their own thinking and writing.	**Teacher models: Chunk 1** Ask students to read the first text chunk silently. You will then read it aloud, stopping as soon as you can identify the idea the author has chosen to write about. Record the answer on the "What ideas develop and interact" row of the organizer (figure 11.4, page 139). Ask students to look at column A on the organizer as you discuss the items on the list and explain how this list will serve as a reference and resource for how ideas are developed—what you will now model identifying. Armed with these examples, start reading aloud from the beginning of the chunk again, this time to identify examples in the text to answer "how" the author is developing the idea. Record the answers on the organizer and continue to think aloud as you process and record answers for the rest of this chunk. Next, tell students it is time to analyze why the author is developing these ideas—what is the author's purpose? Ask students to refer to column B on the organizer, and explain the items from the list. Armed with this information, start reading the chunk aloud again from the beginning and think aloud as you process and write reasons that relate to the author's purpose on the organizer. **Students work with teacher: Chunk 2** After students read the second chunk silently and you read it aloud to them, tell students you want them to see if they can identify and underline examples in the text related to how the author is developing ideas (column A). Call on students to share their answers. Think aloud, process, and record accurate examples on the organizer. Next, ask students to focus on answering the "why?" question. Give them time to underline sections of the text that might relate to or be important clues regarding the author's purpose or why the author is developing these ideas (column B). Call on students to share their answers. Facilitate a conversation as they discuss and defend their answers. Capture accurate student answers on the organizer. **Students work with peers: Chunk 3** After students read the third chunk silently and you read it aloud to them, tell students you want them to work independently to identify how and why the author is developing ideas in this chunk of text. Have students work interdependently with a peer to agree on their answers for "how?" in this chunk. Next, have partners discuss, agree on, and record possible answers for the "why?" question.

5. Teacher formatively assesses student work.	Call on partners to display their answers to "how?" and "why?" for chunk 3. Facilitate a conversation as students discuss the merits of the work that is displayed. Record accurate models on the organizer. Formatively assess as many students as possible from the work that is displayed and discussed.
	NOTE: At this point, you have two options: (1) conclude this lesson by going directly to steps 6 and 7, temporarily skipping the +feature (schedule the +feature for a later class period using the same text and organizers students have completed up to this point), or (2) extend this lesson by incorporating the +feature followed by steps 6 and 7.

What-How-Why (Ideas)+

Teacher models

Ask students to follow along as you read the +prompt (figure 11.4, page 139) aloud. Tell students that in order to provide a well-written response to the prompt, they will need to embed words and phrases (evidence) from the text into their answers. Use figure 9.3 (page 117) as a guide for showing them how to effectively embed textual evidence into their writing. Next, tell students they will need to go to the planning area on their organizers, where they will work to complete the sentence stem.

Students work with teacher

Tell students that the stem requires them to do some synthesizing and narrowing of information from the text. Ask students to think about what criteria they can use to narrow their choices in order to answer the stem. Write accurate examples on the board. Ask students to work independently to apply the criteria to narrow their "how" and "why" choices and be prepared to defend them.

Students work with peers

Next, as students work interdependently with a peer, ask them to reach consensus on their answers and complete the sentence stem that will guide them as they write the constructed response. Finally, ask students to move from the simple completion of the sentence stem to writing a more developed and elaborate response to the +prompt—one that will include embedded textual evidence. Give partners work time. As students work, circulate to answer questions and give feedback.

Teacher formatively assesses students

Call on several pairs of students to display their answers to the prompt. Ask students to compare displayed answers and facilitate a discussion about the merits of each. Students can either identify one answer as exemplary or can write an entirely new exemplary answer as a class with your guidance.

6. Teacher returns to the content standard to identify progress in understanding and retaining new content.	In order to identify student progress with the new content, ask students to write an exit ticket in response to this stem:
	In what ways did the reading, thinking, and writing you did today help you understand the content standard? Explain.

continued →

Lesson Step	Explanatory Notes for the Teacher
7. Closure	Ask students to reflect on their current level of understanding of the content standard(s) and the literacy skill(s) they worked with today by using "fist to five" hand signals to the following questions as you display them, read them aloud, and ask for student responses:
	On a scale of fist to five, where making a fist means not at all and holding up all five fingers means so completely that you could be the teacher, rate your understanding of the following content standard: _____
	On a scale of fist to five, where making a fist means not at all and holding up all five fingers means so completely that you could be the teacher, rate your level of understanding of the following CCSS literacy skill: _____

Visit **go.solution-tree.com/commoncore** to download and print this figure.

PART II:
Overview of Craft and Structure

Academic vocabulary is the true language of power and that is particularly true for our English Language Learners and a wide variety of kids we care about most.

—COLEMAN (2011)

Part II presents a set of literacy strategies designed to help your students meet the standards found in the second section of the Common Core College and Career Readiness Anchor Standards for Reading titled *Craft and Structure*. It is one of four broad categories set forth to describe the critical skills of reading comprehension that independent and highly proficient readers use during the reading of complex informational texts.

The big idea of Craft and Structure is this: *students must go beyond merely understanding what the text is about to acquiring the skills needed to dig more deeply into the text, particularly regarding academic vocabulary.* If you have not already discovered the glossary, turn to it now. It contains over sixty words and terms that students must understand before they can give voice to their thinking processes, understand the directions their teachers are giving, and write about what they have read in a constructed response according to the directions. In too many cases, even when students do understand what the text is about, they do not understand the directions. Figure P2.1 presents an overview of the five elements of an author's style that will be explored in this section.

FIGURE P2.1: Elements of Style*

Diction: How the author chooses words to create a certain effect	
Types of Diction	**Definitions of the Types of Diction**
Formal diction (language)	Uses many polysyllabic words, contains no slang, idioms, colloquialisms, or contractions
Informal or colloquial language	Relaxed and conversational; may contain colloquial expressions that are appropriate in certain regions of the country
Academic language	Scholarly writing such as what would be found in research journals
Concrete or abstract nouns	Nouns that indicate objects, places, or people (concrete) or nouns that indicate concepts or ideas (abstract)
Denotative or connotative words	Words with literal meanings or words used in a nonliteral way
Syntax: How the author arranges the chosen words and various grammatical elements	
Types of Syntax	**Definitions of the Types of Syntax**
Active voice	Emphasize the responsibility of the person, the one doing the action, the subject of the sentence
Passive voice	Emphasize what is happening rather than who did it
Simple sentences	Contain a subject and a verb; express a complete thought
Compound sentences	Contain two independent clauses, joined by a conjunction with a comma preceding it
Complex sentences	Contain subordinate clause or clauses

*Style: The writer's characteristic manner of employing language.   *continued* →

Figurative Language: How the author uses words and phrases to compare things in unique and imaginative ways	
Types of Figurative Language	**Definitions of the Types of Figurative Language**
Analogy	A comparison to show the relationship or similarities between ideas
Simile	A directly stated comparison using the word *like* or *as*
Metaphor	An implied comparison of two things often using helping verbs such as *is*, *are*, *was*, and *were*
Personification	A kind of metaphor that gives human characteristics to lifeless objects or abstract ideas
Imagery: How the author uses words and phrases to represent persons, objects, actions, feelings, and ideas in descriptive ways by appealing to the senses	
Visual	Use of words that appeal to what one can see in the imagination
Auditory	Use of words that appeal to sounds one can hear in the imagination
Tactile	Use of words that give the reader a feeling of physically touching something
Olfactory	Use of words that produce the scent in the imagination
Sound Devices: How the author uses words to heighten auditory imagery and repetition	
Onomatopoeia	Words that imitate sounds
Alliteration	Using several words in a series with the same beginning consonant (consonance) or using several words in a series having the same vowel sound (assonance)
Repetition	The intentional use of words, phrases, sentences, grammatical patterns, or rhythmical patterns more than once

In this section, students will be challenged to go beyond figuring out what the text explicitly means to the next level: interpreting and analyzing the text. This may sound like an impossible undertaking if you have never demanded this kind of deeper reading from the majority of your students in the past. We will show you (and your students) how to do it step by step.

Quick-REACH Vocabulary Toolkit

The Gist of the Quick-REACH Vocabulary Toolkit

Students use Quick-REACH Questions to decide what vocabulary tools will be most helpful for interpreting words and phrases as they are used in the text. In the +feature of the lesson, students complete the constructed response matrix identifying the merits and possible drawbacks of the vocabulary tools they identify as being most helpful.

CCR Anchor Standard 4 for Reading: *Interpret words and phrases as they are used in text, including determining technical, connotative, and figurative meanings, and analyze how specific word choices shape meaning or tone.*

The Quick-REACH Vocabulary Toolkit provides five sets of tools for tackling the meanings of unknown vocabulary encountered in text. REACH is a mnemonic, with each letter standing for one of the following five categories:

1. **R**esources-in-print tools such as a dictionary or glossary

2. **E**lectronic tools such as a smartphone, translator, or the Internet

3. **A**ssociation-connection tools students can make between the word and world knowledge they may already have and the unknown words they encounter in text

4. **C**lues in the text (context) from which students can make inferences

5. **H**elp from an adult, an expert, a classmate, or the teacher if other tools have been tried and the meaning is still unavailable to the student

Background Knowledge

Most teachers at any grade level are prone to assume that being able to figure out word meanings independently is a skill that has been taught and mastered at a prior grade level. However, students will not generally adopt the tools suggested in this strategy unless their teachers consistently suggest, model, encourage, and motivate them to do so. Each of the following sections provides background knowledge to help you understand the tools more completely so that you can explain and model them for your students in the context of whatever text you are reading.

Resources-in-Print Tools

The resources in print enumerated in this first set of REACH tools are the typical print tools found in all school media centers and even in some classrooms. Do not assume, however, that your students have been directly taught how to access the glossary, index, and even the immediate pages of the text on which definitions and explanations can be found in boxes, notes, and other features in the text. Give your students a quick review of how to use these resources with the expectation that they will use them to actually seek out unfamiliar words and apply what they discover in the comprehension of text.

Electronic Tools

Most classrooms have at least one desktop computer with Internet access. All students can benefit from a tutorial on how to conduct a search on the Internet and, more importantly, how to prioritize and sift through the results to find precisely what one is looking for. Ask your media specialist/librarian to work with small groups of students on these important search skills.

Association-Connection Tools

Association–connection tools are based on students using the word and world knowledge they have already acquired. The first, the big word strategy, for example, walks students through the steps of figuring out how to pronounce (decode) an unknown word in order to determine if the word is part of the student's listening vocabulary. Once students are able to approximate the pronunciation of the word (either whispered or aloud), they may immediately recognize it as a word they know.

A second tool in the association-connection set of tools is to make a prediction. This is easy to model for students until they catch on to the big idea: read aloud a sentence containing the unknown word. Then read the sentence a second time and see if you can think of a word or two that you know that would make perfect sense in the context of the sentence. Likely the words you thought of to insert in the place of the unknown word will come very close to giving you enough of the word meaning to keep your comprehension on track.

The third tool is focused on morphological awareness: knowledge about *morphographs*—word parts that change the meanings of words. Morphographs include real words or root words such as *man* and *can*; nonword Latin and Greek roots, such as *aqua*, meaning "water" (Latin) and *auto*, meaning "self" (Greek); and the twenty most common prefixes and suffixes. Knowledge of these morphographs can help students read, spell, and understand a vast number of words. You may wish to begin collecting scientific root words, prefixes, and suffixes, or a set of social studies, history, and geography root words, prefixes, and suffixes in the sites noted earlier.

The final tool in the association-connection toolkit reminds students of the importance of activating their prior knowledge and experiences in order to take advantage of any word and world knowledge they may have, however remote, that might give them a way to unlock an unfamiliar word.

Clues-in-the-Text (Context) Tools

Using context clues to figure out the meanings of unknown words is a widely recommended strategy in the elementary grades. Students are encouraged to make reasonable guesses both to an unknown word's pronunciation and its meaning. Teachers often give the impression that this is a relatively easy thing to do and that the context will provide all the answers they need. This may be the case when students are reading simple predictable books or children's literature with an abundance of illustrations from which to draw meaning. However, researchers suggest that readers can seldom infer enough meaning from the clues in the context to specifically define a word and use it on their own in speaking and writing (Baumann & Kameenui, 1991; Nagy, 1988).

Our response to this challenge is to spend time with students showing them examples of clues in the text, modeling how we infer the meanings of difficult words when we don't have ready access to computers and dictionaries so they can acquire the context tools and begin to exercise them in class discussions, in cooperative group work, and in their own independent reading.

The key to inferring meanings (particularly in testing situations) lies in the close reading and rereading of text. Absent any of the more obvious clues to word meaning, readers will just have to work for the meaning. Readers are always reluctant to do one or more rereadings of a text, thinking that if they didn't get it the first time, why bother. However, rereading is one of the most powerful comprehension tools readers have. During a first reading, readers may have overloaded working memories as they encounter many unfamiliar words, complex sentence structures, and more figurative language. During the second reading, some of this confusion will dissipate and readers will feel more confident. By the third reading, readers will likely have enough information to figure out what seemed impossible at the outset.

Help From a Person

Encouraging your students to seek help from you, other professionals, and even their peers builds a sense of learning community and a willingness to seek help when other tools have failed. However, your goal is to build independent and self-managed students who don't give up in the face of challenging text and are willing to use the clues they find in the context to at least give them an idea of what the content is about.

Understanding How the Strategy Works

Once you have read the gist of the strategy and understand the categories of the mnemonic, read the sample text in figure 12.1 (Flesch-Kincaid grade level 7.8), making a mental note of the unfamiliar terms you encounter.

FIGURE 12.1: Sample Text for the Quick-REACH Vocabulary Toolkit

"Armadillos Are Armed for Survival"
Chunk 1
Kathy and I were having a pleasant picnic lunch at a state park when we heard a rustling behind us. It was a nine-banded armadillo, common in many Texas parks and often used as a symbol of the state. In fact, armadillo shells and likenesses have been sold as state souvenirs since the late 19th century. Accordingly, the armadillo has been honored as the state small mammal along with the Texas longhorn as the state large mammal and the free-tailed bat as the state flying mammal.
The strange-looking creature didn't start spreading across Texas until after the 1850s. Before then, its range was more or less limited to the Rio Grande Valley. But, wow, did it ever expand its range, which now includes Southern states from Oklahoma to Georgia.
About the size of our 2-foot house cat, the armadillo is layered with a covering of armored plates made up of horn and bone. In the middle of its back are a series of small, hinged plates or bands that allow it to bend at the waist and to arch its back. Bony plates cover the top of its head and sides of its legs, and bony rings surround the tail.
The armored critter cannot roll up into a tight ball, as myth would have it. Only the three-banded armadillo of South America can do that.
Tiny scales cover the armadillo's face from snout to ears, and its ears stand erect. The long snout capped with a soft pink nose sniffs out food like beetles and insects, and the long, sticky tongue laps them up.
But the armadillo's tiny, barely noticeable eyes allow only limited vision. That's why our picnic guest sauntered toward us despite Kathy's quick movements to photograph it.

Instead of being intimidated by us, the armadillo went about busily scooping up clods of ground or digging holes with sharp, stubby claws and then rooting through the torn-up soil with its snout to snatch up such tasty morsels as grubs, earthworms, insects, beetles and fruit.

Upended sections of soil in a neighborhood are a sign that an armadillo is in the vicinity. The critter needs the soft soils found in neighborhoods from the Rio Grande Valley to the Hill Country and the Piney Woods. But the harder, rockier soils of the Trans-Pecos and the Panhandle make armadillo presence there less common.

Chunk 2

More Information
DID YOU KNOW?
The nine-banded armadillo (Dasypus novemcinctus) is member of the Xenarthra order that includes anteaters and sloths.

Water crossings: It ingests air and becomes buoyant in order to swim across large bodies of water. Or it sinks to the bottom of a small stream, holds its breath and walks to the opposite bank.

Quirks: It has peglike teeth. It can run fast to escape a predator. It's often hit by cars due to poor eyesight. It is sensitive to cold because of the lack of fur (except for scraggly strands of hair under bony armor).

Chunk 3

Find them: They can be found in warm grasslands, warm forests with soft soil and muddy stream bottoms. They create burrows as underground dens in soft ground. In the Hill Country, they may use a limestone crevice as a burrow.

Reproduction: They breed July–August. Delayed implantation of a fertilized egg over most winter months. Identical quadruplets are born in spring.

Medical research: They are used to research the diagnosis and treatment of leprosy. They have a poor immune system due to low body temperature that makes them susceptible to a virulent strain of leprosy.

Source: Gary Clark. Copyright 2011 Houston Chronicle Publishing Company. Reprinted with permission. All rights reserved.

Now review the sample organizer in figure 12.2, which illustrates how meanings of important words from the text can be figured out by using one or more of the Quick-REACH tools.

FIGURE 12.2: Sample Organizer for the Quick-REACH Vocabulary Toolkit

Text title: "Armadillos Are Armed for Survival"
Name:
Directions: Record unfamiliar but important words from the text on the organizer in column 1. Use the Quick-REACH Questions in column 2 (see also figure 12.4, page 156) to determine which vocabulary tools are most helpful. In column 3, identify which tools you used and explain your new or evolving understanding of what the words mean or most likely mean after using the tool.

continued →

Column 1	Column 2	Column 3
Identify words that are important and require the use of a specific vocabulary tool.	**Use the Quick-REACH Questions to identify the most helpful tools.**	**Identify the tools you used and explain your new understanding of the meaning of the words from column 1.**
Chunk 1		
Range	**R**esources? **E**lectronics? **A**ssociations? **C**lues? **H**elp?	**Tools:** Clues in the text **Meaning:** Where armadillos might be found
Armored plates		**Tools:** Association-connection clues in the text **Meaning:** The horn and bone that cover the animal
Myth		**Tools:** Clues in the text **Meaning:** Something that is not true
Snout		**Tools:** Clues in the text **Meaning:** Soft pink nose
Chunk 2		
Xenarthra order	**R**esources? **E**lectronics? **A**ssociations? **C**lues? **H**elp?	**Tools:** Clues in the text; electronic tools **Meaning:** A grouping of animals
Buoyant		**Tools:** Association-connection clues in the text **Meaning:** Floats in the water
Predator		**Tools:** Association-connection clues in the text **Meaning:** A hunter
Chunk 3		
Burrows	**R**esources? **E**lectronics? **A**ssociations? **C**lues? **H**elp?	**Tools:** Electronic tools; association-connection tools **Meaning:** Places to live
Quadruplets		**Tools:** Associations-connection tools; resources in print **Meaning:** Four offspring
Leprosy		**Tools:** Help from a person; resources in print **Meaning:** A skin disease
Virulent		**Tools:** Help from a person; resources in print **Meaning:** Something that is severe

Quick-REACH Vocabulary Toolkit+		
Directions: In the constructed response matrix that follows the teacher model, identify two of the tools that you found most helpful, explain their merits, and list any possible drawbacks.		
Tool	**Merits**	**Drawbacks**
Teacher Model: Electronics—smartphone	If you have a smartphone and know how to use a search engine, it is quick and easy to type a word and do a search. Within seconds, you will be able to access a lot of definitions.	Schools usually have policies that ban the use of electronics and cell phones—even when there is an educational purpose involved. If you are able to use a smartphone when you do a search, you are still going to have to narrow down the meaning from all of the definitions you will get.
1. Context Clues	After you know what to look for, you begin to recognize the clues many authors use to help define or explain the most challenging words.	Not every challenging word is surrounded by clues. In addition, it takes a lot of time to use some clues to figure out the meanings of words.
2. Resources in Print	The author or book publisher provides a lot of resources to help you understand the more challenging words or concepts in a passage. Resources like a glossary are right there in the textbook.	It takes time to stop reading and look a word up in a dictionary or glossary. At times, without knowing anything about the word to begin with, the definition alone is not as helpful as it could be.

Items to Prepare

There are seven reproducible resources to support you and your students in the acquisition of the Quick-REACH Toolkit: (1) figure 12.3, Student-Friendly Definitions (page 156); (2) figure 12.4, Quick-REACH Questions (page 156); (3) figure 12.5, Quick-REACH Vocabulary Toolkit (page 157); (4) figure 12.6, Big Word Strategy (page 159); (5) figures 12.7a and 12.7b, Sample Set of Prefixes and Suffixes (page 160); (6) figure 12.8, Steps for Using Clues in the Context (page 161); and (7) figure 12.9, Reproducible Organizer for the Quick-REACH Vocabulary Toolkit (page 161). Each figure plays a unique role in scaffolding what is often a very challenging reading task: figuring out the meanings of words from context.

Figure 12.3 contains the student-friendly definitions students need to navigate this strategy. Each of the resources also contains multiple terms and definitions in student-friendly language.

FIGURE 12.3: Student-Friendly Definitions for the Quick-REACH Vocabulary Toolkit

> **Context:** The words and sentences around a word or phrase you don't know
>
> **Context clues:** Information you find in the context to help you make logical inferences about what a word means

Visit **go.solution-tree.com/commoncore** to download and print this figure.

Figure 12.4 lists the five Quick-REACH Questions you will routinely ask your students in order to create a habit of working for word meanings they do not know rather than shrugging their shoulders and skipping unfamiliar words. The routine use of the Quick-REACH Questions is the precursor to the skillful use of figure 12.5, the Quick-REACH Toolkit. Note that the Quick-REACH Questions are used during the completion of the organizer and referred to once again in the lesson plan.

FIGURE 12.4: The Quick-REACH Questions

Tool Numbers	Acronym	Quick-REACH Questions
1–5	R	Would the resources in print work for this word—a glossary, index, dictionary, or encyclopedia?
6–8	E	How about any of the electronic tools we have available—a computer, iPad, translator, or smartphone?
9–12	A	Will any of the association-connection tools work—a word part you might recognize?
13–19	C	Would any of the clues in the context help us figure out the meaning—examples, details, or explanations? Antonyms or synonyms? Deciding if the word or phrase is being used figuratively?
20	H	Do we need to seek help from someone we know?

Visit **go.solution-tree.com/commoncore** to download and print this figure.

Figure 12.5 is the Quick-REACH Toolkit containing twenty tools for students to use in figuring out the meanings of unknown words in text. This handout will be most useful to your students if you spend some time front-loading information from each of the toolkits before you put a copy of the entire toolkit in their hands. When students have been introduced to the categories and you have provided some mini-modeling lessons for the first three categories, photocopy this reproducible form so students can have it handy when they are closely reading text to extract meaning. You will go more in-depth with the toolkit as we tackle more challenging words in Strategy 13, Weigh the Words.

FIGURE 12.5: The Quick-REACH Toolkit

Resources-in-Print Tools		
Print tools in which you can find definitions and information about unfamiliar words		
Search Question	**The Best Tool to Use**	**Description of Tools**
Do I want to find the meaning of a technical word from a content textbook?	1. Glossary 2. Index 3. The page on which the word occurs	Glossaries and indexes are found at the back of textbooks. Definitions are often found in special boxes or in notes at the bottom of pages.
Do I want to find the meaning of a technical or academic word, or unknown word not in a content textbook?	4. Dictionary	A book that lists words in alphabetical order and their various meanings.
Do I want to find an article about a word or subject that will give me related words and background knowledge?	5. Encyclopedia	A set of alphabetized volumes with articles about important concepts, events, and individuals
Electronic Tools		
Tools with batteries, power cords, and possibly Internet connections with which you can locate definitions and information about unfamiliar words		
Do I want to find information about a word as quickly as possible? Do I want to see an image or picture?	6. Smartphone 7. Classroom computers, laptops, or iPads	Multiple versions of dictionaries, encyclopedias, and other content resources are available on the Internet
Do I want to find the meaning of an English word using my first language?	8. Electronic translator	A battery-operated tool that provides definitions in two or more languages
Association-Connection Tools		
Tools that provide connections to word and world knowledge you already have		
Do I need to figure out how to pronounce the word before I can determine its meaning?	9. Big word strategy	A set of steps to follow when you get stuck on a big word (see figure 12.6, page 159)
When you read the sentence containing the unknown word, can you replace it with a word you already know that might make sense?	10. Make a prediction	Figuring out whether you know a word that would fit the context that might give you a connection to the meaning of your unknown word
Does the word have any prefixes, suffixes, or root words that would help me figure out the word's meaning?	11. Prefixes, suffixes, and root words that every student needs to know	A set of word parts that helps you figure out the meanings of words (see figures 12.7a and 12.7b, page 160)
Can I think of any experiences I've had or knowledge I've learned from life, school, or other texts that would help me figure out the word's meaning?	12. Word and world knowledge from prior learning and experiences	Information you already know about the meanings of related words and background knowledge about the content

continued →

Clues in the Text (Context)
Tools to find clues for technical, connotative, and figurative language

Search Question	The Best Tool to Use	Description of Tools
Does the author actually define the word for you or provide an explanation?	13. A literal definition in the sentences around the word	The parts of the text that come right before or right after the unknown word in which the author gives a definition or explanation.
Does the author provide examples, details, or explanations about the topic of the text from which you might be able to infer the meaning of a word?	14. Examples, details, and explanations in the immediate context	The parts of the text that come before or right after the unknown word in which the author provides inferential clues and you have to figure out what they mean.
Does the author provide information about a word by contrasting it to something?	15. Contrast statements or antonyms of the word in the immediate context	Inferential clues that come in the form of contrast statements and antonyms.
Does the author provide information about a word by restating the meaning of the word in different language and providing a synonym?	16. Restatements or synonyms of the word in the immediate context	Inferential clues that come in the form of restatements and synonyms of the word.
Does the word appear to be a very technical term without any clues to its meaning from the author? Are you on your own without access to other tools?	17. Rereadings of the words around the term	The clues to the word's meaning involve closely reading the text to extract meaning while also thinking about the unknown word.
Could the word or phrase have a connotative or implied meaning with an emotional weight, or importance, that goes beyond the literal meaning?	18. Thinking about what the connotative meaning might be and how it impacts the content	The clues to the word's meaning involve figuring out how the connotative meaning adds an emotional weight that requires a subtle level of interpretation and goes beyond the dictionary definition; it is the difference between *house* and *home*.
Could the word or phrase be figurative language in which the author uses devices like similes and metaphors to compare ideas, events, or individuals in the text to things completely outside of the text?	19. Rereadings of the text to understand the comparison	See figure P2.1 (page 147) for help with understanding figurative language.

Help From a Person		
Tools that give you immediate access to a word meaning in the form of a knowledgeable individuals		
Search Question	**The Best Tool to Use**	**Description of Tools**
Have I encountered a major and very frustrating roadblock in determining the meaning of a word that is essential to understanding the text?	20. A person	Individuals in your environment who can help you.

Visit **go.solution-tree.com/commoncore** to download and print this figure.

Figure 12.6 is a big word strategy. This tool will be especially helpful for ELs, students with special needs, and other struggling readers. However, don't be surprised to find that many of your seemingly better students have difficulty dividing big words into syllables so they can be pronounced. It's never too late to acquire this strategy. If you believe that your students may feel this strategy is too babyish, model using it with some new big words you have encountered in your reading of professional journals or in readings for a graduate course. Or take time to divide a couple of the words from the student-friendly definitions into syllables, modeling for students how this simple step-by-step process can unlock many of the big words they have been skipping during their reading.

FIGURE 12.6: A Big Word Strategy

Step	Directions
1.	Circle the prefixes at the beginning of the word.
2.	Circle the suffixes at the end of the word.
3.	Underline the letters that represent vowel sounds in the rest of the word.
4.	Say the syllables of the word.
5.	Say the syllables fast.
6.	Figure out if there is a word you know that sounds very similar to the one you said, and then correct your pronunciation to match the word you already know.

Visit **go.solution-tree.com/commoncore** to download and print this figure.

Figures 12.7a and 12.7b (page 160) contain the most common prefixes and suffixes with examples. You may wish to begin collecting content-specific examples. For example, you could look for scientific root words, prefixes, and suffixes at www.biologyjunction.com/prefixes%20and%20suffixes.pdf.

FIGURE 12.7A: Twenty Most Common Prefixes

Prefix	Definition	Examples
anti-	against	anticlimax
de-	opposite	devalue
dis-	not, opposite of	discover
en-, em-	cause to	enact, empower
fore-	before, front of	foreshadow, forearm
in-, im-	in	income, impulse
in-, im-, il-, ir-	not	indirect, immoral, illiterate, irreverent
inter-	between, among	interrupt
mid-	middle	midfield
mis-	wrongly	misspell
non-	not	nonviolent
over-	over, too much	overeat
pre-	before	preview
re-	again	rewrite
semi-	half, partly, not fully	semifinal
sub-	under	subway
super-	above, beyond	superhuman
trans-	across	transmit
un-	not, opposite of	unusual
under-	under, too little	underestimate

Source: McEwan-Adkins, 2010.

Visit **go.solution-tree.com/commoncore** to download and print this figure.

FIGURE 12.7B: Ten Most Common Suffixes

Suffix	Definition	Examples
-able -ible	is, can be	affordable, sensible
-al, -ial	having characteristics of	universal, facial
-ed	past-tense verbs, adjectives	the dog walked, the walked dog
-en	made of	golden
-er, -or	one who, person connected with	teacher, professor
-er	more	taller
-est	the most	tallest

-ful	full of	helpful
-ic	having characteristics of	poetic
-ing	verb forms, present participles	sleeping

Source: McEwan-Adkins, 2010.

Visit **go.solution-tree.com/commoncore** to download and print this figure, including ten additional suffixes.

Figure 12.8 is a reproducible resource containing a set of steps for using clues in the text to figure out the meaning of an unknown word. This resource will be a helpful scaffold for ELs, students with special needs, and struggling readers who are not quite ready to tackle that level of difficulty.

FIGURE 12.8: Steps for Using Clues in the Context to Infer the Meaning of an Unfamiliar Word

Step	Directions
1.	Underline the unfamiliar word.
2.	Read the sentences before and after the sentence containing the unfamiliar word.
3.	Explain what you know so far.
4.	Use what you know about the text and the sentence containing the unfamiliar word to infer (predict) what the word might mean.
5.	Read the sentence again and substitute your new word for the unfamiliar word.
6.	Decide if the word you substituted makes sense in the sentence.
7.	Your word may not have the exact meaning of the unfamiliar word, but by using the clues in the context, knowing about what the word means can help you keep reading so as not to forget what you have already read.

Visit **go.solution-tree.com/commoncore** to download and print this figure.

Figure 12.9 is the reproducible organizer that you and your students will use when working with your selected content text.

FIGURE 12.9: Reproducible Organizer for the Quick-REACH Vocabulary Toolkit

| **Text title:** |
| **Name:** |
| **Directions:** Record unfamiliar but important words from the text on the organizer in column Use the Quick-REACH Questions in column 2 (see also figure 12.4, page 156) to determine which vocabulary tools are most helpful. In column 3, identify which tools you used and explain your new or evolving understanding of what the words mean or most likely mean after using the tool. |

continued →

Column 1	Column 2	Column 3
Identify words that are important and require the use of a specific vocabulary tool.	Use the Quick-REACH Questions to identify the most helpful tools.	Identify the tools you used and explain your new understanding of the meaning of the words from column 1.

Chunk 1

	Resources?	Tools: Meaning:
	Electronics?	Tools: Meaning:
	Associations?	Tools: Meaning:
	Clues?	Tools: Meaning:
	Help?	

Chunk 2

	Resources?	Tools: Meaning:
	Electronics?	Tools: Meaning:
	Associations?	Tools: Meaning:
	Clues?	Tools: Meaning:
	Help?	

Chunk 3

	Resources?	Tools: Meaning:
	Electronics?	Tools: Meaning:
	Associations?	Tools: Meaning:
	Clues?	Tools: Meaning:
	Help?	

Quick-REACH Vocabulary Toolkit+		
Directions: In the constructed response matrix that follows the teacher model, identify two of the tools that you found most helpful, explain their merits, and list any possible drawbacks.		
Tool	**Merits**	**Drawbacks**
Teacher Model:		
1.		
2.		

Visit **go.solution-tree.com/commoncore** to download and print this figure.

Lesson Plan

The lesson plan for showing your students how to become more skilled at using various tools to find the meanings of unknown words they encounter in text is found in figure 12.10.

FIGURE 12.10: Lesson Plan for Quick-REACH Vocabulary Toolkit

Lesson Step	Explanatory Notes for the Teacher
1. Teacher prepares and assembles the necessary materials.	1a. Choose content-related and standards-aligned text for teacher modeling and student reading, then: • Chunk text into three parts as shown in the sample text (figure 12.1, page 152). • Complete the reproducible organizer (figure 12.9, page 161) as a key for modeling with the text you selected in preparation for teaching the lesson. 1b. Prepare photocopies for students of your selected text, the student-friendly definitions (figure 12.3, page 156), the Quick-REACH Questions (figure 12.4, page 156), Quick-REACH Toolkit (figure 12.5, page 157), and the reproducible organizer (figure 12.9, page 161). 1c. As appropriate, assemble technology to use in modeling the strategy for students (for example, document camera, PPT slides, SMART Board, overhead transparencies, or posters).
2. Teacher identifies the content standards from state or district standards for students.	Display the content-specific standard you want students to understand and retain as a result of their reading, thinking, and writing. Discuss the standard with students.
3. Teacher shares an advance organizer, reviews the student-friendly definitions, and distributes teacher-prepared materials.	Share the following advance organizer or one of your own choosing: Recently, the idea of using checklists has become popular as a way to improve the outcomes of everything from surgery to airplane safety. What if we were to apply a similar idea to vocabulary by using Quick-REACH (vocabulary) questions in the form of an acronym to consider the best approach for figuring out words we don't know—and seem important to know—in a text? Could we improve our outcomes when it comes to adding new vocabulary to our personal mental dictionaries?

continued →

Lesson Step	Explanatory Notes for the Teacher
4. Teacher models and provides rehearsal opportunities, gradually releasing responsibility to students for doing more of their own thinking and writing.	**Teacher models: Chunk 1** Have students read the chunk silently. As you read aloud, stop at the first word that is important and that they may not know in this chunk. Write the word in column 1 of the organizer and then reread the sentence or sentences around the word aloud again. Tell students that you are going to use the Quick-REACH Questions (figure 12.4, page 156) to help them narrow down a category of tools that could help them determine the meanings of words. As you discuss each letter of the acronym and read the questions associated with it, you are thinking about whether you could, should, or would use a particular category of tools with the word. Finally, select the categories of tools that would be most reasonable or helpful, and refer to the Quick-REACH Toolkit (figure 12.5, page 157) to select the specific tools to use. Write your new or evolving understanding of the word in column 3 along with one or two of the tools that were most helpful in figuring out the meaning. Continue working through the first text chunk. Try to limit the number of words to the three or four most important words in the chunk. **Students work with teacher: Chunk 2** Ask students to underline words in this chunk that are important but unfamiliar as they read the text silently. After you read the text aloud, call on students to share the words they have underlined. Think aloud about which words are important to understanding what the text is mainly about, and select the three or four most important words to write on the organizer. As you begin to tackle the first identified word, reread the sentence or sentences around the word. Call on students to help as you begin asking the Quick-REACH Questions (figure 12.4, page 156). Ask the students to select the one or two categories that are most likely to be helpful to use. Refer to the toolkit to review those categories and select the tools to apply to the word. Record these tools in column 3 of the organizer. Call on students to share their new or evolving understanding of the meaning and write a model response on the organizer in column 3. Continue to work through this process until all of the words from column 1 are defined. **Students work with peers: Chunk 3** Ask students to read the text silently before you read it aloud. Ask students to work independently to identify and underline the words that they do not know and think are important to know. Have students work interdependently with a partner to reach consensus on the words. Call on students to share their lists so that you can help them select three or four words to put in the organizer.

4.	Teacher models and provides rehearsal opportunities, gradually releasing responsibility to students for doing more of their own thinking and writing. *(continued)*	Ask partners to work together rereading the sentences around the first word. Tell students to ask the Quick-REACH Questions to find categories that will help them build their personal mental dictionaries. Have them select the one or two tools that seem most reasonable and apply them to the word. Record these tools in column 3 of the organizer. Tell students to record their new or evolving understanding in column 3. Have students continue this process until all of the words in column 1 are defined.
5.	Teacher formatively assesses student work.	Call on several pairs to share their definitions and the tools they selected. If definitions need to be clarified, use the other students as resources for finding a more accurate definition. Write model definitions on the organizer as well as a consensus of which strategies were most helpful. Use the work that is shared and students' responses to formatively assess as many students as possible. NOTE: At this point, you have two options: (1) conclude this lesson by going directly to steps 6 and 7, temporarily skipping the +feature (schedule the +feature for a later class period using the same text and organizers students have completed up to this point), or (2) extend this lesson by incorporating the +feature followed by steps 6 and 7.

Quick-REACH Vocabulary Toolkit+

Teacher models

Tell students that you will model completing the constructed response matrix on the organizer by choosing the tool that you think students are least likely to choose. Write the name of the tool in the "tool" box. Share some of the merits of that tool then ask students to brainstorm to add suggestions. Armed with that short bit of brainstorming, complete the constructed response for merits.

Students work with teacher

Now, ask students to help you by repeating the same process as you think about drawbacks. After brainstorming, call on and help students as they think about and offer suggestions for completing the constructed response. Record an exemplary model of the response for drawbacks on the organizer.

Students work with peers

Ask students to work with a partner to identify and agree on their top two most useful tools. Students will complete both portions—merits and drawbacks—of the matrix for the first tool, then partner with another group. Together in their group, each pair will discuss their matrix, ask the other pair to review their work for accuracy and quality, and provide any other helpful feedback. Students will then return to working with partners to make any revisions before moving on to complete the rest of the matrix by writing the merits and drawbacks for the second tool.

Teacher formatively assesses student work

Have several partners display their completed matrix, and as you facilitate a conversation about the merits of the work, formatively assess as many students as possible. Ask students to either select one matrix as the exemplary class model or facilitate the process as they write an entirely new response as a class.

continued →

Lesson Step	Explanatory Notes for the Teacher
6. Teacher returns to the content standard to identify progress in understanding and retaining new content.	In order to identify student progress with the new content, ask students to write an exit ticket in response to this stem: In what ways did the reading, thinking, and writing you did today help you understand the content standard? Explain.
7. Closure	Ask students to reflect on their current level of understanding of the content standard(s) and the literacy skill(s) they worked with today by using "fist to five" hand signals to the following questions as you display them, read them aloud, and ask for student responses: On a scale of fist to five, where making a fist means not at all and holding up all five fingers means so completely that you could be the teacher, rate your understanding of the following content standard: _____ On a scale of fist to five, where making a fist means not at all and holding up all five fingers means so completely that you could be the teacher, rate your level of understanding of the following CCSS literacy skill: _____

Visit **go.solution-tree.com/commoncore** to download and print this figure.

Weigh the Words

The Gist of Weigh the Words

Students read a text and show their understanding of the author's craft by focusing on the importance, or "weight," of the words in the text. In the +feature of the lesson, students identify the single most important element of the author's craft in relation to this text, discuss, and explain their choice in a constructed response.

CCR Anchor Standard 4 for Reading: *Interpret words and phrases as they are used in a text, including determining technical, connotative, and figurative meanings, and analyze how specific word choices shape meaning or tone.*

Strategy 13, Weigh the Words, builds on the previous strategy in which readers learned how to retrieve specific tools from the Quick-REACH Vocabulary Toolkit to help them identify the meanings of challenging words in the text they are reading. Weigh the Words quickly notches up expectations for students and demands that they become more analytical and inferential in their analysis of how specific kinds of words (technical, connotative, and figurative) directly impact the meaning and tone of a text they are reading.

The title of this standard is based on the expression "weigh your words," meaning you should be careful to choose exactly the right words when you speak or write to someone, especially an important person like the boss, someone you love, or a newspaper reporter who will quote your words in an article. The literal meanings of some words may feel totally appropriate while we are saying or writing them. However, their connotative meanings may send an entirely different message to a listener or reader. Text with many of these "weighted words" will be challenging to read and require readers to not only make logical inferences from the overall text itself, but also to come up with higher-level inferences about the underlying meanings of these words, which impact the central idea of the text. Achieving this standard requires a great deal of word and world knowledge. How do students acquire that kind of knowledge? By reading a lot—not only in classrooms but independently on their own in the library, cafeteria, and at home.

Background Knowledge

There are three categories of words that can interfere with students' reading comprehension and eventually their understanding and retention of critical content standards: (1) technical, (2) connotative, and (3) figurative.

Technical Vocabulary

Teachers are tempted to rely on glossary and dictionary definitions to "teach" highly technical vocabulary as if one can understand technical terms like *photosynthesis* by simply memorizing its definition. Students learn important concepts or acquire the specialized vocabulary found in content texts in three ways (Novak, 1998; Novak & Gowin, 1984):

1. Hearing words explained and used in conversation and context at least three to five times

2. Seeing words brought to life with pictures, models, and diagrams

3. Constructing graphic organizers that show relationships between words

One of our favorite organizers for helping students organize important information about technical terms is the Frayer model. The Frayer model is a graphic organizer designed by Dorothy Frayer and colleagues at the University of Wisconsin (Frayer, Frederick, & Klausmeier, 1969). This model uses a four-square format to distinguish the essential characteristics from those that are only marginally associated with a word. This variation from the traditional model prompts students to think about words in terms of examples, essential characteristics, nonexamples, and nonessential characteristics. Figure 13.1 shows a sample of a Frayer model.

Connotative Vocabulary

Many words in the English language have two kinds of meanings: literal and connotative. The literal or denotative meaning of a word refers to its specific dictionary definition. The connotative meaning of a word includes all of the emotional associations, both positive and negative, that a word carries with it—the weight of that word. Recall the sample text found in figure 6.2 on page 85, "Vietnam Revisited: I Was a Refugee Long Before Katrina." The author repeats the word *home* sixteen times throughout the article. Sometimes she is referring to the literal meaning of the word: a physical structure where

FIGURE 13.1: Sample Frayer Model

Essential Characteristics	Non-essential characteristics
Not much rainfall	Does not have to be hot
Rough terrain	Does not have to have sand
Extreme temperatures	Does not have to be barren
	Can have plants and animals

Word
Desert
Student-Friendly Definition
Dry land without much rain

Examples	Non-examples
Sonoran Desert in southwestern USA	Beaches
Sahara Desert in Northern Africa	Arboretums
	Rain forests

Source: McEwan & Bresnahan, 2008.

one lives, as when she states: "I wept for all those who lost their homes." But, in other instances, she uses the word to convey one of its connotative meanings: "I suppose I will always be searching for my home, but I am also certain that I will never find it," "I don't have a home," or in referring to her parents, "They would never return home." This particular text offers multiple opportunities for examining the variety of connotative meanings of just a single word and serves to remind us of the importance of constantly talking about the important words of our disciplines, teaching both the literal and connotative meanings as often as we can.

Figurative Language

Figurative language consists of words or phrases that lead the reader to compare something in the text to an idea, object, or experience from outside of the text. Authors use figurative language to make their descriptions more meaningful and to help the reader make connections to other experiences they may have had. Figure P2.1 (page 147), Elements of Style, provides additional definitions and examples to illustrate other types of figurative language.

Understanding How the Strategy Works

In order to appreciate how this strategy works, spend some time with the sample text in figure 13.2 on page 170 (Flesch-Kincaid grade level 11.9) and then follow the steps of the completed organizer (figure 13.3, page 171), which replicates the process you and your students will use. The text is divided into three chunks in order to make the steps more manageable.

FIGURE 13.2: Sample Text for Weigh the Words

"Time for Some Innovative Thinking in the War on Cancer"

Chunk 1

In her book *Innovation Generation*, Dr. Roberta Ness, the dean of the University of Texas School of Public Health, says innovative thinking can be taught. One teachable skill is framing, putting a problem in its proper context to create previously unimagined solutions.

One of Dr. Ness's examples of poor framing is the war on cancer begun in 1971 when President Nixon signed the National Cancer Act after saying:

"The time has come in America when the same kind of concentrated effort that split the atom and took man to the moon should be turned toward conquering this dread disease."

But is the martial metaphor an apt one? Cancer cells are more like normal cells than they are like invading strangers (e.g., bacteria). Cancer probably starts as a malfunctioning of multiple genes setting off a cascade of molecular missteps. The primary event is unclear, but it is probably part of the natural processes of aging in the face of environmental stressors, plus a contribution from innate genetic cancer proclivities.

Cancer could be like climate change on the cellular level. The abnormal genes resembling rising seas and wandering polar bears are the effects, not the causes, of a problem. Framing our quest to lessen its impact on people might be better considered in the words of Walt Kelly's Pogo: "We have met the enemy and he is us." Cancer, unfortunately, is part of life.

Chunk 2

Thus the cancer problem is not like the space race or the Manhattan Project. Getting to the moon and harnessing the destructive power of the atom required few new scientific insights to be reduced to practice. Those successes were due to the application of sufficient resources to problems with known technical barriers. The underlying principles needed to solve the cancer problem have not yet been elucidated, making the best technical route to a solution unclear.

The war on cancer currently is a single-minded national, big-science research strategy of completely identifying all the potential molecular aberrancies in clinical cancer, so as to target aberrant gene products and exploit an individual tumor's vulnerabilities. For the most part, in the common cancers that plague Americans—breast, lung, colon and prostate—therapeutic progress has been very slow. Screening, early detection and prevention strategies have been more successful.

Instead of concentrating all of our funding on research to develop weapons of mass destruction against cancer, we could use more funds to identify the risk factors that lead to cancer's development and ways to intervene before cancer arises. And we know many of these already: smoking, obesity, radiation, sexually transmitted diseases and asbestos exposure far outweigh innate genetic syndromes as causes of human cancer.

Chunk 3

We have some choices to make. We could spend a billion dollars on more lung cancer research or pay the college tuition of all 18-year-olds who have never smoked. We could analyze the genetics of thousands of human lung cancers yielding a great deal of new scientific information that may or may not extend the survival or quality of life of a single cancer patient, or we could pay tobacco farmers to switch to different crops and decrease the supply of the only FDA-regulated product that when used as designed, will kill human beings.

I am proposing that we reframe the cancer problem from one of waging war to one of using what we already know works and research ways to prevent as well as treat this very therapeutically resistant set of diseases.

Framing the cancer problem as a war for the past 40 years hasn't really gotten us all that far compared with the rapidity of the success of the Manhattan Project or the triumph of NASA reaching the moon a mere eight years after President Kennedy expressed our national goal to do so.

That's because the cancer problem is harder than splitting the atom or landing on the moon. Maybe it's time for some innovative thinking. Maybe it's time for a frame shift.

FIGURE 13.3: Sample Organizer for Weigh the Words

Text title: "Time for Some Innovative Thinking in the War on Cancer" Name:		
Directions: Identify words or phrases with weight in the text and list them in column 1. Use the Quick-REACH Questions (figure 12.4, page 156), the Quick-REACH Toolkit (figure 12.5, page 157), and information from figure P2.1 (figurative language) on page 147 to identify specific tools to help you figure out the meanings of these words or phrases. Write the name of the tool and explain how it helped you in column 2. Write your understanding of the term and its importance to the text in column 3.		
Column 1 **Identify words/phrases that have weight or importance (technical, connotative, figurative).**	**Column 2** **Use the Quick-REACH Questions and Toolkit to choose the best tool for unlocking the meaning of the words/phrases. Explain how the tool specifically helped you.**	**Column 3** **Write your understanding of the meaning of the word or phrase.**
Chunk 1		
The war on cancer (figurative language)	**Tool:** Clues in the text: figurative language **Explanation:** The author uses this analogy as the glue that holds his argument for "framing" together. The "war on cancer" mentality promotes fighting against the disease and not focusing on the prevention.	The "war" on cancer means that we have focused our battle on the treatment of cancer—after the enemy (cancer) has been diagnosed.
Cancer could be like climate change (figurative language)	**Tool:** Clues in the text: figurative language **Explanation:** The abnormal genes are possibly the result of either genetics or the environment—just like rising water is the result of climate change.	"Cancer could be like climate change" means that cancer is the result of a problem, not the cause of a problem.

continued →

Chunk 2		
Aberrancies—aberrant (technical)	**Tool:** Clues in the text: examples, explanations, details **Explanation:** One sentence refers to a "strategy of completely identifying all the potential molecular aberrancies in clinical cancer, so as to target aberrant gene products . . ." In explaining that scientists want to target aberrant gene products, I infer that the "target" is what they want to get rid of.	Aberrancies must be abnormal cells.
Therapeutic progress (technical)	**Tool:** Clues in the text: contrast statements **Explanation:** One sentence laments that "therapeutic progress has been very slow." That is contrasted with the next sentence where "screening, early detection and prevention strategies have been more successful."	Therapeutic must have to do with the cure and not the prevention.
Weapons of mass destruction (figurative language)	**Tool:** Clues in the text: figurative language **Explanation:** The author uses this analogy to allude to the problems that result from declaring a "war on cancer." The funding for research tends to focus on a cure instead of on prevention.	Although developing "weapons of mass destruction" may be one way to end a war, and developing "weapons of mass destruction" against cancer may be helpful if you already have the disease, it is not the best approach. Focusing on prevention is the best approach.
Chunk 3		
The only FDA-regulated product that . . . will kill human beings (connotation)	**Tool:** Clues in the text: rereading the text to identify the word as having an emotional weight **Explanation:** The use of the word *kill* is a strong word to choose in relation to the federal government. The point the author makes is dramatic.	To kill someone is to murder him or her—which is what the author thinks tobacco is doing.

Weigh the Words+	
+Directions: Consider the weight of each word or phrase identified on the first part of the organizer, and select a few of the words with the most weight or impact to process. List those in the column on the left. Decide what effect the use of that word or phrase has on the overall meaning and effectiveness of the text, and record your answer in the column on the right.	
Words/Phrases	**How does the word/phrase contribute to the effectiveness of the text?**
Cancer could be like climate change	Helps make clear the author's points about cause and effect in reference to cancer
Therapeutic progress	Understanding this concept helps support the author's point about the need to focus on prevention
Weapons of mass destruction	This analogy supports the author's point that we have to reframe our "war on cancer" approach to research and funding
The only FDA-regulated product that . . . will kill human beings	This detail adds an emotional component to the author's ideas about prevention and makes the text more memorable

+ Prompt: Now, focusing on the author's craft (style of writing), identify the one word or phrase from the text that most strongly impacts the author's message; identify it as an example of a technical term, a word with connotative meaning, or an example of figurative language; and explain how the weight of the word or phrase—its importance and impact—contributes to the overall effectiveness of the text.

Constructed Response

The author's connotative use of the word *kill* has the strongest overall impact on this text. The emotional weight of the word contributes to the overall effectiveness of the text because it is with the use of this word—*kill*—that the author squarely focuses on one of the causes of cancer (smoking) and stops short of blaming the FDA directly for the deaths of those who die because of lung cancer as a result of smoking. It is the most memorable idea in the text and therefore adds to the overall effectiveness of the text.

Items to Prepare

There are two reproducible figures that support the Weigh the Words strategy. Figure 13.4 contains student-friendly definitions of the terms you will explain as you show your students how to execute this strategy during their reading.

FIGURE 13.4: Student-Friendly Definitions for Weigh the Words

Craft: The way an author writes; a unique style
Analyze: Explain or describe how something works
Tool: In reading, something you do to help you solve a comprehension problem
Weight of a word: How important a word is to the overall meaning of the text

continued →

> **Technical word:** A word that has a specific meaning for the text or the content
>
> **Connotative word:** A word used in a nonliteral way
>
> **Figurative language:** Words or phrases used to make comparisons between ideas, events, or individuals referred to in the text and similar ideas, events, or individuals not in the text

Visit **go.solution-tree.com/commoncore** to download and print this figure.

The second reproducible, figure 13.5, is an organizer for you to record your thinking as you model and for students to record their thinking during their initial encounter with the strategy and in subsequent rehearsals in various content text selections.

FIGURE 13.5: Reproducible Organizer for Weigh the Words

Text title: Name:		
Directions: Identify words or phrases with weight in the text and list them in column 1. Use the Quick-REACH Questions (figure 12.4, page 156), the Quick-REACH Toolkit (figure 12.5, page 157), and information from figure P2.1 (figurative language) on page 147 to identify specific tools to help you figure out the meanings of these words or phrases. Write the name of the tool and explain how it helped you in column 2. Write your understanding of the term and its importance to the text in column 3.		
Column 1 Identify words/phrases that have weight or importance (technical, connotative, figurative).	**Column 2** Use the Quick-REACH Questions and Toolkit to choose the best tool for unlocking the meaning of the words/phrases. Explain how the tool specifically helped you.	**Column 3** Write your understanding of the meaning of the word or phrase.
Chunk 1		
	Tool: Explanation:	
	Tool: Explanation:	
	Tool: Explanation:	
Chunk 2		
	Tool: Explanation:	
	Tool: Explanation:	
	Tool: Explanation:	

Chunk 3		
	Tool: **Explanation:**	
	Tool: **Explanation:**	
	Tool: **Explanation:**	

Weigh the Words+

+Directions: Consider the weight of each word or phrase identified on the first part of the organizer, and select a few of the words with the most weight or impact to process. List those in the column on the left. Decide what effect the use of that word or phrase has on the overall meaning and effectiveness of the text, and record your answer in the column on the right.

Words/Phrases	How does the word/phrase contribute to the effectiveness of the text?

+ Prompt: Now, focusing on the author's craft (style of writing), identify the one word or phrase from the text that most strongly impacts the author's message; identify it as an example of a technical term, a word with connotative meaning, or an example of figurative language; and explain how the weight of the word or phrase—its importance and impact—contributes to the overall effectiveness of the text.

Constructed Response

Visit **go.solution-tree.com/commoncore** to download and print this figure.

Lesson Plan

The lesson plan for showing your students how to execute the Weigh the Words strategy is found in figure 13.6. We are assuming in the design of this lesson that you and your students have thoroughly digested the contents of Strategy 12, the Quick-REACH Questions, and the Quick-REACH Toolkit.

FIGURE 13.6: Lesson Plan for Weigh the Words

Lesson Step	Explanatory Notes for the Teacher
1. Teacher prepares and assembles the necessary materials.	1a. Choose content-related and standards-aligned text for teacher modeling and student reading, then: • Choose a text that has examples of technical, connotative, and figurative meanings as defined and described in earlier text. • Chunk text into three parts as shown in the sample text (figure 13.2, page 170). • Complete the reproducible organizer (figure 13.5, page 174) as a key for modeling with your text in preparation for teaching the lesson. 1b. Prepare photocopies for students of your selected text, the student-friendly definitions (figure 13.4, page 173), the strategy's reproducible organizer (figure 13.5, page 174), and the tools to help unlock the meanings of words: Quick-REACH Questions (figure 12.4, page 156), Quick-REACH Toolkit (figure 12.5, page 157), and figure P2.1, Elements of Style, on page 147. 1c. As appropriate, assemble technology to use in modeling the strategy for students (for example, document camera, PPT slides, SMART Board, overhead transparencies, or posters).
2. Teacher identifies the content standard from state or district standards for students.	Display the content-specific standard you want students to understand and retain as a result of their reading, thinking, and writing. Discuss the standard with students.
3. Teacher shares an advance organizer, reviews the student-friendly definitions, and distributes teacher-prepared materials.	Share the following advance organizer or one of your own choosing: If we were about to analyze a painting, we would focus our attention on the artist's choices in relation to color, treatment of space, and perhaps even brushwork. These choices make up the artist's craft. Like artists, authors make choices as well. We can attend to the author's craft by focusing our attention on the author's deliberate use of words. Today, we are going to focus on understanding the author's craft as conveyed in a piece of text through the weight and importance of words and phrases the author deliberately uses.
4. Teacher models and provides rehearsal opportunities, gradually releasing responsibility to students for doing more of their own thinking and writing.	**Teacher models: Chunk 1** Ask students to read the text chunk silently before you read it aloud to them. As you read it aloud, stop to identify and jot down in column 1 examples of words with weight and importance, including technical words that are critical to the meaning of the text, words with strong connotative meanings, and words and phrases used in figurative ways—all parts of author's craft.

4. Teacher models and provides rehearsal opportunities, gradually releasing responsibility to students for doing more of their own thinking and writing. *(continued)*	After identifying two to four total examples from this chunk (if possible, try to locate one of each), go back to the first word or phrase listed on the organizer, reread the sentences around the word or phrase, and using the Quick-REACH Questions (figure 12.4, page 156), ask students to help you identify the most appropriate category of tools (for example, resources in print, electronic tools) to unlock the meaning of the word or phrase. Then use the Quick-REACH Toolkit (figure 12.5, page 157) to choose the most appropriate tool. Record the tool in column 2. Do a think-aloud as you record an explanation on the organizer to show the results of your efforts to extract and construct meaning from the weighted words. Finally, complete the "write your understanding" box in column 3 by calling on students to help you as you think aloud about what to write for your new or more precise understanding of the term as a result of your effortful processing. Repeat this process for each identified word or phrase on the organizer. **Students work with teacher: Chunk 2** Ask students to read the chunk silently before you read it aloud. As you are reading, have students underline words with weight that relate to the author's craft (technical terms, words with connotative meaning, words or phrases used in figurative ways). Call on students to share what they underlined as you jot down examples on the organizer—try to limit the number of examples and try to have an example of each type of word or phrase that relates to an author's craft represented on the organizer for this chunk. Next, ask students to reread the sentences around the first word or phrase listed and refer to the Quick-REACH Questions (figure 12.4, page 156) and the Quick-REACH Toolkit (figure 12.5, page 157) in order to identify and record the most appropriate tool that will most likely help them extract and construct the meaning of the recorded word or phrase. Call on students to share the tool they have identified. Record accurate examples on the organizer. Ask students to complete the explanation of how that tool specifically helped as they applied it to a specific word or phrase. Call on students, review their answers, and record models on the organizer. Finally, ask students to complete the "write your understanding" box in column 3 for each term listed in this chunk. Call on students to share their answers and record accurate models on the organizer. Repeat this process for each identified word or phrase. **Students work with peers: Chunk 3** Ask students to read the chunk silently before you read it aloud. Ask students to independently underline the words with weight that most importantly contribute to the author's craft. Working interdependently with a partner, students should limit and agree on the word/phrases they will include on their organizer.

continued →

Lesson Step	Explanatory Notes for the Teacher
4. Teacher models and provides rehearsal opportunities, gradually releasing responsibility to students for doing more of their own thinking and writing. *(continued)*	After rereading the sentences around each word or phrase, have students use the Quick-REACH Questions and the Quick-REACH Toolkit to identify the most appropriate tool to help them extract a deeper meaning from the recorded words or phrases. Partners should identify the tool and write an explanation of how the tool specifically helped them as they applied it to the words or phrases. Finally, students should complete the "write your understanding" box in column 3. Repeat this process for each term.
5. Teacher formatively assesses student work.	Call on several partners to display their work for chunk 3. Facilitate a conversation in order to review the examples and check for accuracy. Have the class select an exemplar organizer as a model for chunk 3. Use the work that is shared and the students' responses to formatively assess as many students as possible. NOTE: At this point, you have two options: (1) conclude this lesson by going directly to steps 6 and 7, temporarily skipping the +feature (schedule the +feature for a later class period using the same text and organizers students have completed up to this point), or (2) extend this lesson by incorporating the +feature followed by steps 6 and 7.

Weigh the Words+

Teacher models

Now that students have exerted effort to process and understand the text, it's time to analyze the effect the author's choices have on the overall text. Refer students to the two columns on the Weigh the Words+ portion of the organizer. Tell them that you want them to reduce the words/phrases listed in column 1 of the original organizer by choosing just three or four with the most weight and importance. Call on students to share their choices and record several of these on your organizer. Now, shift your focus to the "effectiveness of the text" column on the right. Think aloud as you process the impact that the weight of the first word or phrase listed has on the text and record your thinking in the column.

Students work with teacher

Ask students to continue to work to identify the effect that the words and phrases with weight have on the text for each word they selected in the column on the left. Call on students to share their answers and think aloud as you process and select models to add to the organizer.

Students work with peers

Tell students that they will now use all of the work they have done in order to complete a constructed response for which they will have to show how the weight of one word or phrase contributes to the overall effectiveness of the text.

Students will work interdependently with a partner to address the constructed response prompt by essentially combining and explaining their ideas from the "words/phrases" column and the "effectiveness of the text" column.

Teacher formatively assesses student work

Call on students to display their constructed response. As you facilitate a conversation about the merits of the work, formatively assess as many students as possible. Ask students to select—and justify their selection—of an exemplary model or work with the class to construct an entirely new response to serve as an exemplary model.

6.	Teacher returns to the content standard to identify progress in understanding and retaining new content.	In order to identify student progress with the new content, ask students to write an exit ticket in response to this stem: In what ways did the reading, thinking, and writing you did today help you understand the content standard? Explain.
7.	Closure	Ask students to reflect on their current level of understanding of the content standard(s) and the literacy skill(s) they worked with today by using "fist to five" hand signals to the following questions as you display them, read them aloud, and ask for student responses: On a scale of fist to five, where making a fist means not at all and holding up all five fingers means so completely that you could be the teacher, rate your understanding of the following content standard: _____ On a scale of fist to five, where making a fist means not at all and holding up all five fingers means so completely that you could be the teacher, rate your level of understanding of the following CCSS literacy skill: _____

Visit **go.solution-tree.com/commoncore** to download and print this figure.

Identify-Analyze-Relate (Problem-Solution)

The Gist of Identify-Analyze-Relate

Students turn sentences into headlines as they analyze the problem-solution structure of a text. In the +feature of the lesson, they write a constructed response describing how each chunk of the text contributes (relates) to the overall structure of the text.

CCR Anchor Standard 5 for Reading: *Analyze the structure of texts, including how specific sentences, paragraphs, and larger portions of the text (e.g., a section, chapter, scene, or stanza) relate to each other and the whole.*

Identify-Analyze-Relate consists of three steps: (1) read a text and identify its text structure; (2) analyze that structure, that is, break it down and closely examine its individual sentences as well as paragraphs or a larger section in the context of the whole text; and (3) describe how these sentences are related to each other and to the whole text in a constructed response. This strategy and its companion, Strategy 15, use the same lesson design to show students how to analyze two of the most problematic structures for students: problem-solution and cause–effect.

We will describe six of the most common text structures and provide word and content clues to help students identify specific text structures. The first selected text structure for modeling this strategy is problem-solution. Although we focus on informational text to demonstrate how students can use their knowledge of the problem-solution text structure to understand and retain what they read, they will encounter this structure in nearly every piece of literary fiction they read as well. Becoming skilled at identifying problems and solutions will improve students' reading comprehension as well as their writing abilities. Knowing how a specific text is organized (structured) can help your students in their reading, understanding, and retention of content.

Background Knowledge

The expectations of CCR Anchor Standard 5 are daunting to be sure: "analyze the structure of texts, including how specific sentences, paragraphs, and larger portions of the text . . . relate to each other and the whole." In order to achieve this standard, students need an understanding of a concept called *text structure*. Text structure refers to the various ways authors write (construct or build) text. The term *text* as used in the context of this book refers to two kinds of informational text: content textbooks and materials (informational text) and literary informational text. We have deliberately featured informational text throughout the book, and as you have already discovered, there are examples of both informational (nonfiction) and literary informational texts (literary nonfiction). In contrast, narrative texts (fiction) have a very different type of text structure that includes but is not limited to characters, setting, theme, and a plot.

If you have been accustomed to categorizing texts as expository (nonfiction) and narrative (fiction), you will find the terminology of the standards to be somewhat different. Although you will not find the term *expository* used in the main standards document (CCSSI, 2010a), you will find references to it in the CCSS's Appendix A (CCSSI, 2010b).

Locating information about text structure on the Internet is fraught with possibilities for confusion. First, finding a definitive list of text structures is impossible. You will find dozens of compilations, some using different terms. To further complicate the issue, you may find references to *expository structure*. This term could lead you to believe that there is a discrete text structure called expository, which is not the case. The term *expository structure* is used in some states and districts to refer to one of three types of essays students are expected to write on their state assessment. The other two are persuasive (which is a text structure) and narrative (which is the term used to refer to fiction in most textbooks and research). *Expository*, *persuasive*, and *narrative* are used in the context of writing in which students are taught to write for three different purposes: (1) inform or explain in an expository essay, (2) entertain in a narrative essay, and (3) convince or explain in a persuasive essay. If these terms are not used in your context, do not worry about them. However, if your students have been well taught using these terms, you may need to point out the subtle differences to them.

If the kind of textual analysis found in this strategy is a completely new concept for you, one option for gaining a deeper understanding of text structures is to ask an ELA teacher to give your content team or department a crash course in text structure with a specific emphasis on content texts and supplementary materials. If you are comfortable with the concept of text structures, read on.

Understanding How the Strategy Works

In order to appreciate and understand how this strategy works to scaffold Standard 5 of the CCR Anchor Standards for Reading, spend some time with the sample text in figure 14.1 (Flesch–Kincaid grade level 11.8) and the completed organizer in figure 14.2 (page 184). Note that the text is divided into three chunks in order to make the identify-analyze-relate steps more manageable.

FIGURE 14.1: Sample Text for Identify-Analyze-Relate (Problem-Solution)

"In Teen Sex Education Debate, Both Sides Ahead"

Chunk 1

(1) For years, a war has been waged between advocates of teaching teenagers to abstain from sex and those advocating a comprehensive sex education. (2) It looks like both sides are winning.

(3) The National Center for Health Statistics released a study this month about sexual activity among 15- to 19-year-olds. (4) It shows that although the change since 2002 is not significant, since 1988 there has been a dramatic drop in the percentage of sexually active teens. (5) In 1988, 51 percent of teen girls said they had engaged in sexual intercourse, compared with only 43 percent in 2006–10. (6) For boys, it dropped from 60 percent to 42 percent over the same period.

(7) Among teens who have had sex, there has been a steady increase in the use of contraception at their first intercourse. (8) For girls, it rose from 67 percent in 1988 to 78 percent now. (9) And for boys, it went from 71 percent to 85 percent.

(10) In other words, during the past 20 years, we have simultaneously seen a lower rate of teens having sex and a higher rate of contraceptive use among those who are sexually active. (11) This is noteworthy because critics of comprehensive sex education fear that promoting contraception increases the likelihood that teens will have sex. (12) Conversely, critics of abstinence-only education fear that depriving teens of information about contraception increases the likelihood that sexually active teens won't use it.

(13) Perhaps the vociferous arguments from two distinct sides have allowed teens to get both messages clearly and more effectively than if there had been no war in the first place. (14) Perhaps opponents' criticism has caused each side to temper its message, offering better balance and accuracy, and thus, efficacy.

Chunk 2

(15) Hopefully, teens have learned accurate information about condom effectiveness (and ineffectiveness), as well as skills for resisting peer pressure and developing healthy dating relationships. (16) Hopefully, adults have realized that giving clear-cut expectations to youths does influence their behavior.

---

continued →

(17) Faith-based organizations actively promote the idea that sex should be reserved for marriage. (18) Interestingly enough, moral or religious beliefs topped the list of reasons that abstinent teens gave for their choice. (19) Other top reasons included fear of pregnancy and not having found the right person.

(20) Clear-cut messages that sexually active teens should protect themselves against disease and pregnancy also seem to be getting through. (21) Since 1988, the number of teens simultaneously using condoms and a hormonal contraceptive at their last intercourse has risen.

Chunk 3

(22) So we've made a lot of progress, but we still have a long way to go. (23) Many of the positive trends that occurred from 1988 to 2002 have leveled off.

(24) Furthermore, the data suggest that other factors play a significant role. For example, only 35 percent of teen girls who live with both of their parents have had sex, compared with 54 percent of those living in other arrangements. (25) Maybe if we grappled with teen sexuality from that angle we would find additional solutions.

(26) But it's worth celebrating the solutions we've already devised. (27) Prior to 1988, there had been a steady rise in the percentage of sexually active female teens, a rise that many people thought was irreversible. (28) But now we know that it was reversible, because we reversed it.

(29) We know that it is realistic to expect teens to wait (the majority do) and to expect those who don't to use protection. (30) The war is working, and both sides are winning.

Source: Reprinted by permission of Ashley Sánchez. Sánchez has been a regular contributor to the opinion page of the Austin American-Statesman *for sixteen years. She lives with her husband and three daughters in Cedar Park, Texas. This article originally appeared in the* Austin American-Statesman, *October 23, 2011.*

FIGURE 14.2: Sample Organizer for Identify-Analyze-Relate (Problem-Solution)

Text title: "In Teen Sex Education Debate, Both Sides Ahead" Name:			
Directions: Record the specific sentence number(s) in column 1 that contain either a direct or implied statement of the problem. Write the headline in column 2. Record sentences containing information about solutions in column 3 and headlines in column 4.			
Problems		**Solutions**	
Column 1 Sentence number	**Column 2** Problem headline	**Column 3** Sentence number	**Column 4** Solution headline
Chunk 1			
Implied in sentences 1–9	Sexually active teens not using contraception consistently	13–14	Vociferous "war" results in tempered yet effective message about contraception and abstinence
11	Does promoting contraception increase teen sex?		
12	Does "abstinence-only" decrease use of contraception?		

Chunk 2			
Implied in sentence 15	Teens lack skills to prevent pregnancies	15	Adults hopeful teens have learned lessons
		16	Clear-cut expectations from adults influence teen behavior
		17–18	Moral beliefs top reasons for abstinence
		19	Fear of pregnancy among top reasons for abstinence
		19	Some teens abstain until they find right person
		20–21	Clear-cut messages about protection are getting through
Chunk 3			
22	Progress made with teen pregnancy but long way to go		
23	Positive teen pregnancy trends level off		
24–25	Are we grappling with teen sexuality from all angles?		

Identify-Analyze-Relate (Problem-Solution)+

+Prompt: Write a constructed response that shows your understanding of how each chunk relates to the overall structure of the text as a whole as well as to each other. Well-written constructed responses will effectively weave text-specific evidence into the response.

Chunk 1—Model for examining the relationship of this chunk to the text

This chunk of text introduces the "war" between two sides advocating different solutions for the problem of teen pregnancy, sets up the author's overall problem-solution organizational structure, introduces the National Center for Health Statistics to support the author's assertions of improvement, and states the thesis.

Constructed Response Answer

Chunk 1

Chunk 1 introduces the "war" between the two sides advocating very different solutions for the problem of teen pregnancy, which sets up the problem-solution structure of the text. The author introduces the research on which she bases her beliefs that "both sides are winning" and leads to her thesis that the decrease in sexual activity among teens and increase in use of contraception are a result of both the "vociferous" and "tempered" arguments from the two distinct sides.

Chunk 2

The author continues to support her thesis that the decrease in teen pregnancy is the result of the work of both groups. Adults giving "clear-cut expectations to youth," whether those expectations include the use of contraception to protect against disease and pregnancy or expectations that promote the idea that "sex should be reserved for marriage" does influence their behavior.

continued →

> **Chunk 3**
>
> The author continues to explore how additional factors could play a significant role in the problem of teen pregnancy, like whether or not a female teen lives with both parents, and suggests that we still need to "grapple with teen sexuality" from all angles.

Items to Prepare

There are four reproducible figures that support this strategy. Figure 14.3 lists student-friendly definitions of the terms you will explain as you show your students how to execute this strategy during their reading. Recall that all of the student-friendly definitions are found in the glossary. Many of the terms will be encountered in subsequent strategies, so there will be opportunities to reteach and remind students of the definitions in the context of acquiring other strategies.

FIGURE 14.3: Student-Friendly Definitions for Identify-Analyze-Relate (Problem-Solution)

Identify: Recognize or point out something in a text
Analyze: Read the text closely to determine its structure
Text: In the classroom, any printed material you are expected to read
Text structure: The way an author decides to organize text
Problem-solution: A type of text structure in which the author defines a problem and presents a solution to that problem
Relate: Make (figure out) a connection between two or more things
Problem: Something that needs to be fixed
Solution: A way to solve a problem

Visit **go.solution-tree.com/commoncore** to download and print this figure.

The second reproducible, figure 14.4, is an organizer for you to record your thinking as you prepare to model the strategy and for students to record their thinking during their initial encounter with the strategy and in subsequent rehearsals in various content text selections.

FIGURE 14.4: Reproducible Organizer for Identify-Analyze-Relate (Problem-Solution)

Text title:
Name:
Directions: Record the specific sentence number(s) in column 1 that contain either a direct or implied statement of the problem. Write the headline in column 2. Record sentences containing information about solutions in column 3 and headlines in column 4.

Problems		Solutions	
Column 1 Sentence number	Column 2 Problem headline	Column 3 Sentence number	Column 4 Solution headline
Chunk 1			
Chunk 2			
Chunk 3			

Identify-Analyze-Relate (Problem-Solution)+

+Prompt: Write a constructed response that shows your understanding of how each chunk relates to the overall structure of the text as a whole as well as to each other. Well-written constructed responses will effectively weave text-specific evidence into the response.

Chunk 1—Model for examining the relationship of this chunk to the text

Constructed Response Answer

Chunk 1

continued →

Chunk 2
Chunk 3

Visit **go.solution-tree.com/commoncore** to download and print this figure.

The third reproducible, figure 14.5, is a mini-lesson on how to write head-lines. Students will write headlines in both this strategy and the following one as a way of capturing the essence of a problem–solution and cause–effect.

FIGURE 14.5: A Mini-Lesson for Writing Headlines

1. Use active voice with strong present-tense verbs.
2. Capitalize only the first word in a headline unless the headline contains proper nouns.
3. Use short, familiar words when possible.
4. Avoid the use of articles *a*, *an*, *the*.
5. Make the first word in your headline an important, information-carrying word.
6. Never start a headline with a verb.
7. Use a comma to stand in for the word *and*.
8. Keep the length of your headline to no more than fifteen words.
9. Make your headline memorable if you can, but avoid being cute or humorous.
10. Remember that the headline is a contract you are making with the reader to share what the text is mainly about.

Visit **go.solution-tree.com/commoncore** to download and print this figure.

The fourth and final reproducible, figure 14.6, describes six of the most common text structures found in informational text. The text examples in column 1 of the organizer are provided for your information. They will be removed in the reproducible found at **go.solution-tree.com/commoncore**. If your state or district does not require that text structures be taught, under-stood, and tested at lower grade levels, then you may need to spend additional time with this figure to nail down students' understanding of text structures and how important they are to reading comprehension.

FIGURE 14.6: Types of Text Structures and How to Identify Them

This chart displays six different text structures—ways an author can organize the text he or she writes. In addition to these six text structures, there are many others. However, if you understand these, you will be able to identify the text structure in most of the texts you read. Knowing the text structure is essential to understanding what you read. More importantly, the text structure will help as you organize your thoughts to write about a text as well as retain the information and ideas you read about.

Type of Text Structure and Example	Word Clues to Help You Identify a Text Structure	Content Clues to Help You Identify a Text Structure
Descriptive "In the Courtyard" (page 126)	Look for the following words or terms: *one, two, three;* or *first, second, third; to begin with;* or *finally.* The author may also use terms like *for example, for instance, including,* or *to illustrate.*	The author provides details, examples, and descriptions in order to show the importance of, explain, show evidence for, or interpret meanings.
Comparison-Contrast "Vietnam Revisited" (page 85)	Look for words or terms such as *however, nevertheless, on the other hand, in comparison, in contrast, different, alike, same as, in the same way, just like, just as,* and *also.*	The author makes comparisons and points out contrasts in order to explain, make information clear, show evidence of, or make a case for something.
Cause-Effect "We Lost the War on Drugs" (page 196)	Look for words or terms such as *therefore, so, this led to, as a result of, because, since, may be due to, effect of, for this reason, consequently,* and *if . . . then.*	The author describes a cause-and-effect relationship between individuals, events, or ideas in order to draw a conclusion, support an inference, or show evidence for something.
Problem-Solution "In Teen Sex Education Debate, Both Sides Ahead" (page 183)	Look for words or terms such as *question, dilemma, mystery, problem, solution, answer, reason, outcome,* or *denouement.*	The author defines a problem and presents a solution to that problem in order to explain, show outcomes or results, support an inference, or make a case for or about something.
Time-Sequence-Order "The History of the Internet" (page 49)	Look for actual calendar dates or flashbacks. Also pay attention to words such as *earlier, later, previously, now, before, then, next,* and *after.*	The author presents examples, details, anecdotes, and descriptions in order to explain or show outcomes or results.
Argument or Persuasion "We Lost the War on Drugs" (page 196)	Look for words or terms such as *proves, supports, substantiates, verifies, corroborates, confirms, backs up,* and *bears out.*	The author provides details, statistics, examples, illustrations, and anecdotes to give evidence for or make a case about something.

Visit **go.solution-tree.com/commoncore** to download and print this figure.

Lesson Plan

The lesson plan for showing your students how to execute Identify–Analyze–Relate is found in figure 14.7.

FIGURE 14.7: Lesson Plan for Identify-Analyze-Relate (Problem-Solution)

Lesson Step	Explanatory Notes for the Teacher
1. Teacher prepares and assembles the necessary materials.	1a. Choose content-related and standards-aligned text for teacher modeling and student reading, then: • Chunk text into three parts and number the sentences as shown in the sample text (figure 14.1, page 183). • Complete the reproducible organizer (figure 14.4, page 186) as a key for modeling with your text in preparation for teaching the lesson. 1b. Prepare photocopies for students of your selected text, the student-friendly definitions (figure 14.3, page 186), the strategy's reproducible organizer (figure 14.4, page 186), rules for writing headlines (figure 14.5, page 188), and types of text structures and how to identify them (figure 14.5). 1c. As appropriate, assemble technology to use in modeling the strategy for students (for example, document camera, PPT slides, SMART Board, overhead transparencies, or posters).
2. Teacher identifies the content standards from state or district standards for students.	Display the content-specific standard you want students to understand and retain as a result of their reading, thinking, and writing. Discuss the standards with students.
3. Teacher shares an advance organizer, reviews the student-friendly definitions, and distributes teacher-prepared materials.	Share the following advance organizer or one of your own choosing: When builders look at a blueprint, they very quickly understand the essential structures of that building. When readers begin to attack a piece of text, however, they are usually on their own to figure out the author's blueprint for that particular text—the text structure. The sooner readers learn the importance of identifying text structure and learn the types of structures, the sooner they can use that information to their advantage in understanding the text. Today, we will rehearse the skill of identifying and understanding text structures.

1.	Teacher models and provides rehearsal opportunities, gradually releasing responsibility to students for doing more of their own thinking and writing.	**Teacher models: Chunk 1** Ask students to read the first chunk silently. As you read the text aloud, ask students to listen to see if they can identify the text structure—the underlying organizational principle of this chunk. Call on students to give you the answer. Either verify or tell students that the text structure is problem-solution and explain that knowing that structure helps empower them as readers. Share figure 14.6, page 189, with students to review this structure and the value of knowing a text's structure. Tell students that you will model the process of identifying the problems and solutions for this chunk. Reread the chunk aloud again and stop when you can identify either the problem or solution (stated or implied) in the text. Record the number(s) of the sentence(s) in column 1 or 3 of the organizer—depending on whether the example is a problem or solution. Next, tell students that instead of just copying and pasting the sentences from the text to the organizer, you are going to do a little bit of additional processing in the form of turning the information from the text into a headline before copying it onto the organizer. Tell students that there are some rules that you will review with them about writing headlines (figure 14.5, page 188). After reviewing the figure, go back to the sentence numbers you have recorded on the organizer, read the sentence(s) aloud, and share ideas for a headline. With the help of students, write a model headline and record it in either column 2 or column 4 of the organizer—depending on whether it is a problem or solution. As you reread the rest of this chunk, repeat this process with each problem-solution you encounter. **Students work with teacher: Chunk 2** Ask students to read chunk 2 silently and then read it aloud. Ask students to go back into the text to underline sentences related to the problem with a solid line and sentences related to the solution with a dotted line. Call on students to share the sentences they have identified. Facilitate a discussion as students verify accurate answers. Record accurate sentence numbers on the organizer. Call on students to share ideas for headlines (remind them of the headline rules as necessary) and record model examples on the organizer. **Students work with peers: Chunk 3** Ask students to work independently to identify sentences related to problems or solutions using the same underlining system as was used in chunk 2. Ask students to work interdependently to agree on the sentences that are related to the problem or the solution. After they have reached consensus, students will write headlines together. Circulate to answer questions and offer feedback.

continued →

5. Teacher formatively assesses student work.	Ask students to share the sentence numbers that relate to problems and solutions and record accurate answers on the organizer. Call on students to share headlines for the sentences. Record models on the organizer. Formatively assess as many students as possible as you review their work and listen to their discussions.
	NOTE: At this point, you have two options: (1) conclude this lesson by going directly to steps 6 and 7, temporarily skipping the +feature (schedule the +feature for a later class period using the same text and organizers students have completed up to this point), or (2) extend this lesson by incorporating the +feature followed by steps 6 and 7.

Identify-Analyze-Relate (Problem-Solution)+

Teacher models

Ask students to follow along as you read the +prompt in figure 14.4, page 186, aloud. Tell students that in order to complete this prompt, they will need to be able to examine and identify the relationship of each chunk to the text. In order to move forward with that understanding, display the organizer for chunk 1 with the headlines and model answering this question: What do we learn about the problem-solution of this issue in chunk 1? Tell students that those answers will help them as they prepare to explain the relationship of this chunk to the overall structure of the text.

Students work with teacher

Ask students to look at the "Chunk 1—Model" on their organizer and follow along as you read aloud. Tell students that this model will help as you work together to respond to the prompt for chunk 1. It will also serve as a model for chunks 2 and 3 as well. With this model in mind, think aloud as you (with solicited help from students) complete the constructed response for chunk Record your answer on the organizer in the constructed response answer area.

Students work with peers

As students work interdependently with a peer, ask them to look at the headlines for chunk 2 and see if they can verbally discuss and answer this question: What do we learn about the problem-solution of this issue in chunk 2? Next, tell students to refer to the "Chunk 1—Model," perhaps even jotting down some similar notes before they begin to write. With this model in mind, students should work together to complete the constructed response for chunk 2. Circulate around the room to answer questions or give feedback. As students finish, display their work and facilitate a conversation about the merits. Choose a model to record on your organizer.

Students work alone

Ask students to work independently to complete the constructed response for chunk 3.

Teacher formatively assesses student work

As students are working, circulate to read as many responses as possible. As students finish, call on several students to display their work. Facilitate a conversation to discuss the merits of the responses. Students will either agree on a model that represents the class or will write an entirely new response as a class.

Lesson Step	Explanatory Notes for the Teacher
6. Teacher returns to the content standard to identify progress in understanding and retaining new content.	In order to show what they learned from the text, ask students to write an exit ticket in response to this stem: In what ways did the reading, thinking, and writing you did today help you understand the content standard? Explain.
7. Closure	Ask students to reflect on their current level of understanding of the content standard(s) and the literacy skill(s) they worked with today by using "fist to five" hand signals to the following questions as you display them, read them aloud, and ask for student responses: On a scale of fist to five, where making a fist means not at all and holding up all five fingers means so completely that you could be the teacher, rate your understanding of the following content standard: _____ On a scale of fist to five, where making a fist means not at all and holding up all five fingers means so completely that you could be the teacher, rate your level of understanding of the following CCSS literacy skill: _____

Visit **go.solution-tree.com/commoncore** to download and print this figure.

Identify-Analyze-Relate (Cause-Effect)

The Gist of Identify-Analyze-Relate (Cause-Effect)

Students turn sentences into headlines as they analyze the cause-effect structure of a text. In the +feature of the lesson, they write a constructed response describing how each chunk of the text contributes (relates) to the overall structure of the text.

CCR Anchor Standard 5 for Reading: *Analyze the structure of texts, including how specific sentences, paragraphs, and larger portions of the text (e.g., a section, chapter, scene, or stanza) relate to each other and the whole.*

This strategy and its companion, Strategy 14, use the same lesson design to show students how to analyze two of the most problematic text structures for students: problem–solution and cause–effect. If you have not already worked with Strategy 14, you will benefit from skimming through it. There are two figures and some background knowledge that will not be repeated in this strategy. The lesson designs for these strategies are virtually identical. Only the actual text structure of our sample text and the text you choose for students to read differ. In this strategy, the focus is on cause and effect. We will aid you in showing your students how to read text, identify and analyze its structure, and then show the relationship of the various parts of the text to its whole in a text in which the author describes a cause-effect relationship between individuals, events, or ideas in order to draw a conclusion.

Background Knowledge

If you did not read the Background Knowledge section in Strategy 14, you may find the information there helpful for the implementation of Strategy 15. The lesson design used in Strategies 14 and 15 can also be adapted to the remaining four text structures shown in figure 14.6 (page 189).

The text structure we selected for modeling in this strategy is one of the most problematic for students at every grade level. The concept of *causation* or *causality* refers to a relationship between two things. Students seem to have no problem with identifying cause and effect when it comes to their personal lives or experiences at school. They can easily tell teachers their version of why a homework assignment was not completed or the why they have a broken arm but often are powerless to tease out cause and effect in text they are reading. Show them how it works with this strategy.

Understanding How the Strategy Works

If you have already used Strategy 14, you will already have a sense of how the strategy works. However, in order to see how the strategy works with a cause–effect text structure, review the sample text in figure 15.1 (Flesch–Kincaid grade level 12.2) and the completed organizer in figure 15.2 (page 198) that replicates the process you and your students will use. Note that the text is divided into three chunks in order to make the identify–analyze–relate steps more manageable and the sentences are consecutively numbered to help students refer to them in their organizers.

FIGURE 15.1: Sample Text for Identify-Analyze-Relate (Cause-Effect)

"We Lost the War on Drugs"
Chunk 1
(1) When President Richard Nixon created the Drug Enforcement Administration by executive order 40 years ago, the promise was a diminishing market for illegal drugs and a decrease in crime and violence. (2) The reality has been much different.
(3) In the early 1970s very few Americans had ever used an illegal drug. (4) Now nearly half of us have. (5) Illegal drugs are available to anyone willing to pursue them.
(6) The violence in producing countries in Central and South America and transit countries such as Mexico and the Caribbean has increased to the point that it threatens the stability of some governments.
(7) We have spent over $1 trillion on the ever escalating drug war. (8) Ironically, the only drug that has decreased in use is tobacco.
(9) The United Nations and the United States work to force all countries to adhere to the same drug laws and policies regardless of logic or outcome. (10) Nevertheless, a few countries have tried different approaches.

Chunk 2

(11) From the beginning, the Netherlands tolerated sales of marijuana for personal use in their famous "coffee shops." (12) The Dutch now use marijuana at about half the rate of Americans. (13) The rates of cocaine and heroin use in the Netherlands are far lower than here.

(14) In 1994, the Swiss began giving injectable doses of heroin to addicts at certified medical centers. (15) Crime among the addicts decreased markedly, employment increased and their health improved dramatically.

(16) Portugal decriminalized all drugs in 2001 and put the money saved on law enforcement into education and medical treatment. (17) Crime, drug use by teenagers, HIV, overdoses and heroin use all declined.

(18) Fifteen U.S. states have decriminalized possession of marijuana. They have about the same rates of cannabis use as the other states. (19) Sixteen states and the District of Columbia have voted to allow use of marijuana as a medicinal herb. (20) They have not experienced an increase in use among the young or increased crime.

Chunk 3

(21) In spite of evidence that alternative approaches can be useful drug prohibition laws remain entrenched.

(22) Nixon appointed the National Commission on Marihuana and Drug Abuse, then ignored its recommendations, as well as this prescient observation: "Perhaps the major consequence of . . . well-meaning efforts to do something about drug use . . . has been the creation of a vested interest in the perpetuation of the problem among those dispensing and receiving funds."

(23) Forty years later the funds have increased exponentially and the vested interests distort public policy in a myriad of ways.

(24) Federal anti-drug grants and asset forfeiture policies have made pursuing low-level drug dealers and users a top priority for police departments.

(25) Meanwhile, clearance rates for violent crimes are abysmally low. Homicide clearance has dropped from 91 percent in 1965 to 65 percent today.

(26) Defense contractors lobbied vigorously for the Andean Counterdrug Initiative and the Mérida Initiative. (27) These programs pay for transport helicopters, surveillance aircraft and other military equipment as well as spraying crops with herbicide. (28) More than $10 billion has been spent.

(29) Private security contractors hire multiple lobbying firms and receive billions from the federal government to carry out global counternarcotics activities.

(30) Since the early 1970s, the United States has built the largest prison system in the history of the world. (31) Americans are imprisoned at seven times the rate of Europeans. (32) The liquor industry financed the opposition to California's Proposition 19 in 2010 which would have legalized marijuana for adult use. (33) The pharmaceutical industry does a massive amount of lobbying. (34) It has a strong financial interest in making cannabis legal only as a pharmaceutical product, not as a plant.

(35) The "War on Drugs" is more disruptive and destructive than the drugs themselves. (36) It has increased drug use, eroded our civil rights, skewed policing and funding priorities, put control of dangerous drugs in the hands of criminals and threatened democracy throughout our hemisphere.

continued →

(37) Reform organizations, religious groups, medical associations, the NAACP and leaders such as President Jimmy Carter, Kofi Annin and the former presidents of Brazil, Colombia and Mexico have all advocated for changes in drug policy.

(38) The responsible course of action for the federal government is to allow countries and states to adopt the policies their citizens deem appropriate and just.

Source: Reprinted by permission of the author, Suzanne Wills. This article originally appeared in the Austin American-Statesman *on December 8, 2011.*

FIGURE 15.2: Sample Organizer for Identify-Analyze-Relate (Cause-Effect)

Text title: "We Lost the War on Drugs" Name:			
Directions: Record the specific sentence number(s) in column 1 that contains either a direct or implied statement of the causes. Write the headline in column 2. Record the numbers for sentences containing information about effects in column 3 and headlines in column 4.			
Causes		**Effects**	
Column 1 Sentence number	**Column 2** Cause headline	**Column 3** Sentence number	**Column 4** Effect headline
Chunk 1			
1, 2	DEA reality different than promise made 40 years ago	3, 4, 5, 6	Illegal drug use increases; violence increases
7	1 trillion spent in escalating drug war	8	Irony? War on drugs decreases use of tobacco
Chunk 2			
11	Netherlands tolerates sale and personal use of marijuana	12	Dutch use of marijuana about half the rate of Americans
		13	Rates of cocaine and heroin use in Netherlands lower than here
14	Heroin given to Swiss addicts	15	Among Swiss addicts: decrease in crime; increase in employment; improved health
16	Portugal decriminalizes drugs; moves money from enforcement to education and treatment	17	Portugal sees drop in crime, drug use, HIV, and overdoses
18	15 U.S. states decriminalize possession of marijuana	18	States with decriminalized marijuana possession see no increase in use

19	16 states allow medical use of marijuana	20	States allowing medical marijuana see no increase in use of crime
Chunk 3			
22	Nixon appoints National Commission on Marihuana and Drug Abuse	22	Nixon ignores commission's recommendations
23	Increased funds for DEA in last 45 years	23	Vested interests distort public policy
24	Federal antidrug grants make pursuing dealers a priority	24	Homicide clearance rates drop 26% since 1965
26, 27	Defense contractors lobby for counterdrug initiatives		
29	Private contractors, lobbyists receive billions		
		35, 36	"War on Drugs" increases drug use, erodes civil rights
37	Reformers advocate drug policy changes		

Identify-Analyze-Relate+

+Prompt: Write a constructed response that shows your understanding of how each chunk relates to the overall structure of the text as a whole as well as to each other. Well-written constructed responses will effectively weave text-specific evidence into the response.

Chunk 1—Model for examining the relationship of this chunk to the text

This chunk introduces the cause-effect organizational pattern and the contrasts between the promises of the DEA and the realities, indirectly reveals the thesis, and sets up the author's discussion about how other countries approach drugs.

Constructed Response Answer

Chunk 1

Chunk 1 introduces the cause-effect text structure that will enable the author to discuss the differences between the "promises" of the DEA and the "much different" reality. The author shows the actual effects of the executive order Nixon signed forty years ago, which resulted in an increase in illegal drug use and "violence in producing . . . and transit countries." The chunk ends with the author's introduction to the idea that there are "different approaches" to the issue of drugs that she will discuss in the next chunk. The author alludes to her thesis—which she ultimately reveals at the end of the text: the federal government should allow for "different approaches" to policies related to drugs.

Chunk 2

The author continues to use the cause-effect text structure to show the "different approaches" taken by countries where drugs are tolerated or decriminalized (the cause) and the use of drugs (the effect). In the Netherlands, where sales and personal use of marijuana are tolerated, the Dutch use the drug "at about half the rate of Americans." U.S. states where possession has been decriminalized have "about the same rates of cannabis use as the other states."

continued →

> **Chunk 3**
>
> Chunk 3 focuses on the "vested interests" of defense contractors and private security contractors who vigorously seek money (the cause) and the amounts of money they receive (the effect). After showing the causes and effects, the author ultimately draws the conclusion that the "war on drugs" is worse than the "drugs themselves." She definitively states her thesis—that the federal government should allow countries and states to "adopt policies" based on what their citizens want.

Items to Prepare

Note that figures 14.5, A Mini-Lesson for Writing Headlines (page 188), and 14.6, Types of Text Structures (page 189), will serve the same purpose for this strategy as they did in Strategy 14. In addition to those two reproducible figures that are carried forward from the prior strategy, there are two new figures to support instruction for Strategy 15. Figure 15.3 contains student-friendly definitions of the terms you will explain as you show your students how to execute this strategy during their reading. Some of the definitions will be duplicates of those in the previous strategy, but there is a student-friendly definition for the cause–effect text structure that you will want to share with students.

FIGURE 15.3: Student-Friendly Definitions for Identify-Analyze-Relate (Cause-Effect)

Identify: Recognize or point something out in a text
Analyze: Read the text closely to determine its structure
Relate: Make (figure out) a connection between two or more things
Text: Anything you read (for example, textbooks, articles)
Text structure: The way an author decides to organize text
Purpose: The reason for which an author writes a text
Cause: To make something happen
Effect: A change that happens as a result of a cause
Cause-effect text structure: The author describes a causal relationship or connection between two things

Visit **go.solution-tree.com/commoncore** to download and print this figure.

The second reproducible, figure 15.4, is an organizer for you to record your thinking as you prepare to model the strategy and for students to record their thinking during their initial encounter with the strategy and in subsequent rehearsals in various content text selections.

FIGURE 15.4: Reproducible Organizer for Identify-Analyze-Relate (Cause-Effect)

Text title:			
Name:			
Directions: Record the specific sentence number(s) in column 1 that contains either a direct or implied statement of the causes. Write the headline in column 2. Record the numbers for sentences containing information about effects in column 3 and headlines in column 4.			
Causes		**Effects**	
Column 1 Sentence number	**Column 2** Cause headline	**Column 3** Sentence number	**Column 4** Effect headline
Chunk 1			
Chunk 2			
Chunk 3			
Identify-Analyze-Relate+			
+Prompt: Write a constructed response that shows your understanding of how each chunk relates to the overall structure of the text as a whole as well as to each other. Well-written constructed responses will effectively weave text-specific evidence into the response.			
Chunk 1—Model for examining the relationship of this chunk to the text			

continued →

Constructed Response Answer
Chunk 1
Chunk 2
Chunk 3

Visit **go.solution-tree.com/commoncore** to download and print this figure.

Lesson Plan

The lesson plan for showing your students how to execute Identify–Analyze–Relate (Cause–Effect) is found in figure 15.5.

FIGURE 15.5: Identify-Analyze-Relate (Cause-Effect) Lesson Plan

Lesson Step	Explanatory Notes for the Teacher
1. Teacher prepares and assembles the necessary materials.	1a. Choose content-related and standards-aligned text for teacher modeling and student reading, then: • Chunk text into three parts and number the sentences as shown in the sample text (figure 15.1, page 196). • Complete the reproducible organizer (figure 15.4, page 201) as a key for modeling with your text in preparation for teaching the lesson. 1b. Prepare photocopies for students of your selected text, the student-friendly definitions (figure 15.3, page 200), and the strategy's reproducible organizer (figure 15.4, page 201). 1c. As appropriate, assemble technology to use in modeling the strategy for students (for example, document camera, PPT slides, SMART Board, overhead transparencies, or posters).
2. Teacher identifies the content standards from state or district standards for students.	Display the content-specific standard you want students to understand and retain as a result of their reading, thinking, and writing. Discuss the standard with students.
3. Teacher shares an advance organizer, reviews the student-friendly definitions, and distributes teacher-prepared materials.	Share the following advance organizer or one of your own choosing: Understanding how something is organized—from the files on a computer to the aisles of the local pet store—gives us a tremendous advantage. As a reader, one of the initial challenges with any new piece of text is understanding how it is organized. Knowing the various text structures and being able to recognize them can be quite useful.

4.	Teacher models and provides rehearsal opportunities, gradually releasing responsibility to students for doing more of their own thinking and writing.	**Teacher models: Chunk 1** Ask students to read the first chunk silently. As you read the text aloud, ask students to listen to see if they can identify the text structure—the underlying organizational principle of this chunk. Call on students to give you the answer. Either verify or tell students that the text structure is cause-effect and explain that knowing that structure helps empower them as readers. Share figure 14.6, page 189, with students to review this structure and explain the value of knowing a text's structure. Tell students that you will model the process of identifying the causes and effects for this chunk. Reread the chunk aloud again and stop when you can identify either the causes or effects (stated or implied) in the text. Record the number(s) of the sentence(s) in column 1 or 3 of the organizer—depending on if the example is a cause or effect. Next, tell students that instead of just copying and pasting the sentences from the text to the organizer, you are going to do a little bit of additional processing in the form of turning the information from the text into a headline before copying it onto the organizer. In order to do that, tell students that there are some rules that you will review with them about writing headlines (figure 14.5, page 188). After reviewing the figure, go back to the sentence numbers you have recorded on the organizer, read the sentences aloud, and share ideas for a headline. With the help of students, write a model headline and record it in either column 2 or column 4 of the organizer—depending on whether it is a cause or effect. As you reread the rest of this chunk, repeat this process with each cause-effect you encounter. **Students work with teacher: Chunk 2** Ask students to read chunk 2 silently and then read it aloud. Ask students to go back into the text to underline sentences related to the cause with a solid line and sentences related to the effect with a dotted line. Call on students to share the sentences they have identified. Facilitate a discussion as students verify accurate answers. Record accurate sentence numbers on the organizer. Call on students to share ideas for headlines (remind them of the headline rules as necessary) and record model examples on the organizer. **Students work with peers: Chunk 3** Ask students to work independently to identify sentences related to cause-effect using the same underlining system as was used in chunk 2. Ask students to work interdependently to agree on the sentences that are related to the cause or the effect. After they have reached consensus, students will write headlines together. Circulate to answer questions and offer feedback.

continued →

Lesson Step	Explanatory Notes for the Teacher
5. Teacher formatively assesses student work.	Ask students to share the sentence numbers that relate to causes and effects and record accurate answers on the organizer. Call on students to share headlines for the sentences. Record models on the organizer. Formatively assess as many students as possible as you review their work and listen to their discussions.
	NOTE: At this point, you have two options: (1) conclude this lesson by going directly to steps 6 and 7, temporarily skipping the +feature (schedule the +feature for a later class period using the same text and organizers students have completed up to this point), or (2) extend this lesson by incorporating the +feature followed by steps 6 and 7.

Identify-Analyze-Relate+

Teacher models

Ask students to follow along as you read the +prompt aloud. Tell students that in order to complete this prompt, they will need to be able to examine and identify the relationship of each chunk to the text. In order to move forward with that understanding, display the organizer for chunk 1 with the headlines and model answering this question: What do we learn about the causes and effects of this issue in chunk 1? Tell students that those answers will help us as we prepare to explain the relationship of this chunk to the overall structure of the text.

Students work with teacher

Ask students to look at the "Chunk 1—Model" on their organizer and follow along as you read aloud. Tell students that this model will help as you work together to respond to the prompt for chunk 1. It will also serve as a model for chunks 2 and 3 as well. With this model in mind, think aloud as you (with solicited help from students) complete the constructed response for chunk 1. Record your answer on the organizer in the constructed response answer area.

Students work with peers

As students work interdependently with a peer, ask them to look at the headlines for chunk 2 and see if they can verbally discuss and answer this question: What do we learn about the causes and effects of this issue in chunk 2? Next, tell students to refer to the "Chunk 1—Model," perhaps even jotting down some similar notes about this chunk before they begin to write. With this model in mind, students should work together to complete the constructed response for chunk 1. Circulate around the room to answer questions or give feedback. As students finish, display their work and facilitate a conversation about the merits. Choose a model to record on your organizer.

Students work alone

Ask students to work independently to complete the constructed response for chunk 3.

Teacher formatively assesses student work

As students are working, circulate to read as many responses as possible. As students finish, call on several students to display their work. Facilitate a conversation to discuss the merits of the responses. Students will either agree on a model that represents the class or write an entirely new response as a class.

6.	Teacher returns to the content objective to identify progress in understanding and retaining new content.	In order to identify student progress with the new content, ask students to write an exit ticket in response to this stem: In what ways did the reading, thinking, and writing you did today help you understand the content standard? Explain.
7.	Closure	Ask students to reflect on their current level of understanding of the content standard(s) and the literacy skill(s) they worked with today by using "fist to five" hand signals to the following questions as you display them, read them aloud, and ask for student responses: On a scale of fist to five, where making a fist means not at all and holding up all five fingers means so completely that you could be the teacher, rate your understanding of the following content standard: _____ On a scale of fist to five, where making a fist means not at all and holding up all five fingers means so completely that you could be the teacher, rate your level of understanding of the following CCSS literacy skill: _____

Visit **go.solution-tree.com/commoncore** to download and print this figure.

Purpose-Content-Style

The Gist of Purpose-Content-Style

Students read a text to identify the author's purpose, the development of the content of the text, and the author's style. In the +feature of the lesson plan, students complete a constructed response to explain how purpose shapes content and style.

CCR Anchor Standard 6 for Reading: *Assess how point of view or purpose shapes the content and style of a text.*

The CCR Anchor Standard 6 for Reading, which inspired this strategy, suggests two perspectives from which to examine the content and style of a text: *point of view* and *purpose.* We have selected *purpose* as the focus of Strategy 16.

Students will likely be familiar with the term *purpose* since it is widely used in elementary literacy instruction during reading to identify an author's reason for writing a specific text or for planning to write an essay designed to serve a specific purpose. *Purpose* is why the author has written a text or what he or she hopes to accomplish by writing the text. As you and your students work with a new text for the first time, the question is: Why is the author writing this text?

Likewise, *content* is a familiar term to students. Content is what the text is about. *Central idea* is the term you will find in the organizer to describe content. In addition to identifying the central idea of the text, students will also be asked to describe how the text is developed. In order to do this, they must be ready to list the key details and ideas that have something important to say about this central idea and how the author uses them to accomplish his or her purpose.

So, as you and your students consider content in the context of the Purpose-Content-Style strategy, you will be asking a two-part question: What is this text about (that is, its central idea), and how does the author develop that idea (what supporting details and information are provided) to accomplish his or her purpose?

The term *style* may be a new one for students. It refers to how an author uses language. Two authors could have similar purposes for writing, choose to write about the same content, and even select similar kinds of ideas and details to develop that content, but write in remarkably different ways. Figure P2.1, Elements of Style (page 147), describes five categories one can use to identify the various ways authors employ language in their writing: diction, syntax, figurative language, imagery, and sound devices. However, there is nothing like a good analogy to help you understand what style is. The following comes from a teacher friend, Christopher Schmidt (personal communication, March 9, 2012):

> Consider, for example, Louis Armstrong's rendition of "What a Wonderful World" and compare it to an orchestral rendition of Vivaldi's "Spring" from *Four Seasons*. Both compositions are written to entertain and possibly even inspire [*purpose*]. Both are about green leaves and birds and bees [*content presented in a similar text structure, a musical score*]. Both are written from the perspective of a grateful and joyful human observer of nature [*point of view*]. But they have *very* different styles. The two songs sound different, and they appeal to different audiences, because they have different styles. Analyzing an author's style is like analyzing the style of a piece of music—like remarking that Louis Armstrong's hobbled vocal chords remind you of a bee buzzing around a flower or remarking that the pulsing downbeat behind Vivaldi's melody resembles the awakened life of springtime [*blood and water coursing through the veins of beast and fern*].

Background Knowledge

It's time to do a little recursive teaching and review several key concepts that are essential to understanding the CCR Anchor Standards for Reading. Print out a copy of figure P1.3, Types of Informational Text (page 25), and figure P2.1, Elements of Style (page 147). While you have these two figures in front of you, consider these big ideas related to your implementation of the CCR Anchor Standards for Reading thus far:

- The standards and assessments that will measure your students' mastery of the standards are heavily weighted toward expository informational (content materials) and literary informational (opinion pieces, essays, historical, scientific, and technical accounts written for a broad audience) texts.

- Both kinds of informational texts are written for a similar set of purposes (column 2 of figure P1.3).

- The content of informational texts can be organized for the reader in a variety of different ways called text structures (column 3 of figure P1.3). Strategies 14 and 15 demonstrated how to analyze problem-solution texts and cause-effect texts. We have only listed the most basic text structures in figure 14.6 (page 189). This is not an exhaustive or definitive list.

- The purpose an author has for writing a piece of text shapes both the content (what the text is about, including its central idea and supporting details and ideas) as well as the style of the text (the various ways the author chooses to use words, phrases, and sentences).

- The elements of style may be a brand-new topic for discussion in content classrooms, and many content textbooks are entirely devoid of style. The reason for this, in our opinion, is that their authorship is often by committee. However, you can readily find literary informational text related to your content that will show your students that reading science and history, for example, can be a lively and engaging experience. The elements of style are described (in a somewhat limited fashion) in figure P2.1. You will discover how they are used and teased out of text in the sample organizer in figure 16.4 (page 214).

Understanding How the Strategy Works

Figure 16.1 is a sample text (Flesch-Kincaid grade level 12.8) selected to show you how Purpose-Content-Style works, and the sample organizer in figure 16.2, page 211, is your on-ramp to understanding this strategy.

FIGURE 16.1: Sample Text for Purpose-Content-Style

"Giffords Case Raises Awareness of Traumatic Brain Injury"
Chunk 1
The tragic circumstances surrounding the incident in which U.S. Rep. Gabrielle Giffords was shot in the head have significantly increased awareness of traumatic brain injury (TBI). I believe her decision to resign from her congressional seat was the right thing to do. Rather than go through the rigors of a re-election campaign, she has chosen to continue to go through the rigors of rehabilitation. This is a good choice, not only for herself but also for the 5.4 million other Americans who live with the consequences of a TBI.
In the U.S. it is estimated that there are 1.7 million new cases of TBI per year and many more that go unreported. In contrast, there are estimated to be up to 11,000 new cases of multiple sclerosis and approximately 40,000 new cases of Parkinson's disease each year.
Fortunately, most TBIs are considered mild. However, a concussion, which is considered a mild brain injury, was once thought to have little to no residual effects.

continued →

We are just now learning about the long-term effects on cognition and behavior. Post-mortem studies of professional football players are finding that multiple hits to the head result in changes in the brain that resemble Alzheimer's disease.

Chunk 2

There have been tremendous advances in the treatment of TBI but we still have a long way to go in the area of post-acute and long-term rehabilitation. Robotic interventions are being explored in which isolated arm, wrist or hand movements are facilitated mechanically and even electrically. Leg movements and body weight can be controlled by a robotic device to help regain the ability to walk. While it is still early, some evidence suggests that a robotic intervention does not require enough effort on the part of the patient and the patient plays a less active role in the therapy session. The more the patient actively participates, the more likely there are to be long-term gains as the brain responds and adapts in a more normal fashion.

Our own research suggests that some individuals can benefit from high-intensity, long-duration physical therapy even years after the injury. Our preliminary studies have shown that a properly prescribed aerobic conditioning program can improve the cardiorespiratory fitness of a person with a TBI. Improved cardiorespiratory fitness has physiologic, biochemical and psychological benefits in many patients, and certainly we should all strive to be more physically active to help prevent cardiovascular disease, Type 2 diabetes and early onset dementia, just to name a few chronic disabling conditions.

Chunk 3

Rep. Giffords' injury was serious and could have lifelong effects. It has been more than a year since she was injured, and she is fortunate to have the resources available that enable her to continue her rehabilitation. If you watched the YouTube video on her website where she announced her resignation, you could see she still has challenges that hopefully she will be able to overcome.

Rep. Giffords is fortunate that her costs are covered by the workers' compensation plan available to all federal employees. Unfortunately, not everyone is going to receive the kind of care that Giffords has and will continue to receive. If we assume you were covered by Medicare (total coverage is capped at $1,880 per year for physical and speech therapy combined), your number of one-hour sessions would be significantly less than what the congresswoman is receiving. Additional sessions would have to be paid for by other third-party payers or out-of-pocket.

The kind of care the average American can expect is dependent on the insurance plan (if any), state of residence and, probably most importantly, how strongly they or family members/caregivers advocate for their needs.

Rep. Giffords' office has made it known that not everyone has been as fortunate as she in receiving the full spectrum of treatment. Our biggest challenges are funding for research and access to high-quality treatment.

As she continues her therapy, Rep. Giffords will teach us all about the potential for improvement long after the initial event. Her world changed in an instant, and it could happen to anyone.

FIGURE 16.2: Sample Organizer for Purpose-Content-Style

Text title: "Giffords Case Raises Awareness of Traumatic Brain Injury" Name:		
Directions: Read to identify the author's purpose, the content of the text, and author's style for each chunk. Record responses in the appropriate boxes.		
Column 1 **Purpose, or why the author writes**	**Column 2** **Content, or what the text is about**	**Column 3** **Style, or how the author uses language**
Chunk 1		
To get the attention of the reader by conveying information about U.S. Representative Giffords' recent traumatic brain injury (TBI) and increase awareness about TBI by informing the reader of the frequency with which traumas occur	**Central Idea:** Frequency and impact of traumatic brain injuries **Key supporting details/ideas:** There are a greater number of new cases of TBI a year (7 million) than multiple sclerosis (11,000) and Parkinson's (40,000). **Key supporting details/ideas:** Mild brain injuries, like multiple "hits to heads" of football players, result in "long-term effects."	**Example of Style:** The author uses the sound device of alliteration with the repetition of the "r" sound in "rather than go through the rigors of a re-election campaign, she has chosen to continue to go through the rigors of rehabilitation." **Example of Style:** The author uses the sound device of alliteration with the repetition of the "h" sound in "hits to the head." **Example of Style:** The diction is both academic: "post-mortem," "residual effects"; and informal: "shot in the head," "multiple hits to the head," "I believe."
Chunk 2		
To explain the differences in the preliminary advances in the treatment of TBI	**Central Idea:** Treatment advances are tremendous and preliminary. **Key supporting details/ideas:** There are differences in the solutions that are being studied in the area of post-acute and long-term rehabilitation, including (a) robotic interventions and (b) high-intensity, long-duration physical therapy.	**Example of Style:** The diction is academic: "physiological," "biochemical," and "psychological." **Example of Style:** The author uses an active voice (first-person): "Our own research suggests . . ."

continued →

Chunk 3		
To explain the most important aspects of recovery from a TBI and provide a subtle appeal for better funding for research	**Central Idea:** Recovery is dependent on resources. **Key supporting details/ideas:** There are differences in the kind of care someone who is "fortunate" to have resources will receive versus the kind of care someone who is on, for example, Medicare will receive. **Key supporting details/ideas:** There are differences in the kind of care someone will receive if he or she has an advocate.	**Example of Style:** The author uses repetition of the words "fortunate" and "unfortunate." **Example of Style:** The author uses an active voice (first person): "Our biggest challenges are funding . . ."

Purpose-Content-Style+

+Prompt: Write constructed responses for each chunk that identify (1) how the author's purpose shapes the content and (2) how the author's purpose shapes the style. Well-written constructed responses will effectively weave the text-specific evidence together seamlessly in the response.

Planning Model

What is the relationship between the author's purpose, content, and style?	Content	Purpose (to inform about TBIs) shapes the central idea (frequency and impact of the injuries) and the key supporting details and ideas (7 million new TBIs a year).
	Style	Purpose (to inform about TBIs) shapes the author's style (academic language) in order to achieve an impact (credibility for the author).

Constructed Responses

Chunk 1

How does the author's purpose (to inform) shape:

Content?

The author chooses to inform the reader about the magnitude of the problem of traumatic brain injuries by comparing the differences between the number of new cases of TBI per year, approximately 7 million, with the 11,000 new cases of multiple sclerosis and 40,000 new cases of Parkinson's disease. The author continues to provide information about the importance of the problem by explaining how even a mild brain injury can result in "long-term effects."

Style?

The author uses alliteration to draw attention to the important choice that Giffords made between the "rigors of a re-election campaign" and the "rigors of rehabilitation." The author's continued use of alliteration ("hits to the head") draws attention to the sound that is increasingly associated with a TBI on the football field. The author uses diction that is academic to explain the effects of a TBI and to create credibility for himself as someone who is able to speak with authority on this subject. His diction is also, at times, informal to show his personal involvement with and sensitivity to the subject.

Chunk 2

How does the author's purpose (to explain) shape:

Content?

The author explains the differences as he compares the two "advances in the treatment of TBI" and cautions that there is still "a long way to go" in terms of research. Although it is "still early," the author points out that evidence suggests a robotic intervention "does not require enough effort on the part of the patient" to produce the kind of long-term gains that will more likely occur from "high-intensity long-duration" therapy.

Style?

The author continues to use diction that is academic to explain the advances in treatment and create credibility for himself as someone who speaks with authority about the advances. His use of an active voice from the first-person point of view ("our own research suggests") connects him personally and quite directly to the research on the benefits of long-term physical therapy.

Chunk 3

How does the author's purpose (to explain) shape:

Content?

The author chooses to explain how resources can impact recovery from a TBI by showing the differences in the kind of care individuals may receive. "Fortunate" individuals have both insurance and "probably most importantly . . . family members/care-giver advocates."

Style?

The author chooses to use repetition of the word "fortunately" as a way of contrasting the potential for recovery of those who have access to resources—in this case, Giffords—to those who do not. The author uses an active voice ("our biggest challenges") from the first-person point of view to connect himself personally and directly to those facing challenges with funding for research.

Items to Prepare

There are three reproducible figures to support Purpose–Content–Style. The first reproducible, figure 16.3, displays student-friendly definitions of the terms that relate to the various aspects of the strategy.

FIGURE 16.3: Student-Friendly Definitions for Purpose-Content-Style

Purpose: Why the author writes the text (what the author hopes to accomplish in the text)
Content: What the text is about
Develop: The way an author tells more and more about the content of a text in order to make the reader understand more clearly
Style: How the author uses language

Visit **go.solution-tree.com/commoncore** to download and print this figure.

The second reproducible, figure 16.4, is an organizer on which to record your thinking as you process your chosen text prior to modeling for students. Your students will also complete this organizer, recording their thinking as they execute the strategy.

FIGURE 16.4: Reproducible Organizer for Purpose-Content-Style

Text title: Name:		
Directions: Read to identify the author's purpose, the content of the text, and author's style for each chunk. Record responses in the appropriate boxes.		
Column 1 **Purpose, or why the author writes**	**Column 2** **Content, or what the text is about**	**Column 3** **Style, or how the author uses language**
Chunk 1		
	Central Idea:	Example of Style:
	Key supporting details/ideas:	Example of Style:
	Key supporting details/ideas:	Example of Style:
		Example of Style:
Chunk 2		
	Central Idea:	Example of Style:
	Key supporting details/ideas:	Example of Style:
	Key supporting details/ideas:	Example of Style:
		Example of Style:

Chunk 3		
	Central Idea:	**Example of Style:**
	Key supporting details/ideas:	**Example of Style:**
	Key supporting details/ideas:	**Example of Style:**
		Example of Style:

Purpose-Content-Style+
+Prompt: Write constructed responses for each chunk that identify (1) how the author's purpose shapes the content and (2) how the author's purpose shapes the style. Well-written constructed responses will effectively weave the text-specific evidence together seamlessly in the response.

Planning Model		
What is the relationship between the author's purpose, content, and style?	**Content**	Purpose (_____) shapes the central idea (_____) and the key supporting details and ideas (_____).
	Style	Purpose (_____) shapes the author's style (_____) in order to achieve an impact (_____).

Constructed Responses
Chunk 1
How does the author's purpose shape:
Content?
Style?
Chunk 2
How does the author's purpose shape:
Content?
Style?
Chunk 3
How does the author's purpose shape:
Content?
Style?

Visit **go.solution-tree.com/commoncore** to download and print this figure.

The third reproducible, figure 16.5, contains a set of questions for students to ask while they are initially reading a text. The answers they discover as they read will help them determine the author's purpose, the content of the text, and how the author uses language in various ways—style.

FIGURE 16.5: Questions to Ask When Assessing How Purpose Shapes Content and Style

Purpose: Why the Author Is Writing the Text	
Is the author writing to. . .	a. Inform or teach to help the reader understand something about the information?
	b. Explain his or her thoughts about a topic?
	c. Entertain or amuse?
	d. Describe how something works, what it looks like?
	e. Show how something works or why a certain perspective is accurate or inaccurate?
	f. Persuade, convince, or appeal to someone to agree with a stance, position, or idea?
	g. Show or prove why something is true or false?
Content: What the Text Is About	
What is the author writing about?	What is the text mainly about (central idea)?
	What are the key supporting details and ideas?
Do the author's key supporting details and ideas . . .	a. Point out similarities and/or differences?
	b. Use statistics or data?
	c. Discuss problems and solutions?
	d. Share anecdotes or tell stories?
	e. Provide definitions?
	f. Give explanatory details?
	g. Show cause and effect?
Style: How the Author Uses Language	
How does the author . . .	a. Use diction?
	b. Use syntax?
	c. Use figurative language?
	d. Use imagery?
	e. Use sound devices?

Visit **go.solution-tree.com/commoncore** to download and print this figure.

Lesson Plan

The lesson plan for showing your students how to execute the Purpose-Content–Style strategy is found in figure 16.6.

FIGURE 16.6: Lesson Plan for Purpose-Content-Style

Lesson Step	Explanatory Notes for the Teacher
1. Teacher prepares and assembles the necessary materials.	1a. Choose content-related and standards-aligned text for teacher modeling and student reading, then: • Chunk text into three parts as shown in the sample text (figure 16.1, page 209). • Complete the reproducible organizer (figure 16.4, page 214) as a key for modeling with your text in preparation for teaching the lesson. 1b. Prepare photocopies for students of your selected text, the student-friendly definitions (figure 16.3, page 213), and the strategy's reproducible organizer (figure 16.4). 1c. As appropriate, assemble technology to use in modeling the strategy for students (for example, document camera, PPT slides, SMART Board, overhead transparencies, or posters).
2. Teacher identifies the content standard from state or district standards for students.	Display the content-specific standard you want students to understand and retain as a result of their reading, thinking, and writing. Discuss the standard with students.
3. Teacher shares an advance organizer, reviews the student-friendly definitions, and distributes teacher-prepared materials.	Share the following advance organizer or one of your own choosing: Purpose determines everything. If your purpose when driving is to get to your destination quickly as opposed to getting to your destination safely, you may speed or fail to come to a complete stop at the stop sign. A writer's purpose determines everything as well. Purpose shapes everything from the content of the text to the way the author chooses to use language. Our goal as readers is to pay attention to the author's purpose to determine how it shapes content and style. Today, we will rehearse those skills.
4. Teacher models and provides rehearsal opportunities, gradually releasing responsibility to students for doing more of their own thinking and writing.	**Teacher models: Chunk 1** Ask students to read the first chunk silently before reading it aloud to them. Ask students to reflect on what they already know about the concept of "author's purpose" and facilitate a discussion—capturing accurate ideas on the board. If it is necessary to deepen their understanding, display figure 16.5 and review the questions for purpose. Think aloud as you process this chunk to determine the author's purpose for writing. Construct and record a response in column 1 for chunk 1.

continued →

Lesson Step	Explanatory Notes for the Teacher
4. Teacher models and provides rehearsal opportunities, gradually releasing responsibility to students for doing more of their own thinking and writing. *(continued)*	Next, consider content (the central idea of this chunk) by asking, "What is the information in this chunk mainly about?" Think aloud as you record the central-idea statement on the organizer. Refer to the questions for content on figure 16.5 (page 216) to review the ways in which key supporting details and ideas can be developed. Reread the chunk aloud again to identify the supporting details and ideas the author has used, and record your answers in column 2. Refer once again to figure 16.5. Read the questions for style. (Refer to figure P2.1, page 147, for more details if needed.) Read the text aloud again to identify examples of style—while soliciting the help of students. Record the examples of style in column 3 of the organizer. **Students work with teacher: Chunk 2** Ask students to read the text silently before you read it aloud to them. Ask students to identify the author's purpose for writing this chunk—using the questions from figure 16.5, page 216, as needed. Record accurate answers on the organizer. Ask students to work with you to agree on a central idea and record it on the organizer. Next, ask students to consider the key supporting details/ideas of chunk 2—referring to figure 16.5, as needed. Read the text aloud again if necessary. Call on students and record accurate answers on the organizer. Call on students to consider the style of chunk 2—referring to 14.6, page 188, and P2.1 as needed. Record accurate answers on the organizer. **Students work with peers: Chunk 3** Tell students to read the text silently before you read it aloud to them. Have students work with a partner to identify purpose, the central idea, supporting details and ideas, and style for this chunk. Circulate and offer help and feedback as students work to answer questions.
5. Teacher formatively assesses student work.	Ask several pairs to display their work for chunk 3. Facilitate a conversation with students as they discuss the merits of the work that is displayed. Record accurate models on the organizer. Use the work displayed and students' responses to formatively assess as many students as possible. NOTE: At this point, you have two options: (1) conclude this lesson by going directly to steps 6 and 7, temporarily skipping the +feature (schedule the +feature for a later class period using the same text and organizers students have completed up to this point), or (2) extend this lesson by incorporating the +feature followed by steps 6 and 7.

Purpose-Content-Style+

Teacher models

Ask students to refer to the +prompt (figure 16.4, page 214) for the constructed response. Read the prompt aloud. Ask students to reflect on the meaning of "shapes" as it is used by the standard and as it is used here. Call on students to help you make a list of possible synonyms on the board. These might include: *influences, determines, controls, forms,* and *dictates.* With a clearer understanding in mind, tell students that you want them to work with you as you write a response to the prompt.

Students work with teacher

The first task involves showing the relationship between purpose and content. Refer students to the Planning Model in the +prompt of the organizer. Read the model related to content. Explain that this is a planning model to analyze how purpose shapes content. With this model in mind, think aloud (with solicited help from students) as you record your constructed response on the organizer for chunk 1 in reference to content.

When you have finished answering the prompt related to content, begin to address the next task, showing the relationship between purpose and style. Refer students once again to the Planning Model on the organizer. Read the model related to style. Explain that this is a planning model to analyze how purpose shapes style. With this model in mind, think aloud (with solicited help from students) as you record your response on the organizer for chunk 1 in reference to style.

Students work with peers

Ask students to work with a partner to complete the constructed responses for chunk 2. Ask students to use the stems to complete a Planning Model for chunk 2 before they begin to write. Circulate around the room to answer questions and formatively assess students as they work interdependently. Display finished work and facilitate a conversation about the merits. Choose a model to record on your organizer.

Students work alone

Ask students to work independently to complete the constructed responses for chunk 3.

Teacher formatively assesses student work

As students are working, circulate throughout the room to read as many responses as possible. As students finish, call on several students to display their work. Facilitate a conversation to discuss the merits of the responses. Students will either agree on model responses to represent the class or write entirely new responses as a class.

6.	Teacher returns to the content standard to identify progress in understanding and retaining new content.	In order to identify student progress with the new content, ask students to write an exit ticket in response to this stem: In what ways did the reading, thinking, and writing you did today help you understand the content standard? Explain.
7.	Closure	Ask students to reflect on their current level of understanding of the content standard(s) and the literacy skill(s) they worked with today by using "fist to five" hand signals to the following questions as you display them, read them aloud, and ask for student responses: On a scale of fist to five, where making a fist means not at all and holding up all five fingers means so completely that you could be the teacher, rate your understanding of the following content standard: _____ On a scale of fist to five, where making a fist means not at all and holding up all five fingers means so completely that you could be the teacher, rate your level of understanding of the following CCSS literacy skill: _____

Visit **go.solution-tree.com/commoncore** to download and print this figure.

PART III:
Integration of Knowledge and Ideas

There may one day be modes and methods of information delivery that are as efficient and powerful as text, but for now there is no contest. To grow, our students must read lots, and more specifically they must read lots of 'complex' texts—texts that offer them new language, new knowledge, and new modes of thought.

—ADAMS (2009)

Part III presents a set of literacy strategies designed to help your students meet the standards found in the section of the Common Core College and Career Anchor Standards for Reading titled *Integration of Knowledge and Ideas*. As Marilyn Adams points out in the epigraph, when students don't read lots of complex texts, they end up with word and world knowledge deficits that in turn lead to a downward spiral of comprehension difficulties and a diminishing motivation to read. This is a vicious cycle that must be broken and sooner rather than later.

If the CCR Anchor Standards for Reading are a mountain to climb, Strategies 17–19 are at the stage of the climb where you feel as though you've been hiking forever, and rather than feeling a rush of confidence and adrenalin to carry you through the final push up the jagged cliffs that remain, you suddenly realize that everything up to this point has been easy compared to what is left. You wonder why you thought it was a good idea to even start the climb.

The big idea of the Integration of Knowledge and Ideas category is this: *students must be prepared to read critically, delineating and evaluating arguments, analyzing how authors develop themes and topics in their writing, and comparing two or more texts to build their knowledge.*

Comparative analysis is the peak of the mountain. Reading complex texts and understanding them is one thing, but now your students are being asked to analyze and compare them. This type of comparative analysis is usually the purview of teachers who teach AP or Honors English. Critical thinking is often reserved for literature read only by a select few students who are already pretty good and highly motivated hikers. The CCR Anchor Standards for Reading expect all teachers and students to climb this mountain—a daunting, but not impossible, task for you and your students. Strategies 17–19 will show you how to scaffold the process and steps of comparative analysis so that you can model it for your students in applicable content text. The text you use will not be literature but informational texts related to your content.

Navigate-Integrate-Evaluate

The Gist of Navigate-Integrate-Evaluate

Students navigate through and summarize content presented in diverse formats. Students then integrate the information in order to draw a conclusion. In the +feature of the lesson, students write a constructed response using embedded textual evidence to support their conclusion.

CCR Anchor Standard 7 for Reading: *Integrate and evaluate content presented in diverse formats and media, including visually and quantitatively, as well as in words.*

The Navigate-Integrate-Evaluate strategy consists of a several-step process in which students first *navigate* several different types of media, all focused on the same topic. Students continue to navigate as they move back and forth between their sources, thinking about how best to summarize each in one sentence as well as coming up with possible text-to-text connections or commonalities among them. This aspect of navigating is a way of compelling students to determine the central idea of what they have read before moving on to the next step. Absent this aspect of navigating, many students will skip through the various documents, assure themselves that they do understand, and come up frustrated in the second step when they are tempted to say as Cris Tovani (2000) says in the book titled *I Read It, But I Don't Get It.*

In the second step, students *integrate* the sources by reviewing their one-sentence summaries, recalling what they have read, and selecting two sources of information from which they can draw a conclusion supported by evidence in those sources. In the +feature of the lesson, students move to step 3, *evaluate,* in which they write a constructed response that includes embedded textual evidence. If you anticipate that large numbers of students will have difficulty with the independent writing of a one-sentence summary of each of the diverse resources you choose, plan for additional rehearsals of the summary writing process based on the Snapshot Summary strategy (page 95). Figure 7.6 (page 102) is a checklist for evaluating summaries. If students do not have copies of this reproducible, make them available or put up a poster-size version. Recall that in Strategy 9 there is a mini-lesson showing students how to embed textual evidence in the responses they write. Figure 9.3 (page 117) is a reproducible figure for reteaching or reviewing this process.

Background Knowledge

This strategy puts the spotlight on a critical literacy skill for the 21st century—the ability to integrate and evaluate information from diverse formats and media. The Internet has become the primary research tool for students looking for information about various topics in anticipation of completing school assignments or writing research reports, and while most teachers include an activity like this search and select activity in their classrooms, the final product is often just a poster with fancy graphics that tells little about the thinking and understanding of students. Donald J. Leu, Charles K. Kinzer, Julie Coiro, and Dana W. Cammack (2004) suggest five discrete types of reading skills needed to survive in a technological age: (1) identifying the essential questions, (2) locating information, (3) analyzing information, (4) synthesizing information, and (5) communicating information. All of these skills are a part of Navigate-Integrate-Evaluate.

Many districts are hyper-focused on technology and a concept that is becoming the new buzz phrase: *21st century learning*. They expect students to be able to integrate ideas and knowledge from many diverse sources to include quantitative charts and graphs as well as video. However, there is almost a blind faith in the power of laptops, notebooks, and devices like iPods to suddenly transform students into 21st century learners, skipping lightly over the compendium of challenging thinking "habits" that are required to understand and retain the big ideas of science and the social sciences: interpreting sources, evaluating evidence and competing claims, problem solving, and integrating the knowledge and ideas of the various disciplines into coherent mental scaffolds (Conley, 2005, 2007).

Each of the strategies in the book thus far has employed scaffolding. Our goal has been to provide scaffolded lesson designs and instructional resources that enable your students to tackle challenging reading and writing processes that would not have been possible for them to do at all without support. While Strategy 17 assumes that the majority of your students will be able to independently write a one-sentence summary about the central idea of each of the five different media sources you select for them to use, we do not assume that they can search for and select five credible media sources on a specific topic absent teacher support.

Although contemporary students would seem to be expert in navigating the Internet, they often have weak searching and selecting skills, particularly if you factor in the need for evaluation skills. John T. Guthrie and Irwin S. Kirsch (1987) describe searching and selecting as "the finding of text, browsing through information, or collecting resources for the purpose of answering questions, solving problems, or gathering information" (p. 220). Although searching–selecting is widely cited as both an essential workplace skill and a vital academic strategy, most students have not been expected to demonstrate their abilities to integrate the knowledge and ideas they find on the Internet with relevant print resources.

Understanding How the Strategy Works

Figure 17.1 is a completed sample organizer for this strategy. It introduces a variety of media examples similar to those you might choose for your students. We have encouraged you throughout the book to choose text that is not only related to the content you teach but also to the specific standards your students are expected to meet. The sample texts we have selected may or may not have any relevance for your specific content. You are the content expert. Therefore, we strongly suggest that you immediately begin collecting diverse media related to your course content and the standards.

FIGURE 17.1: Sample Organizer for Navigate-Integrate-Evaluate

Name:	
Part A **Directions:** Write a one-sentence summary for each of the sources.	
Column A **Sources**	**Column B** **One-sentence summary**
Figure 17.2 Editorial Cartoon "Why isn't smoking prevention working?"	The tobacco companies are spending more money to entice people to smoke than the government is spending to prevent people from starting to smoke or help those who are smoking to quit.
Figure 17.4 Op-Ed Piece "Innovative thinking in the war on cancer"	Until we "reframe" the way we approach cancer and use some innovative thinking, we will continue to make slow progress on lessening cancer's impact on people.

continued →

Figure 17.5 Letter to Editor "Salient Points"	The environment, our lack of physical activity, and our diets are contributing to the soaring incidences of cancer.
Figures 17.6a and 17.6b Cancer Trend Charts Male and Female	In relation to stomach and pancreatic cancer death rates, deaths associated with lung and bronchus cancers are much higher.
Figure 17.7 Cigarette Warning Label	There is a link between smoking and cancer.

Part B

Directions: Based on all of the information you have reviewed, what is one conclusion that you can draw that could be supported by information from at least two of the sources?

Conclusion	If we want to lessen cancer's impact on people, especially the impact from smoking, we should focus on campaigns to prevent people from starting to smoke in the first place.
Sources	Op–Ed Piece, "Innovative thinking in the war on cancer"
	Editorial cartoon, "Why isn't smoking prevention working?"

Navigate-Integrate-Evaluate+

+Prompt: Write a constructed response that includes or improves on the conclusion you have already written, supported by embedded textual evidence from the two sources you have already identified.

Before writing, use the constructed response planning area to record the evidence that you select for your response after evaluating all of the possible evidence you could use from the two sources.

Planning Area

Sources	Selected Evidence
Source 1 Op-Ed—"Innovative thinking in the war on cancer"	"We could spend a billion dollars on more lung cancer research or pay the college tuition of all 18-year-olds who have never smoked."
Source 2 Editorial cartoon—"Why isn't smoking prevention working?"	"Amount spent by tobacco companies marketing tobacco products: 28 million dollars a day." "Amount spent by the states to prevent smoking and to help smokers quit: 4 million dollars a day."

Constructed Response:

If we want to lessen cancer's impact on people, especially the impact of smoking, we should focus on campaigns to prevent people from starting to smoke in the first place. One idea is to have the states spend more money to prevent people from starting to smoke. The "4 million dollars a day" currently spent to keep people from smoking isn't enough to make an impact in relation to the "28 million dollars a day" the tobacco companies spend enticing them to smoke. Another prevention idea, promoted by Leonard Zwelling, a doctor in Houston, is to take the "billion dollars" currently spent on lung cancer research and use that money as an incentive by paying the college tuition of "all 18-year-olds who have never smoked."

Once you have read through the sample organizer, take a brief look at each of the media examples. Figure 17.2 is an editorial cartoon. This cartoon relates to the featured topic in these sample texts: cancer and its causes.

FIGURE 17.2: Editorial Cartoon

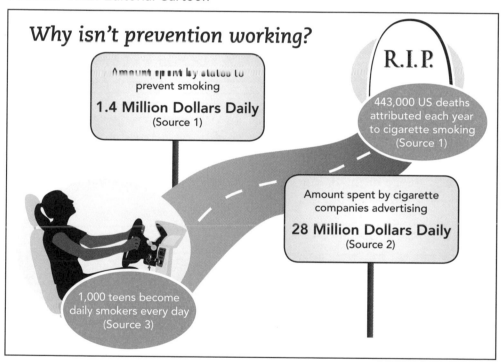

No doubt you have used political–editorial cartoons to enliven your lessons in the past, but many students, particularly ELs or students with insufficient background knowledge, need additional help with interpreting cartoons. Figure 17.3 (page 230) provides a mini-lesson for how to interpret a political–editorial cartoon.

FIGURE 17.3: How to Interpret a Political-Editorial Cartoon

1.	Read the caption (headline) on the cartoon and see if you can identify the central idea. Try to put that central idea into your own words. Here's a stem to help you: "This cartoon is mainly about . . . "Keep in mind that this is only a rough draft of the central idea. Next follow steps 2–8 to see if you discover any ideas or information that changes your thinking about what the central idea is.
2.	What historical or contemporary event or issue was the inspiration or motivation for this cartoon?
3.	Do you need more information about a topic to understand what the cartoon means? Use the resources in figure 12.5, Quick-REACH Toolkit, on page 157.
4.	Are any of the people shown in the cartoon real people (living or dead)?
5.	A caricature is an exaggerated drawing of a physical feature of an actual person. If a person has ears that stick out slightly, the cartoonist will draw the ears of that person in the cartoon to be the first thing you see when you look at the cartoon. Does the cartoonist use caricatures in the cartoon you are viewing?
6.	Symbols are objects pictured in the cartoon that stand for an idea. For example, an elephant stands for the Republican Party and a donkey stands for the Democratic Party. Are there any symbols in the cartoon you are viewing?
7.	What opinion or message do you think the cartoonist is trying to convey?
8.	Does the cartoonist seem to have any biases for or against a certain position or idea?
9.	Has your idea about the central idea of the cartoon changed as you have considered all of the different parts of the cartoon? Take a moment to quickly write down what you now think the central idea of the cartoon is.

Visit **go.solution-tree.com/commoncore** to download and print this figure.

The next piece of media, figure 17.4, is an op-ed piece about the topic of cancer (Flesch-Kincaid grade level 11.9).

FIGURE 17.4: An Op-Ed Piece

"Time for Some Innovative Thinking in the War on Cancer"
Chunk 1
In her book, *Innovation Generation*, Dr. Roberta Ness, the dean of the University of Texas School of Public Health, says innovative thinking can be taught. One teachable skill is framing, putting a problem in its proper context to create previously unimagined solutions.
One of Dr. Ness's examples of poor framing is the war on cancer begun in 1971 when President Nixon signed the National Cancer Act after saying:
"The time has come in America when the same kind of concentrated effort that split the atom and took man to the moon should be turned toward conquering this dread disease."
But is the martial metaphor an apt one? Cancer cells are more like normal cells than they are like invading strangers (e.g., bacteria). Cancer probably starts as a malfunctioning of multiple genes setting off a cascade of molecular missteps. The primary event is unclear, but it is probably part of the natural processes of aging in the face of environmental stressors, plus a contribution from innate genetic cancer proclivities.

Cancer could be like climate change on the cellular level. The abnormal genes resembling rising seas and wandering polar bears are the effects, not the causes, of a problem. Framing our quest to lessen its impact on people might be better considered in the words of Walt Kelly's Pogo: "We have met the enemy and he is us." Cancer, unfortunately, is part of life.

Chunk 2

Thus the cancer problem is not like the space race or the Manhattan Project. Getting to the moon and harnessing the destructive power of the atom required few new scientific insights to be reduced to practice. Those successes were due to the application of sufficient resources to problems with known technical barriers. The underlying principles needed to solve the cancer problem have not yet been elucidated, making the best technical route to a solution unclear.

The war on cancer currently is a single-minded national, big-science research strategy of completely identifying all the potential molecular aberrancies in clinical cancer, so as to target aberrant gene products and exploit an individual tumor's vulnerabilities. For the most part, in the common cancers that plague Americans—breast, lung, colon and prostate—therapeutic progress has been very slow. Screening, early detection and prevention strategies have been more successful.

Instead of concentrating all of our funding on research to develop weapons of mass destruction against cancer, we could use more funds to identify the risk factors that lead to cancer's development and ways to intervene before cancer arises. And we know many of these already: smoking, obesity, radiation, sexually transmitted diseases and asbestos exposure far outweigh innate genetic syndromes as causes of human cancer.

Chunk 3

We have some choices to make. We could spend a billion dollars on more lung cancer research or pay the college tuition of all 18-year-olds who have never smoked. We could analyze the genetics of thousands of human lung cancers yielding a great deal of new scientific information that may or may not extend the survival or quality of life of a single cancer patient, or we could pay tobacco farmers to switch to different crops and decrease the supply of the only FDA-regulated product that when used as designed, will kill human beings.

I am proposing that we reframe the cancer problem from one of waging war to one of using what we already know works and research ways to prevent as well as treat this very therapeutically resistant set of diseases.

Framing the cancer problem as a war for the past 40 years hasn't really gotten us all that far compared with the rapidity of the success of the Manhattan Project or the triumph of NASA reaching the moon a mere eight years after President Kennedy expressed our national goal to do so.

That's because the cancer problem is harder than splitting the atom or landing on the moon. Maybe it's time for some innovative thinking. Maybe it's time for a frame shift.

Figure 17.5, page 232, is a letter to the editor about our focus topic, cancer (Flesch–Kincaid grade level 8.0). It appeared in the *Houston Chronicle* in response to the previous op-ed piece.

FIGURE 17.5: Letter to the Editor

In the decades since the end of the Depression and World War II, the incidence of cancer has soared, and I don't think it is too much of a stretch to attribute that in large part to some significant changes that have happened in the way we live. First is the environment. When I moved to Houston in the 1950s to attend Rice, we never had smog; even then it was rare in Los Angeles. But more than smog, now we are daily bombarded with a soup of petrochemical waste in the air that we breathe. And that is true throughout the country, not just in Houston or Texas. Added to that, our homes are filled with thousands of chemicals that didn't exist 60 years ago; they are in what we eat, what we wear, what we drink and eat, and the air we breathe.

Second is our lifestyle. Physical activity is disappearing from our daily lives; children no longer walk or bike to school; most of the time the grocery store is not within walking distance; we are all way too car-dependent. That leads to a less healthy state for all who live that way, in turn leading to obesity, diabetes, and general poor health.

Finally and to me most important is what we eat; our diets are killing us. Our bodies are not getting the nutrition they need to stay healthy and to fight off disease. Almost all of our processed foods are laden with salt and high fructose corn syrup. Most of the fruits and vegetables are not grown locally, so they have to be harvested way before they reach maturity and therefore full nutritional value. For example, many of the tomatoes available to us have both the taste and the nutritional value of cardboard.

Is it any wonder that cancers attack us? Our bodies have lost the ability to fight for us, to fend off the bad things that are hovering around just waiting to attack. Unless and until we recognize that these are the reasons that we are not winning the war on cancer, unless and until we seriously start looking for prevention rather than cure, and unless and until we realize that our convenient lifestyles are killing us, we will not stop this disease. Actually we have known this for a long time, but there is very little government money devoted to healthier lifestyles and huge amounts devoted to subsidizing just the way we live now—how do you think we got this way?

Source: Daniel B. Barnum. Copyright 2012 Houston Chronicle Publishing Company. Reprinted with permission. All rights reserved.

Smoking causes approximately 90% of all lung cancer deaths in men and 80% of all lung cancer deaths in women.

Nearly one-third of all cancer deaths are directly linked to smoking.

FIGURE 17.7: A Cigarette Package Warning Label

Figure 17.6a is a line graph showing cancer trend levels for males. We adapted information from multiple Internet sites to create this particular graph comparing lung and bronchus cancer to two other types of cancers. Figure 17.6b presents similar information for females.

Figure 17.7 displays another type of media: a cigarette package with a warning label.

Items to Prepare

There are two reproducible figures that support Navigate-Integrate-Evaluate. The first, figure 17.8 (page 234), is a poster with student-friendly definitions of the terms you will explain as you show your students how to execute this strategy during their reading. Note that we define

FIGURE 17.6A: Age-Adjusted Cancer Death Rates, Males by Site, U.S., 1955–2005

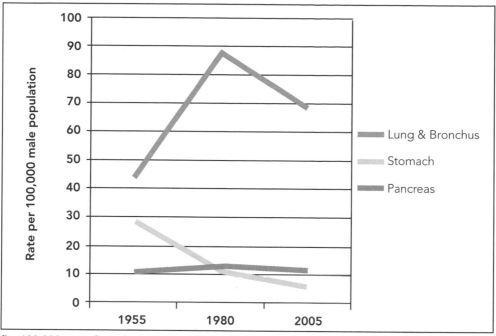

Per 100,000, age adjusted to the 2000 US standard population

Source: US Mortality Volumes 1930–1959, US Mortality Data 1960 to 2008, National Center for Health Statistics, Centers for Disease Control and Prevention. Copyright 2012, American Cancer Society, Inc., Surveillance Research.

FIGURE 17.6B: Age-Adjusted Cancer Death Rates, Females by Site, U.S., 1955–2005

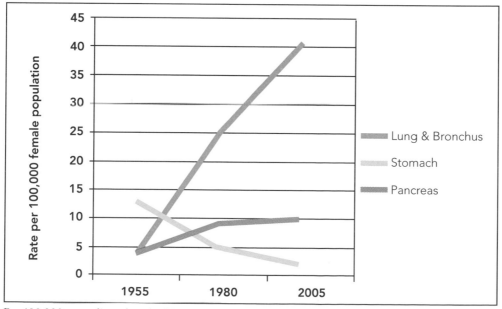

Per 100,000, age adjusted to the 2000 US standard population

Source: US Mortality Volumes 1930–1959, US Mortality Data 1960 to 2008, National Center for Health Statistics, Centers for Disease Control and Prevention. Copyright 2012, American Cancer Society, Inc., Surveillance Research.

the terms in the name of the strategy: navigate, integrate, and evaluate. Recursively teach these terms so that students will have multiple opportunities to see the terms in action as you model them and eventually deeply understand how to put these terms into action in their reading and writing.

FIGURE 17.8: Student-Friendly Definitions for Navigate-Integrate-Evaluate

---

Navigate: To read text in several kinds of media one after the other with understanding about what they mean and how they connect

Integrate: To think about all of the various kinds of media in terms of a single idea

Evaluate: To form an idea about the value or worth of your conclusion, to refine it if you need to, and to write a constructed response citing evidence from the text

Political-editorial cartoon: An illustration drawn in a comic book style that makes a statement about a current event

Letter to the editor: A letter written by a reader to a newspaper to make a point about a current issue or to respond to an article in the paper

Op-ed piece: The "op" stands for opposite, and the "ed" stands for editorial; refers to longer articles or commentaries that appear in the newspaper on the opposite page of the editorial page

---

Visit **go.solution-tree.com/commoncore** to download and print this figure.

The second reproducible, figure 17.9, is the organizer on which you will record your thinking for modeling the strategy. Your students will also use this reproducible to record their thinking during their initial encounter with the strategy and in subsequent rehearsals in various content text selections.

FIGURE 17.9: Reproducible Organizer for Navigate-Integrate-Evaluate

Name:	
Part A **Directions:** Write a one-sentence summary for each of the sources.	
Column A **Sources**	**Column B** **One-sentence summary**

Part B

Directions: Based on all of the information you have reviewed, what is one conclusion that you can draw that could be supported by information from at least two of the sources?

Conclusion	
Sources	

Navigate-Integrate-Evaluate+

+Prompt: Write a constructed response that includes or improves on the conclusion you have already written, supported by embedded textual evidence from the two sources you have already identified.

Before writing, use the constructed response planning area to record the evidence that you select for your response after evaluating all of the possible evidence you could use from the two sources.

Planning Area	
Sources	Selected Evidence
Source 1	
Source 2	
Constructed Response:	

Visit **go.solution-tree.com/commoncore** to download and print this figure.

Lesson Plan

The lesson plan for showing your students how to execute the Navigate-Integrate-Evaluate strategy is found in figure 17.10, page 236.

FIGURE 17.10: Lesson Plan for Navigate-Integrate-Evaluate

Lesson Step	Explanatory Notes for the Teacher
1. Teacher prepares and assembles the necessary materials.	1a. Choose content-related and standards-aligned media about a common topic in diverse formats (four to five) as shown in our sample organizer, then: • Complete the reproducible organizer (figure 17.9, page 234) as a key for modeling with your text in preparation for teaching the lesson. 1b. Prepare photocopies for students of your selected texts in diverse formats, How to Interpret a Political-Editorial Cartoon (figure 17.3, page 230), the student-friendly definitions (figure 17.8, page 234), and the strategy's reproducible organizer (figure 17.9, page 234). 1c. As appropriate, assemble technology to use in modeling the strategy for students (for example, document camera, PPT slides, SMART Board, overhead transparencies, or posters).
2. Teacher identifies the content standard from state or district standards for students.	Display the content-specific standard you want students to understand and retain as a result of their reading, thinking, and writing. Discuss the standard with students.
3. Teacher shares an advance organizer, reviews the student-friendly definitions, and distributes teacher-prepared materials.	Share the following advance organizer or one of your own choosing: Not only will 21st century workers need to have the ability to navigate successfully through both print and visual media, they will also need to be able to integrate and evaluate content from multiple sources in diverse formats in order to gain meaning. Today, you will rehearse the skills you will need in order to thrive in the brave new workplaces you will one day enter.
4. Teacher models and provides rehearsal opportunities, gradually releasing responsibility to students for doing more of their own thinking and writing.	**Teacher models** Tell students that this strategy will initially require them to use a skill they are familiar with—summarizing—as they navigate through quite a number of diverse formats of media, some of which they may never have tried to gain meaning from before. In order to model the process, select one type of media with which the students may not be familiar (we recommend using figure 17.3, page 230, along with a political cartoon), and think aloud to show students how to understand and interpret the information in order to write a one-sentence summary about it. Record the summary on your organizer in column B for the source (column A) you have just processed. **Students work with teacher** Ask students to write one-sentence summaries in Part A of their organizers for the remaining sources you have shared with them. As they finish, call on students to display examples of the summaries. Review and process the summaries—recording models on your organizer for each source.

4. Teacher models and provides rehearsal opportunities, gradually releasing responsibility to students for doing more of their own thinking and writing *(continued)*	**Students work with peers** After reviewing the summaries completed in Part A of the organizer, read aloud and explain the directions for Part B. In order to complete this task, ask students to work interdependently with a partner to review their summaries and draw a conclusion (see figure P1.2, How to Draw a Conclusion column, page 23) based on the integration (connection) of information from at least two different sources. Have partners reach consensus on their answers and complete the conclusion and sources boxes in Part B of the organizer.
5. Teacher formatively assesses student work.	Ask several pairs to display their work for Part B—a conclusion and the two sources that support it. Facilitate a conversation with students as they discuss the merits of the work that is displayed. Record an accurate model on the organizer. Use the work displayed as well as students' responses to formatively assess as many students as possible. NOTE: At this point, you have two options: (1) conclude this lesson by going directly to steps 6 and 7, temporarily skipping the +feature (schedule the +feature for a later class period using the same text and organizers students have completed up to this point), or (2) extend this lesson by incorporating the +feature followed by steps 6 and 7.

Navigate-Integrate-Evaluate+

Teacher models

Read the +prompt (figure 17.9, page 234) aloud to students. To model this process so students will understand the work that it requires, call on a pair of students to display Part B of their organizer—their conclusion along with two identified sources. Tell students that although they have identified the sources that will support the conclusion, they will still need to find the specific evidence within each source. Model locating one piece of specific evidence from one of the sources in order to support the pair's conclusion.

Students work with teacher

Tell all students that they will continue practicing this process by searching for additional specific evidence from the text to support the pair's conclusion. Call on students to share the examples of evidence they have identified. Ask the pair of students whose conclusion you have been working on to evaluate the examples of evidence that have been shared. Facilitate the pair's conversation as they think aloud, select the best evidence, and record it on the organizer.

Students work with peers

Ask students to work with their partner to follow this modeled process with their own conclusions and sources. As students locate and agree on evidence, they should record it on their organizers in the constructed response planning area. As soon as the constructed response planning is complete, ask students to work independently to write their own individual responses in the space provided on their organizer.

Teacher formatively assesses student work

As students are working, circulate throughout the room to read and give feedback to as many students as possible. As they finish, call on several students to display their work. Facilitate a conversation to discuss the merits of the displayed responses. Students will either agree on a model response to represent the class or write an entirely new response as a class. Formatively assess as many students as possible based on the work that is displayed and the discussions that occur regarding the merits of the work.

continued →

Lesson Step	Explanatory Notes for the Teacher
6. Teacher returns to the content standard to identify progress in understanding and retaining new content.	In order to identify student progress with the new content, ask students to write an exit ticket in response to this stem: In what ways did the reading, thinking, and writing you did today help you understand the content standard? Explain.
7. Closure	Ask students to reflect on their current level of understanding of the content standard(s) and the literacy skill(s) they worked with today by using "fist to five" hand signals to the following questions as you display them, read them aloud, and ask for student responses: On a scale of fist to five, where making a fist means not at all and holding up all five fingers means so completely that you could be the teacher, rate your understanding of the following content standard: _____ On a scale of fist to five, where making a fist means not at all and holding up all five fingers means so completely that you could be the teacher, rate your level of understanding of the following CCSS literacy skill: _____

Visit **go.solution-tree.com/commoncore** to download and print this figure.

Delineate-Evaluate-Explain

The Gist of Delineate-Evaluate-Explain

Students are required to delineate and evaluate the author's reasoning before interpreting the meaning of the information in the text. In the +feature of the lesson, students are asked to complete a constructed response that requires them to draw a conclusion about issues in the text.

CCR Anchor Standard 8 for Reading: *Delineate and evaluate the argument and specific claims in a text, including the validity of the reasoning as well as the relevance and sufficiency of the evidence.*

There is no educational goal so elusive as that of teaching students how to think critically. There are books, programs, lesson plans, organizations, and foundations, all devoted to advancing the cause of critical thinking in schools, universities, and workplaces. Therefore, we approach the introduction of the Delineate-Evaluate-Explain strategy with a measure of trepidation. We are not so arrogant as to think we can pack all of the facets of critical thinking into a single strategy. For, in order to think critically about a topic or problem, readers must be able to distinguish between fact and opinion, recognize generalizations that must be supported by evidence, test various hypotheses, and determine the relevancy, validity, and sufficiency of the evidence. These are tall orders for secondary students, many of whom still struggle with simply extracting meaning from text. This strategy provides an instructional scaffold to lead your students to critical thinking. We discuss various facets of critical thinking, but our student-friendly definition of critical thinking is simply this: *reading and intensively thinking about the text to determine if the author's reasoning about a claim is valid and if the evidence provided is relevant and sufficient.*

Background Knowledge

The big idea of the Common Core College and Career Readiness Anchor Standard for Reading featured in this strategy is "critical thinking." There are multiple definitions of this concept; however, our favorite comes from *The Teaching of Thinking* in which Raymond S. Nickerson, David N. Perkins, and Edward E. Smith (1985) define it as "the ability to judge the plausibility of specific assertions, to weigh evidence, [and] to assess the logical soundness of inferences" (p. 4). Critical thinking can be examined from various perspectives, to include the writing of a persuasive essay or the preparation of arguments and supporting evidence in the context of a formal debate. In this strategy, critical thinking while reading content text means that students will be closely reading to evaluate the claims made by the author to include assessing the validity of the author's reasoning along with judging the relevance and sufficiency of the evidence. Critical thinking requires approaching text with a questioning mindset. This is a habit of the mind that must be applied whenever students read text in which authors are presenting a thesis, claim, or argument.

Understanding How the Strategy Works

Figure 18.1, sample text (Flesch-Kincaid grade level 14.8), and figure 18.2, a sample organizer, will allow you to test-drive Delineate-Evaluate-Explain.

FIGURE 18.1: Sample Text for Delineate-Evaluate-Explain

"Radical Reform of Higher Education Is Inevitable"
Chunk 1
Radical reform of higher education is coming whether we like it not. Clayton Christensen of the Harvard Business School argues that "disruptive innovation" will inevitably radically reform higher ed. Michael Horn, co-author with Christensen of several studies on higher ed, predicts: "I wouldn't be surprised if in 10 to 15 years, half of the institutions of higher education will have either merged or gone out of business." This change will not seriously affect upper elite colleges and universities because there will always be enough wealthy students to attend these prestigious schools—and image does matter.
What are the causes behind disruptive innovation? Consider the following:
It now costs more to send two kids to a university than to buy a nice home. Students entering, say, the University of Texas at Austin will pay about $160,000 over five years, less any government subsidies. Tuition and fees at the 10 largest universities in Texas have risen by 120 percent over the past decade. Data from the U.S. Department of Education indicate that the average full-time student in a public university in Texas takes more than five years to graduate. And data from the Project on Student Debt projects that students nationwide graduating in 2012 will on average have outstanding loans near $29,000, which with interest approaches $40,000. The Educational Credit Management Corp. reports that about 72,000 federal-loan borrowers filed for bankruptcy in 2008. What's more, a recent Pew Research Center study revealed that 57 percent of potential students said that the higher ed system fails to provide good value for the money, and 75 percent said college is unaffordable.

Chunk 2

But there's another immense cause for disruptive innovation: Universities by de facto action are agents of class warfare. An October study by the American Enterprise Institute (AEI) entitled "Cheap for Whom?" finds: "Average taxpayers provide more in subsidies to elite public and private schools than to the less competitive schools where their own children are likely being educated."

The disparity between rich and poor is shocking. Reports AEI, "Among not-for-profit institutions, the amount of taxpayer subsidies hovers between $1,000 and $2,000 per student per year until we turn to the most selective institutions . . . Among these already well-endowed institutions, the taxpayer subsidy jumps substantially to more than $13,000 per student per year."

It has become a caste system. AEI asserts, "If the country is to retain its competitive edge, it must reverse the current policies that result in providing the lowest levels of taxpayer support to the institutions that enroll the highest percentage of low-income, nontraditional and minority students—the fastest growing segments of the population."

Chunk 3

So if half of all institutions of higher ed either merge or go out of business in 10 to 15 years, having priced themselves out of the market, where will the majority of students be educated? They will be educated at community colleges or for-profit career schools. They will resort to online learning, or to "blended learning," or to "distance learning." These methods are not a second-class education. In a recently released, in-depth study of career schools in Texas, The Perryman Group found, "Private career colleges and schools play a key role in helping prepare Texans for the jobs of the future." It also found, about 70 percent of the most recent graduates from private career colleges and schools were immediately employed in a related field. Furthermore, the total cost of training a typical worker is approximately 20 percent lower in a private career college relative to a public community college.

This process of disruptive innovation is similar to what the economist Joseph Schumpeter called "creative destruction"—ultimately a wider benefit to society. The automobile industry destroyed the horse-and-buggy industry, enabling a vastly wider societal gain. Much of the higher ed establishment will be destroyed, but in its place will come forms of education that will benefit far more students.

Source: Ronald L. Trowbridge. Originally appeared in the Houston Chronicle, December 21, 2011. *Copyright 2011 Houston Chronicle Publishing Company. Reprinted with permission. All rights reserved.*

FIGURE 18.2: Sample Organizer for Delineate-Evaluate-Explain

Article title: "Radical Reform of Higher Education Is Inevitable" Name:
Author's thesis, claim, or argument: Radical reforms are necessary and inevitable
Directions: Read the text to identify the thesis or claim. Then, complete the information in each of the columns.

continued →

Column 1	Column 2	Column 3
Delineate Identify the supporting reasons and outline the evidence.	**Evaluate** Decide if the author's reasoning is valid and evidence provided is relevant and sufficient. Explain your answers.	**Explain** Interpret what the information from columns 1 and 2 means, and explain your ideas.
Chunk 1		
Supporting Reason # 1: The costs of college are "unaffordable." **Evidence:** 5 years of college at UT is $160,000 Tuitions in 10 largest universities in Texas have risen by 120% over the past decade Nationwide, students graduating in 2012 will have on average student loans approaching (with interest) $40,000 72,000 federal-loan borrowers filed for bankruptcy in 2008 57% of potential students said higher ed fails to provide good value for the money 75% said college is unaffordable	**Valid (Defensible) Reasoning:** Yes/No The reasoning strongly supports the claim and can be proven with evidence. **Relevant (Connected) Evidence:** Yes/No All evidence directly relates to the increasing costs of college and the impact those costs are having (and will have) on students attending college. **Sufficient (Enough) Evidence:** Yes/No The author provides a sufficient quantity of evidence to support his claim that college is unaffordable. He uses statistics from multiple sources as well as quotations.	A lot of students my age or their families are either going to incur sizeable debt in order to go to college or won't be able to afford to go at all.
Chunk 2		
Supporting Reason #2: Universities are agents of class warfare **Evidence:** Among not-for-profit institutions, taxpayers subsidize between $1,000 and $2,000 per student per year Among well-endowed selective institutions, the subsidy jumps to more than $13,000 per student per year	**Valid (Defensible) Reasoning:** Yes/No Although the reasoning seems to support the claim, it may need to be qualified in order to sufficiently and fairly strengthen the claim. **Relevant (Connected) Evidence:** Yes/No All evidence is important and directly relates to the different amount of taxpayer subsidies colleges are receiving.	Based on the information from at least one source, if the taxpayer subsidies were more fairly distributed, college might be more affordable for low-income and nontraditional students. I may need more information before deciding that universities are agents of class warfare.

"The country . . . must reverse current policies that result in providing the lowest levels of taxpayer support to the institutions that enroll the highest percentage of low-income, nontraditional and minority students . . . "	**Sufficient (Enough) Evidence:** Yes/No The author provides a quantity of evidence to support his claim from a single source. Because of the emotionally charged "class warfare" claim, it may need to be balanced with additional information from other sources.	
Chunk 3		
Supporting Reason # 3: The majority of students will be educated in community colleges or for-profit career schools . . . forms of education that will benefit far more students. **Evidence:** "Private career colleges and schools play a key role in helping prepare Texans for the jobs of the future." 70% of the most recent graduates . . . were immediately employed in a related field 20% lower cost of training a typical worker in a private career college relative to a public community college	**Valid (Defensible) Evidence:** Yes/No The information is from one source and is verifiable. The author's predictions about where and how the majority of students will be educated in 10 to 15 years seem likely and support the claim. **Relevant (Connected) Evidence:** Yes/No All evidence directly relates to the value of community and career colleges. **Sufficient (Enough) Evidence:** Yes/No The author provides a sufficient quantity of evidence in relation to private career colleges and doesn't provide sufficient evidence regarding community colleges.	Colleges that are more affordable and that enable students to be immediately employed in a related field offer a great alternative for all students. I may need more information about community colleges before deciding on their benefits.

Delineate-Evaluate-Explain+

+Prompt: In a constructed response, based on your interpretation of the information (column 3), draw a conclusion about the most important issues from the text.
Constructed Response In the not-too-distant future, increasing numbers of students faced with the issue of significant debt upon graduation, and without the help of appropriate subsidies, may choose to go to the more affordable community and private career colleges—which may ultimately be a good thing.

Items to Prepare

There are three reproducible figures that support the Delineate-Evaluate-Explain strategy. Figure 18.3 shows a set of student-friendly definitions for the terms that relate to the various aspects of this strategy.

FIGURE 18.3: Student-Friendly Definitions for Delineate-Evaluate-Explain

---

Critical thinking: Reading and intensively thinking about a text to determine if the author's reasoning (thinking) about a claim is valid and the evidence provided is relevant and sufficient

Thesis/Claim/Argument: An idea that is to be proved

Reason: A more specific statement that supports the thesis/claim

Evidence: Facts or information that show something is true

Delineate: Describe (tell about) something explicitly (in detail)

Evaluate: Make up your mind about the value of something

Explain: Give reasons for your decision about what the evidence means

Sufficient: Enough

Valid: Defensible

Relevant: Connected

Visit **go.solution-tree.com/commoncore** to download and print this figure.

The second reproducible, figure 18.4, is an organizer for you to record your thinking prior to modeling for students and then for students to record their thinking as they execute the strategy.

FIGURE 18.4: Reproducible Organizer for Delineate-Evaluate-Explain

Article title:		
Name:		
Author's thesis/claim/argument:		
Directions: Read the text to identify the thesis or claim. Then, complete the information in each of the columns.		
Column 1	**Column 2**	**Column 3**
Delineate	**Evaluate**	**Explain**
Identify the supporting reasons, and outline the evidence.	Decide if the author's reasoning is valid and evidence provided is relevant and sufficient. Explain your answers.	Interpret what the information from columns 1 and 2 means, and explain your ideas.

Chunk 1		
Supporting Reason #1: **Evidence:**	**Valid (Defensible) Reasoning:** Yes/No **Relevant (Connected) Evidence:** Yes/No **Sufficient (Enough) Evidence:** Yes/No	
Chunk 2		
Supporting Reason # 2: **Evidence:**	**Valid (Defensible) Reasoning:** Yes/No **Relevant (Connected) Evidence:** Yes/No **Sufficient (Enough) Evidence:** Yes/No	
Chunk 3		
Supporting Reason #3: **Evidence:**	**Valid (Defensible) Reasoning:** Yes/No **Relevant (Connected) Evidence:** Yes/No **Sufficient (Enough) Evidence:** Yes/No	
Delineate-Evaluate-Explain+		
+Prompt: In a constructed response, based on your interpretation of the information (column 3), draw a conclusion about the most important issues from the text.		
Constructed Response		

Visit **go.solution-tree.com/commoncore** to download and print this figure.

The third reproducible, figure 18.5 (page 246), contains a set of constructed response question stems to stimulate students' critical thinking while they are reading text.

FIGURE 18.5: Constructed Response Stems to Stimulate Critical Thinking While Reading Text

1.	What primary methods does the author use to develop and support the arguments? Explain how one or more of the following are used, giving examples. ● Mainly facts ● Statistical data ● Feelings, opinions, intuition ● Expert opinions ● Definitions
2.	What elements of the author's craft are primarily used to impact the quality of the text? Explain how one or more of the following are used, giving examples. ● Analogies, similes, metaphors ● Connotation ● Technical vocabulary
3.	How effectively does the author maintain objectivity in presenting information? Support your responses by citing examples from the text of the author's objectivity or subjectivity. **Objectivity** ● Does the author support arguments from a variety of sources of information? ● Do the points the author is trying to make follow each other in logical order? ● Is the author's reasoning sound? ● Are there facts provided to support each of the claims the author is making? ● Are those facts from credible sources? **Subjectivity** ● Does the author withhold information? ● Does the author stack the deck with only one side of the issue? ● Does the author offer only arguments that support one position? ● Does the author make assumptions without proving them for the reader?
4.	How effectively does the author present the informed opinion of experts and authorities? Explain by citing examples from the text. ● Explain how the author presents evidence from credible sources. ● Explain how the author uses quotations and citations. ● Explain how the author provides experimental evidence from qualitative or quantitative experiments that support a claim.

Visit **go.solution-tree.com/commoncore** to download and print this figure.

Lesson Plan

The lesson plan for showing your students how to apply Delineate-Evaluate-Explain in their reading and writing of informational text is found in figure 18.6.

FIGURE 18.6: Lesson Plan for Delineate-Evaluate-Explain

Lesson Step	Explanatory Notes for the Teacher
1. Teacher prepares and assembles the necessary materials.	1a. Choose content-related and standards-aligned text for teacher modeling and student reading, then: • Chunk the text into three parts as shown in the sample text (figure 18.1, page 240) with each chunk having at least one new reason. • Complete the reproducible organizer (figure 18.4, page 244) as a key for modeling with your text in preparation for teaching the lesson. 1b. Prepare photocopies for students of your selected text, the student-friendly definitions (figure 18.3, page 244) and the reproducible organizer (figure 18.4, page 244).
2. Teacher identifies the content standard from state or district standards for students.	Display the content-specific standard you want students to understand and retain as a result of their reading, thinking, and writing. Discuss the standard with students.
3. Teacher shares an advance organizer, reviews the student-friendly definitions, and distributes teacher-prepared materials.	Share the following advance organizer or one of your own choosing: Martin Luther King Jr. has been credited with saying that the purpose of education is to teach people to "think intensively and to think critically." The strategy that we will learn today requires us to do both because we are going to have to read someone else's argument, understand it, and explain our evaluation of it.
4. Teacher models and provides rehearsal opportunities, gradually releasing responsibility to students for doing more of their own thinking and writing.	**Teacher models: Chunk 1** Ask students to silently read the first text chunk and then read it aloud to them. Think aloud as you consider whether the author has stated the argument (the thesis or claim) in this first chunk. Continue the process of reading each chunk until you are able to identify and record the thesis or claim on your organizer. Returning to the first chunk, begin to identify the reasons the author uses to support the argument. Record the first reason on the organizer. List the evidence the author uses to support the reason on the organizer. At the end of the chunk, think aloud as you consider whether the reasoning is valid (defensible) and the evidence is relevant (connected) and sufficient (enough). Show your students how you have come to your conclusions as you record and explain them in column 2 of the organizer. Finally, think aloud to interpret the information from column 1 and column 2 of the organizer and jot down your ideas in column 3.

continued →

	Lesson Step	Explanatory Notes for the Teacher
4.	Teacher models and provides rehearsal opportunities, gradually releasing responsibility to students for doing more of their own thinking and writing. *(continued)*	**Students work with teacher: Chunk 2** Ask students to read the second chunk silently and then read it aloud to them. Ask students to underline the first statement from the text that they believe is a new reason supporting the argument. Call on students to identify what they have underlined and think aloud as you verify and record accurate answers. Next, ask students to underline the evidence the author is using to support the reason. Call on students to share the evidence they have identified and think aloud as you verify and record accurate answers. Ask students to consider whether there are any additional reasons supporting the argument in this chunk. If so, process them. If not, give students some think time to consider and evaluate the reasoning and evidence. Call on students to think aloud with you as you work together to consider whether the reasoning is valid (defensible) and the evidence is relevant (connected) and sufficient (enough). Write accurate ideas on the organizer. Finally, call on students to share with you their interpretation of the information from columns 1 and 2. Record model answers on the organizer. **Students work with peers: Chunk 3** After students have first independently read the third text chunk and you have read it aloud to them, ask them to identify and underline any new reasons supporting the author's argument. Students will then work with their partner to reach consensus on the first new supporting reason offered and will record their answers on the organizer. Students will work interpedently to agree on and list the evidence used to support the reason. Ask students to consider whether or not there are additional supporting reasons in this chunk. If so, they will process them. If not, they will move on to evaluate the reasoning and the evidence. Students will discuss and record their answers. Finally, students should discuss and agree on an interpretation of columns 1 and 2 and record their ideas in column 3.
5.	Teacher formatively assesses student work.	Call on several pairs to display their responses to columns 1, 2, and 3 for chunk 3. Process responses and record accurate and exemplary answers on the organizer. Formatively assess as many students as possible from the work that is displayed and discussed. NOTE: At this point, you have two options: (1) conclude this lesson by going directly to steps 6 and 7, temporarily skipping the +feature (schedule the +feature for a later class period using the same text and organizers students have completed up to this point), or (2) extend this lesson by incorporating the +feature followed by steps 6 and 7.

Delineate-Evaluate-Explain+	
Teacher models	
Read the +prompt aloud as students follow along (figure 18.4, page 244). Ask students to consider the criteria that might be used to determine whether the answer to the +prompt is acceptable. Students may say, for example, that the conclusion would have to include information from each of the interpretative explanations in column 3. They may say that an acceptable answer would show the relationship among the ideas discussed in column 3 for each chunk. List the most important criteria on the board. Review figure P1.2, page 23, as an additional resource on drawing conclusions.	
Students work with teacher	
Ask students to consider the information from column 3 that absolutely must be included in a conclusion. After think time, call on students to share ideas as you record accurate information on the board.	
Students work with peers	
Ask students to work interdependently with a peer to write a response to the Delineate-Evaluate-Explain+ prompt.	
Teacher formatively assesses student work	
Call on several pairs to display their answers to the +prompt. Ask students to compare and contrast posted answers, and facilitate a discussion about the merits of each. Students can either identify one answer as being exemplary or can write an entirely new exemplary answer as a class.	
6. Teacher returns to the content standard to identify progress in understanding and retaining new content.	In order to identify student progress with the new content, ask students to write an exit ticket in response to this stem: In what ways did the reading, thinking, and writing you did today help you understand the content standard? Explain.
7. Closure	Ask students to reflect on their current level of understanding of the content standard(s) and the literacy skill(s) they worked with today by using "fist to five" hand signals to the following questions as you display them, read them aloud, and ask for student responses: On a scale of fist to five, where making a fist means not at all and holding up all five fingers means you understand it so completely that you could be the teacher, rate your understanding of the following content standard: _____ On a scale of fist to five, where making a fist means not at all and holding up all five fingers means you understand it so completely that you could be the teacher, rate your level of understanding of the following CCSS literacy skill: _____

Visit **go.solution-tree.com/commoncore** to download and print this figure.

Analyze-Compare-Write

The Gist of Analyze-Compare-Write

Students read and analyze two different texts that address the same topic in order to identify each author's approach. In the +feature of the lesson, students write a constructed response that compares the approaches.

CCR Anchor Standard 9 for Reading: *Analyze how two or more texts address similar themes or topics* in order to build knowledge or *to compare the approaches the author takes.*

The Common Core College and Career Readiness Anchor Standard for Reading upon which this strategy is based looks relatively simple and straight-forward when you read it for the first time. However, mastering this standard requires the execution of five different steps, all of which have been intro-duced in previous strategies in the book. Even skilled readers will find the strategy challenging, especially if they are reading text at their frustration level. Here are the mental processing steps that are required to execute this strategy and ultimately master the standard:

1. Read both of the texts that have been selected. By *reading*, we, of course, mean reading closely to determine what the texts explicitly say, while making logical inferences and becoming gradually aware during reading of various bits of textual evidence.

2. Analyze each text chunk of the two different articles for each of four different aspects of the author's approach: (a) the author's relation-ship to the topic, (b) how the author organizes thoughts and presents information, (c) the author's attitude or posture toward the topic, and (d) the author's purpose for writing. Later we'll provide a resource to more fully define and describe these four aspects of an author's

approach. For our purposes, both of the selected sample texts have been chunked to allow students to conserve working memory for thinking and analyzing by enabling them to think about one chunk at a time and write down their thinking on an organizer. So, two texts times four aspects equals eight processing steps. Be aware that, depending on your time limitations, the stamina of your students, and the text you have chosen, you have the option to consider any two aspects of the authors' approaches at a time.

3. Match up the statements you wrote regarding what was important about the four aspects of the two authors' approaches, and then compare and contrast them.

4. Write a topic sentence that states your opinion about whether the two texts are more alike than different, or more different than alike, based on your findings from number 3.

5. Finally, generate a constructed response using the topic sentence that compares each author's approach to the topic.

As you can see, CCR Anchor Standard 9 involves multiple higher-level thinking skills, each one highly dependent on successfully executing the previous skill. This entire process can go off the rails in the first few minutes if students give up on the close reading of the text because it looks too hard or won't exercise their inferential skills because the meaning isn't readily jumping out at them. You are the key to this strategy. It depends completely on your understanding and modeling to make it work.

Note that Standard 9 has two facets: (1) analyzing two or more texts that address similar topics in order to build knowledge and (2) comparing the approaches the authors take. We are assuming that after your students read the two or more texts closely to determine what they explicitly say, make logical inferences along the way, and then dig deeper to compare the two authors' approaches, they cannot help but build knowledge. The focus of this strategy, therefore, is the *author's approach*—the unique ways that a particular author chooses to communicate ideas through his or her writing. We will delve into just what comprises an author's approach in the next section.

Background Knowledge

Reflect for a moment about your favorite author. That individual may be a popular historian like Doris Kearns Goodwin or a scholar from the sciences such as Stephen Hawking. Perhaps, after the challenges of teaching your discipline to adolescents, you prefer to relax with police procedurals. Regardless, you have an intimate knowledge of your favorite author's approach; you don't need a tutorial in how your favorite author approaches writing. In fact, when some authors decide to use new approaches—forsaking fiction for nonfiction or forsaking a character who has appeared in dozens of previous books—they choose a pseudonym so as not to upset their loyal fans with a complete shift in their approach to writing.

The student-friendly definition of an "author's approach" is simple and straightforward: *the overall way an author decides to write about something.* Some authors may intentionally and consciously plan to write about a topic in a certain way, while others may begin to write in a certain way because they have established a signature approach to writing and do not deviate from it. In either case, their approaches are reflected in the answers to the following questions:

1. What is the author's relationship to the subject?

2. How does the author organize thoughts and present information?

3. What is the author's attitude or posture toward the subject?

4. What is the author's purpose for writing?

Understanding How the Strategy Works

In order to appreciate how the Analyze-Compare-Write strategy works, first review the two sample texts in figures 19.1 (Flesch-Kincaid grade level 10.1) and 19.2 (page 254; Flesch-Kincaid grade level 11.0).

FIGURE 19.1: Sample Text 1 For Analyze-Compare-Write

"Stories of an Attack 70 Years Ago Will Live Forever"
Chunk 1
I was attending a Sunday afternoon youth meeting at church in Baltimore when someone came in with the news. The Japanese had bombed the U.S. Navy base at Pearl Harbor. We rushed home to listen to the radio reports as the story of that momentous event in history began to unfold. The next day at school, the principal called the entire student body into the auditorium and we sat there and listened as President Roosevelt delivered his famous "day that will live in infamy" speech to the nation. I am forever grateful to our school principal for his foresight and leadership in having us all hear that most memorable address by the president. That same day, Dec. 8, Congress, with only one member dissenting, voted to declare war on Japan and a few days later on Germany and other Axis nations.
A lot has unfolded in my life since that fateful day, Dec. 7, 1941. I was 14 and enjoying my first year of high school when the lives of Americans, including mine, were about to change forever. The Selective Service Act had been passed in 1940 and now American males, 18 to 45, were being drafted into the armed services. A teacher whom I liked and admired was the first person I knew to be drafted, and that somehow brought the war closer to home. My brother, Bill, was 18 and subject to the draft while attending Western Maryland College. Initially, college students were given deferments to complete their degrees, but soon the needs of the military brought that exemption to an end, and my brother was drafted a year before graduation.

continued →

As we continued our high school studies we all wondered when our turns would come, and we began to prepare for the inevitable call by the military. I explored a Navy program called radar technician training. I was gaining the educational requirements in high school and began thinking of enlistment in the Navy RT program—a better choice than to be drafted into the Army infantry, I thought.

Chunk 2

With dad at my side I did enlist in January 1945, a few weeks before graduating from high school. Dad was again with me as I waited for my train at Baltimore's Mount Royal station to go to Chicago and the Great Lakes Naval Training Station for boot camp. I was sad to leave my dad, anxious about the future, but excited to board the B&O Railroad's Capitol Limited, a famous train that I had dreamed of someday riding. Sleep in my coach seat did not come easy during that long night.

Many weeks later, I learned that Dad had represented me at my graduation ceremony and had gone up on the stage to receive an honor I had been awarded. I can only guess at his feelings. Looking back, it is hard to imagine what my parents were going through with both of their sons away preparing for or fighting in a war. Just a few weeks later, while I was finishing boot camp, my brother Bill was killed in action in Europe following the Battle of the Bulge. I will never forget that Sunday morning when I opened the letter from home that Dad had painfully written to advise me of my brother's death. It had been impossible for him to reach me by phone.

Chunk 3

But my family's story of sadness was only one of probably millions who were affected by tragedies during the Second World War, the war that started for the United States with Pearl Harbor 70 years ago today.

Yes, there still are many of us who will relive events that began with Pearl Harbor. And many more who will know through family members the stories that have been passed down about the war. The day will come when there are no more first hand accounts, just as has happened with World War I, but the stories will live forever.

For all of us, Pearl Harbor day will be a time to give thanks. Thanks to those who gave their lives and suffered as a result of the war and thanks that our great nation was preserved as a democracy and a land of opportunity.

Source: Tom Potts. Copyright 2011 Houston Chronicle Publishing Company. Reprinted with permission. All right reserved.

FIGURE 19.2: Sample Text 2 for Analyze-Compare-Write

"Remembering the Origins of Veterans Day"
Chunk 1
How many Americans know why we observe what we now call Veterans Day on November 11th? How many know what this national holiday originally commemorated? How many read the presidential proclamations issued yearly to guide our remembrance? World War II veteran Paul Fussell wrote in his award-winning 1975 study of the human significance of World War I, The Great War and Modern Memory, "Every war is ironic because every war is worse than expected." The supreme irony is how easy it is for those of us who are not veterans or do not know veterans to hold onto unrealistic expectations about war.

On Oct. 8, 1954, President Dwight D. Eisenhower signed Proclamation 3071. It informs us that on June 4, 1926, Congress passed a resolution that Americans should observe the anniversary of the end of World War I, Nov. 11, 1918, with appropriate ceremonies. In 1938, Congress made Nov. 11 a legal holiday called Armistice Day. Eisenhower changed Armistice Day into Veterans Day because of "two other great military conflicts in the intervening years," World War II and the Korean War. Eisenhower declared these wars necessary "to preserve our heritage of freedom." He called upon us as American citizens "to reconsecrate ourselves to the task of promoting an enduring peace so that [the] efforts [of veterans] shall not have been in vain."

Chunk 2

Ironically, two years later we began promoting enduring peace with 58,178 official American military casualty deaths in the Vietnam War between June 8, 1956, and May 15, 1975. The start is ironically hard to pinpoint because there was no formal declaration of war. The last casualties occurred two weeks after the war ended with the fall of Saigon on April 30, 1975.

As our troops pull out of Iraq, there will be ironic deaths like these and like British soldier-poet Wilfred Owen's. Owen voluntarily returned to the fighting in France in July 1918 so that he could write about the realities of trench warfare. He was killed on Nov. 4, a week before the armistice. In the preface to his poems, Owen wrote, "My subject is War, and the pity of War. The Poetry is in the pity." Their realism strips away the lofty sentiments about noble sacrifices in most presidential Veterans Day proclamations. His poems and his death remind us instead how long it takes and how much it costs to stop wars once we start them.

The very word "armistice" offers a strong warning. It means "a temporary cessation of the use of weapons by mutual agreement." It reminds us that no war will end all wars.

Chunk 3

Indeed, Kurt Vonnegut, who as an American POW survived the firebombing of Dresden, Germany, grasped the irony of doing away with Armistice Day. Born Nov. 11, 1922, he recalled that, when he was a boy, "all the people of all the nations which had fought in the First World War were silent during the 11th minute of the 11th hour of Armistice Day, the moment when "millions upon millions of human beings stopped butchering one another." Veterans told him that on the battlefield, "the sudden silence was the Voice of God." So it must have seemed.

Obscenely ironic was that, after the armistice had been generally announced at 5 a.m., generals still ordered soldiers into battle. The 11,000 casualties suffered in the war's final six hours exceeded those on D-Day. Henry Gunther, a U.S. Army private from Baltimore, was killed at 10:59 a.m.

These stories don't tell us everything about what makes war so traumatic for veterans. But they continue a long tradition of soldiers trying to tell us. At the start of this tradition, Homer and the Greek tragedians distilled the essence of what veterans have to say: Owen's pity, Fussell's irony, Vonnegut's deep feelings of senseless absurdity and Eisenhower's sincere longing for an enduring peace.

Make Veterans Day meaningful wherever you are.

Source: Tony Palaima. This article originally appeared in the Austin American-Statesman *on November 8, 2011.*

Figure 19.3 is a sample organizer that replicates the process you and your students will follow in learning how to analyze two or more texts to compare the approaches the authors take.

FIGURE 19.3: Sample Organizer for Analyze-Compare-Write

Name:				
Part A **Directions:** Analyze each of the texts to identify the four aspects of the author's approach.				
Text 1: "Stories of an attack 70 years ago will live forever" by Tom Potts (2011)				
Aspects of the author's approach	**Chunk 1**	**Chunk 2**	**Chunk 3**	**What's most important about the aspect?**
(1) What is the author's relationship to the topic?	The author is a high school freshman reacting to the "fateful day" Pearl Harbor was attacked.	The author enlists weeks before graduating from high school.	The author looks back at this time in history on the 70th anniversary of the attack on Pearl Harbor.	The author is a veteran of WWII who is reflecting on the "fateful day" of the attack on Pearl Harbor 70 years ago.
(2) How does the author organize thoughts and present information?	The author begins this personal narrative with the bombing of Pearl Harbor and chronologically organizes the text around the important events that transpire as he attends high school.	The author continues the narrative by focusing on the day he enlisted just weeks prior to his high school graduation and ends with the death of his brother Bill who was killed in action in 1945.	This chunk is present day (2011) and is organized around the author's reflections on the 70th anniversary of the bombing of Pearl Harbor.	The author writes a chronologically organized personal narrative reflecting on important events like his enlistment and the death of his brother who was killed in action.
(3) What is the author's attitude or posture toward the subject?	The author recognizes the importance of "that fateful day" and expresses some anxiety about the draft.	The author is focused on the personal impacts of the war.	In this chunk the author shifts his focus from his family's "story of sadness" to one of thankfulness.	The author's attitude evolves over the 70 years since the attack on Pearl Harbor— ultimately understanding that it resulted in the preservation of democracy.

	Chunk 1	Chunk 2	Chunk 3	
(4) What is the author's purpose for writing?	In this chunk, the purpose seems to be to give a firsthand account of how the bombing began to impact his life.	In this chunk, the purpose seems to be to show how his life is being impacted by the war—primarily through his enlistment and the death of his brother.	In this chunk, the purpose seems to be to reflect on the importance of giving thanks that "our great nation was preserved as a democracy and a land of opportunity" due to the sacrifices that were made.	The author helps the reader personalize the war and reflect on the importance of giving thanks that "our great nation was preserved as a democracy and a land of opportunity" due to the sacrifices made by soldiers and their families.

Text 2: "Remembering the origins of Veterans Day" by Tony Palaima (2011)

Aspects of the author's approach	Chunk 1	Chunk 2	Chunk 3	What's most important about the aspect?
(1) What is the author's relationship to the topic?	The author is a civilian with a great deal of knowledge about American history.	The author, who has not experienced war firsthand, employs lines from soldier-poet Wilfred Owens's preface along with the fact that Owens was killed a week before the armistice to exemplify the ironies of war.	The author continues to share the stories of those who experienced the ironies of war.	Because the author has not experienced war firsthand, he shares the trauma and irony of war through the stories and words of those who have.
(2) How does the author organize thoughts and present information?	In this text, the author's thoughts are organized to answer the three rhetorical questions that begin the text.	The author organizes this chunk around examples of the ironies of war—with a powerful quote from the soldier-poet Wilfred Owens.	The author organizes this chunk around examples of the ironies of war, including those identified by author and veteran Kurt Vonnegut.	The author organizes this text to illustrate the ironies and trauma of war.

continued →

Aspects of the author's approach	Chunk 1	Chunk 2	Chunk 3	What's most important about the aspect?
(3) What is the author's attitude or posture toward the topic?	Through his use of rhetorical questions, the author conveys an attitude of concern that perhaps Americans don't know enough about the origins of Veterans Day.	In this chunk, the author shifts from sharing historical information in an effort to shore up the readers' understanding of the holiday to focusing quite dramatically on the ironies of war.	The author's attitude emerges in this chunk as he conveys that he has tried, through stories, to tell us at least some of "what makes war so traumatic for veterans."	Americans need to understand that war is traumatic and filled with bitter ironies.
(4) What is the author's purpose for writing?	The author is a civilian who wants Americans to know the origins of Veterans Day and appreciate its significance.	To point out the trauma and irony of wars.	The author encourages all readers of his text to "make Veterans Day meaningful."	With an increased understanding of the history of this day, the author ultimately wants each of us to "make Veterans Day meaningful."

Part B

Directions: Take the "What's most important about the aspect?" statements for each text from Part A and place them in the "Text 1" and "Text 2" boxes. After the statements are side by side, compare and contrast the approaches. Record your response in the "compare/contrast" box.

Aspects of each author's approach	Text 1 What is most important about the aspect?	Text 2 What is most important about the aspect?	Compare/ contrast
(1) What is the author's relationship to the topic?	The author is a veteran of WWII who is reflecting on his memories from 70 years ago.	Because the author has not experienced war firsthand, he shares the trauma and irony of war through the stories of those who have.	There is a contrast in that one author is a veteran and the other is a civilian.

(2) How does the author organize thoughts and present information?	The author organizes his thoughts chronologically in this personal narrative honoring the 70th anniversary of the bombing of Pearl Harbor.	The author organizes this text around specific examples of the ironies and trauma of war—specifically Wilfred Owens and Kurt Vonnegut.	There is a contrast in that one author writes a personal narrative about his involvement in war and the other writes a text interpreting the impacts of war on those who were involved.
(3) What is the author's attitude or posture toward the topic?	The author's attitude evolves over the 70 years since the attack on Pearl Harbor—ultimately understanding that the war resulted in the preservation of democracy.	Americans need to understand that war is traumatic and filled with bitter ironies.	There is a contrast in that one author seems to see a value in, at least, one war while the other author focuses on the sacrifices of war.
(4) What is the author's purpose for writing?	To help the reader personalize the war and reflect on the importance of giving thanks that "our great nation was preserved as a democracy and a land of opportunity" due to the sacrifices that were made.	With an increased understanding of the history of this day, the author, ultimately, wants each of us to "make Veterans Day meaningful."	There is a similarity in that both authors want to show gratitude for those who have sacrificed for our country.

Analyze-Compare-Write+

+Prompt: After comparing and contrasting the authors' approaches, take a position on whether they are more alike or more different, and support that position with evidence from the text and your "What's most important about the aspect?" boxes on Part B of the organizer. A well-written constructed response will begin with a strong topic sentence that addresses the prompt and sets up the rest of the response for both texts.

Use the Organizational Structure column on the left as a guide to write your response.

Organizational Structure	Constructed Response Planning and Writing Area
(T) Topic sentence	(T) Although both authors write about the topic of war, their approach is more different than alike. (TAT) In "Stories of an attack 70 years ago," Tom Potts (2011) writes (1) as a veteran reflecting on his memories of the "fatal day" that Pearl Harbor was bombed and the years that followed.
(TAT) Title, author, topic	
(1) Author's relationship	

continued →

(2) Author's organizational structure	(2) He writes this personal narrative chronologically and includes an account of the day he enlisted just weeks before high school graduation and the day he tragically learned of the death of his brother who was killed in action. (3) Potts' attitude toward the war has evolved over the years from thinking of it as a "story of sadness" to one of understanding how the war resulted in the preservation of democracy. (4) Potts writes this narrative to personalize the war for the reader and to reflect on the importance of giving thanks that "our great nation was preserved" due the sacrifices that soldiers and their families made. (TR) Another author, (TAT) Tony Palaima (2011), writes about war from a very different approach in his article titled "Remembering the origins of Veterans Day." (1) Because this author is a civilian who has not experienced war firsthand, he shares the trauma and ironies of war through the stories and words of those who have. (2) The author organizes this text around examples of the specific perspectives of war shared by two important veteran-authors, Wilfred Owens and Kurt Vonnegut. (3) Palaima uses the words of these and other men to convey the need for Americans to understand that war is traumatic and filled with bitter ironies. (4) Palaima writes with the hope that an increased understanding of the history of this day will help each of us to "make Veterans Day meaningful."
(3) Author's attitude/posture	
(4) Author's purpose	
(TR) Transition	
(TAT) Title, author, topic	
(1) Author's relationship	
(2) Organizational structure	
(3) Author's posture/attitude	
(4) Author's purpose	

Items to Prepare

There are numerous figures that support your instruction of this strategy. They are introduced here and referred to again in the context of the lesson plan. Figure 19.4 presents the student–friendly definitions of the terms you will explain as you show your students how to employ this strategy during their reading.

FIGURE 19.4: Student-Friendly Definitions for Analyze-Compare-Write

Analyze: Make up your mind about the importance of something
Compare-contrast: Tell what the similarities and differences are between two things; in the case of this strategy, the two things are the approaches to writing of two different authors
Position: How you feel about something
Evidence: Textual proof that supports an inference
Author's approach: The overall way an author decides to write about something

Visit **go.solution-tree.com/commoncore** to download and print this figure.

The second reproducible, figure 19.5, is an organizer for you to record your thinking prior to modeling the strategy and thereafter for students to record their thinking during your initial lesson or subsequent rehearsals of the strategy.

FIGURE 19.5: Reproducible Organizer for Analyze-Compare-Write

Name:				
Part A **Directions:** Analyze each of the texts to identify the four aspects of the author's approach.				
Text 1:				
Aspects of the author's approach	**Chunk 1**	**Chunk 2**	**Chunk 3**	**What's most important about the aspect?**
(1) What is the author's relationship to the topic?				
(2) How does the author organize thoughts and present information?				
(3) What is the author's attitude or posture toward the subject?				
(4) What is the author's purpose for writing?				
Text 2:				
Aspects of the author's approach	**Chunk 1**	**Chunk 2**	**Chunk 3**	**What's most important about the aspect?**
(1) What is the author's relationship to the topic?				
(2) How does the author organize thoughts and present information?				

continued →

Aspects of the author's approach	Chunk 1	Chunk 2	Chunk 3	What's most important about the aspect?
(3) What is the author's attitude or posture toward the topic?				
(4) What is the author's purpose for writing?				

Part B

Directions: Take the "What's most important about the aspect?" statements for each text from Part A and place them in the "Text 1" and "Text 2" boxes. After the statements are side by side, compare and contrast the approaches. Record your response in the "compare/contrast" box.

Aspects of each author's approach	Text 1 What's most important about the aspect?	Text 2 What's most important about the aspect?	Compare/ contrast
(1) What is the author's relationship to the topic?			
(2) How does the author organize thoughts and present information?			
(3) What is the author's attitude or posture toward the topic?			
(4) What is the author's purpose for writing?			

Analyze-Compare-Write+

+Prompt: After comparing and contrasting the authors' approaches, take a position on whether they are more alike or more different, and support that position with evidence from the text and your "What's most important about the aspect?" boxes on Part B of the organizer. A well-written constructed response will begin with a strong topic sentence that addresses the prompt and sets up the rest of the response for both texts.

Use the Organizational Structure column on the left as a guide to write your response.

Organizational Structure	Constructed Response Planning and Writing Area
(T) Topic sentence	
(TAT) Title, author, topic	
(1) Author's relationship	
(2) Author's organizational structure	
(3) Author's attitude/ posture	
(4) Author's purpose	
(TR) Transition	
(TAT) Title, author, topic	
(1) Author's relationship	
(2) Organizational structure	
(3) Author's posture/ attitude	
(4) Author's purpose	

Visit **go.solution-tree.com/commoncore** to download and print this figure.

The third reproducible, figure 19.6, enumerates the four aspects of an author's approach and provides questions for students to ask and answer as they read and analyze the text.

FIGURE 19.6: Aspects of the Author's Approach

Aspect of the Author's Approach	Questions to Ask and Answer to Discover the Author's Approach
1. **What is the author's relationship to the subject?**	a. Is the author writing as someone who has experienced the subject firsthand?
	b. Is the author writing as an observer?
	c. Is the author writing as both an observer and as someone who has experienced the topic firsthand?
	d. Is the author an expert on the subject?
	e. Does the author have specialized knowledge such as advanced degrees or job experience?

continued →

Aspect of the Author's Approach	Questions to Ask and Answer to Discover the Author's Approach
2. **How does the author organize his or her thoughts and primarily present information?**	a. What kind of text structure does the author use to organize and present his or her thoughts—for example, narrative, descriptive, comparison/contrast, cause-effect, problem-solution, time-sequence-order, or argument or persuasion? b. How does the author primarily present information—for example, using details, descriptions, illustrations, quotations from individuals, or anecdotes?
3. **What is the author's attitude or posture toward the subject?**	a. Does the author seem respectful? b. Does the author have any obvious biases about the subject? c. Does the author have a neutral or objective attitude toward the subject? d. Does the author have an agenda (something specific he or she wishes to accomplish in writing the text)? e. Does the author use a sarcastic or condescending tone? f. Does the author make any assumptions about the text?
4. **What is the author's purpose for writing?**	a. What is the author's primary purpose for writing this text—for example, inform or teach, explain, entertain, describe or give an account of, present, persuade or convince, show or prove? b. Does the author seem to have just one or more than one purpose for writing?

Visit **go.solution-tree.com/commoncore** to download and print this figure.

Three additional reproducibles, figures 19.7 through 19.9 (page 267), support the +feature of the lesson. Figure 19.7 provides a checklist for writing a compare–contrast constructed response.

FIGURE 19.7: Compare-Contrast Checklist

	Model Response	Your Response
	Use this column to complete the checklist for the model paragraph.	Use this column to complete the checklist for your paragraph—one author's approach versus another author's approach.
Section 1 **Background Knowledge:** Remember that a compare-contrast response shows similarities (how aspects are alike) and differences (how aspects are different). In the topic sentence, however, after weighing all of the information, the writer must decide if what's being compared is most importantly alike or most importantly different.		

Checklist Question: Does the topic sentence in this response clearly state a position on whether what's being compared is most importantly alike or different?	Yes No	Yes No

Section 2

Background Knowledge: A goal of a constructed response is to use the information reported in the "What's most important about the aspect" box along with appropriate textual evidence to prove the position stated in the topic sentence.

Checklist Question: Does the response use information from the "what's most important about the aspect" box along with embedded textual evidence to help support the stance taken in the topic sentence?	Yes No	Yes No

Section 3

Background Knowledge: The goal is to write the constructed response using an organizational method called the Block Method. This means that the writer will present all of the selected aspects about the first item being compared followed by a transition and then present all of the parallel aspects of the second item. Writers will not constantly flip back and forth between the first and second items to make comparisons and point out contrasts—that type of structure is called Point by Point.

Checklist Question: Is the information organized in a block format?	Yes No	Yes No
Is there a transition between the two comparisons?	Yes No	Yes No

Visit **go.solution-tree.com/commoncore** to download and print this figure.

Figure 19.8 is a model response for you and your students to use in preparation for writing your own response. Note that we are not providing sample text to accompany the model response. The information in this figure is intended as a model and not as a factual representation of the topic.

FIGURE 19.8: Model Response

Model Comparison/Contrast Response			
Part B: With the statements about each type of car side by side, compare and contrast the different aspects. Record your responses in the "compare/contrast" box.			
Aspects to be compared	Item 1: What's most important about the aspect?	Item 2: What's most important about the aspect?	Compare/ contrast
(1) Car selection	There is a lot of choice in terms of the traditional fueled car (TFC), with new manufacturers entering the marketplace frequently.	There are not a lot of hybrid cars to choose from because fewer manufacturers make hybrids.	There is a contrast in that the TFC has a greater selection than the hybrid.

continued →

Aspects to be compared	Item 1: What's most important about the aspect?	Item 2: What's most important about the aspect?	Compare/ contrast
(2) Average price of car	A new TFC costs, on average $28,400.00.	On average, a hybrid costs between $32,000 and $38,000.	There is a contrast in that the TFC is less expensive.
(3) Cost of maintenance	The cost of maintenance can be lower because any full-service garage can complete the required work.	Hybrid maintenance can be higher because, for the most part, all work on the car must be done by the dealership because few garages are equipped to work on the hybrid.	There is a contrast in that the maintenance of the TFC is generally cheaper.
(4) Fuel cost	The average car on the market gets almost 24 miles per gallon. If the owner drives 10,000 miles per year and gas costs $3.50 per gallon, then the owner is spending $1,458.00 per year.	The average hybrid on the market gets almost 50 miles per gallon. If the owner drives 10,000 per year and gas costs $3.50 per gallon, then the owner is spending $700.00 a year on gas.	There is a contrast in that the TFC gets about half the gas mileage of the hybrid.

Prompt: After comparing the various aspects of a TFC and hybrid, take a position on whether they are more alike or more different and support that position with evidence from the "What's most important about the aspect" boxes.

Organizational Structure	Planning and Writing Area
Topic sentence	Although both the TFC (traditional fueled car) and hybrid are excellent means of transportation, they are more different than alike. (1) The choices for TFC have never been more extensive—with new companies successfully emerging into the market with increased frequency. (2) The price tag for a new TFC is approximately $28,400.00. (3) Maintenance for the TFC is reasonable because it can typically be done at any full-service garage instead of the more-expensive dealership. (4) Even with the cost of gas hitting the $3.50 a gallon mark, the average driver will spend less than $1,500.00 a year filling the tank. Hybrid cars, on the other hand, (1) are built by only a few car manufacturers, so an interested buyer might find that there isn't a lot to choose from. (2) On average, the new hybrid will cost between $32,000.00 and $38,000.00. (3) The cost of maintenance is typically higher because most of the repairs must be completed at a dealership. (4) The average driver of a hybrid will spend only about $700.00 per year to fill the tank.
(1) Car selection	
(2) Price	
(3) Cost of maintenance	
(4) Cost of fuel	
Transition	
(1) Car selection	
(2) Price	
(3) Cost of maintenance	
(4) Cost of fuel	

Visit **go.solution-tree.com/commoncore** to download and print this figure.

Finally, figure 19.9 is a representative sampling of transition stems that you and your students can use as you write your model responses.

FIGURE 19.9: Transition Stems

Transition	Purpose of the Transition
Another	Adding a new idea
In addition to	
Equally important	Showing agreement or similarity with a previous statement
Also	
Similarly	
Specifically	Restating a claim within a paragraph in a more specific way
Consequently	Continuing a line of reasoning
Additionally	
Furthermore	
As a result of	Showing cause and effect
Because of	
Nonetheless	Changing a line of reasoning (contrast)
However	
Nevertheless	
In contrast	
On the one hand . . . on the other hand	
In conclusion	Signaling the conclusion
Finally	
To conclude	
In summary	
Therefore	

Visit **go.solution-tree.com/commoncore** to download and print this figure.

Lesson Plan

The lesson plan for showing your students how to execute the Analyze-Compare-Write strategy is found in figure 19.10.

FIGURE 19.10: Lesson Plan for Analyze-Compare-Write

Lesson Step	Explanatory Notes for the Teacher
1. Teacher prepares and assembles the necessary materials.	1a. Choose two content-related and standards-aligned texts about the same topic for teacher modeling and student reading, then:

continued →

Lesson Step	Explanatory Notes for the Teacher
1. Teacher prepares and assembles the necessary materials. *(continued)*	• Chunk both texts into three parts as shown in the sample texts (figures 19.1 and 19.2, pages 253–254). Identify and label one text as "Text 1" and the other as "Text 2." • Complete the reproducible organizer (figure 19.5, page 261) as a key for modeling with both of your selected texts. 1b. Prepare photocopies for students of your selected texts, the student-friendly definitions (figure 19.4, page 260), the strategy's reproducible organizer (figure 19.5, page 261), questions to ask and answer to discover an author's approach (figure 19.6, page 263), a compare-contrast checklist (figure 19.7, page 264), a model constructed response for Analyze-Compare Write+ (figure 19.8, page 265), and samples of transition stems (figure 19.9, page 267). 1c. As appropriate, assemble technology to use in modeling the strategy for students (for example, document camera, PPT slides, SMART Board, overhead transparencies, or posters).
2. Teacher identifies the content standard from state or district standards for students.	Display the content-specific standard you want students to understand and retain as a result of their reading, thinking, and writing. Discuss the standard with students.
3. Teacher shares an advance organizer, reviews the student-friendly definitions, and distributes teacher-prepared materials.	Share the following advance organizer or one of your own choosing: Many people identify the letters to the editor as their favorite part of the newspaper. Here, concerned citizens write to the editor with the intent of sharing their point of view on a topic—most likely hoping that others will read and find value in their ideas. On any given day, it isn't uncommon to find two or three letters all addressing the same topic—a topic that has been approached differently by each author. Those different approaches—and our ability to identify them—make the letters interesting! Turns out, the ability to identify and analyze different authors' approaches to a topic makes this type of comparative reading interesting for all different kinds of texts. Today, our goal is to work on our ability to identify and analyze the different approaches two authors use in texts that they have written about the same topic in order to compare them.
4. Teacher models and provides rehearsal opportunities, gradually releasing responsibility to students for doing more of their own thinking and writing.	**Teacher models: Text 1** Ask students to notice the title of the text 1 and put it in the appropriate box of their organizers. Ask students to read the first chunk of text 1 silently. Tell students that you are going to work on identifying ways the author has chosen to approach the topic. Briefly display and discuss figure 19.6 (page 263) in order to review the questions to ask to identify the author's relationship to the subject.

| 4. | Teacher models and provides rehearsal opportunities, gradually releasing responsibility to students for doing more of their own thinking and writing.

(continued) | With this in mind, read the chunk aloud. Think aloud as you construct and write a response for the author's relationship to the subject for chunk 1. Repeat the same process as you analyze chunks 2 and 3 of the text for this same aspect—author's relationship. When you have recorded responses to all three chunks for this aspect, think aloud as you explain that your response in the "What's most important" column will not necessarily be a summary or synthesis of the information from all three chunks as much as it will be the result of your weighing all of the information to decide on what's most important to say about the author's relationship to the subject. Construct and write a response to the "What's most important about the aspect?" box. Follow this process with the next three aspects of the author's approach, recording answers on the organizer for all columns. This will complete the processing for text 2.

Students work with teacher: Text 2

Tell students that you will now work with them to explore the author's approach in the second text. Tell students to notice the title of the text and put it in the appropriate box of their organizers. Ask students to read the first chunk of the second text silently. Ask students to refer once again to figure 19.6, page 263. in order to access the questions to ask and answer to discover the author's approach. Ask students to think about how they might respond in the "author's relationship" box for chunk 1 as you read the chunk aloud. Tell students to construct and write a response, then call on students to share what they have written. Process the answers students share to ensure that they are accurate and that you have a good example to record on the organizer. Follow this process for the remaining chunks of this aspect and for the "What's most important" column as well. Follow this same structure for the rest of the aspects of the author's approach for text 2.

Students work with peers: Texts 1 and 2

Ask students to work independently to essentially copy and paste what they have written in the "What's most important about the aspect" boxes in Part A of the organizer into the appropriate boxes of Part B. With the aspect statements for each text side by side, think aloud to model for students how to process the "What's the author's relationship" information from text 1 and text 2 in order to compare/contrast them. Record your answer on the organizer. Ask students to work interdependently with a partner to complete the compare/contrast statements for aspects 2, 3, and 4. |
| 5. | Teacher formatively assesses student work. | Call on pairs to display their compare/contrast responses for aspects 2, 3, and 4. Call on students to discuss the merits of the displayed responses. Think aloud as you process responses. Either select a model response to record on the organizer for each aspect or ask the class to work together to write an exemplary response. Formatively assess as many students as possible as you review their work and listen to their discussions. |

continued →

Lesson Step	Explanatory Notes for the Teacher
5. Teacher formatively assesses student work. *(continued)*	NOTE: At this point, you have two options: (1) conclude this lesson by going directly to steps 6 and 7, temporarily skipping the +feature. Schedule the +feature for a later class period using the same text and organizers students have completed up to this point; or (2) extend this lesson by incorporating the +feature followed by steps 6 and 7.

Analyze-Compare-Write+

Teacher models

Ask students to look at the +prompt (figure 19.5, page 261) and follow along as you read it aloud. Explain to students that because this task is challenging, you want them to see a model (figure 19.8, page 265) and use a comparison/contrast checklist (figure 19.7, page 264) to determine if the model has followed the guidelines for writing this type of paragraph. Review the checklist with students and the specific questions that they will have to respond to both for the model paragraph and, later, for their own. As you discuss section 3 of the checklist, refer students to figure 19.9 (page 267) for examples of transitions that they can use as they write. Next, ask students to review Part B of the organizer for the model response (figure 19.8, page 265) that the student completed in preparation for her paragraph about a different topic—cars. Call attention to the aspects that are being compared for both cars and ask students to silently read the "What's most important about the aspect" boxes for each type of car. Finally, ask students to silently read the model paragraph in the planning and writing area of the organizer that compares hybrid cars to traditional fueled cars.

Students work with teacher

Ask students to now work with you to use the compare-contrast checklist (figure 19.7, page 264). Read section 1 background knowledge aloud followed by the checklist question. Think aloud and facilitate a conversation with students in order to answer yes or no to this question about the topic sentence. Move on to the next two sections in order to arrive at answers as well.

Now that students have seen a model and used the checklist, they are ready to move forward to their specific assignment. Remind students of the paragraph they must write—which begins with a topic sentence that takes a position on whether the authors' approaches are more alike or more different. Refer students to the compare/contrast column of Part B on the organizer (figure 19.5, page 261). Think aloud in order to model for students how to determine, based on what they have compared/contrasted, whether the approaches are more alike or more different. Stress to students that it is not just a matter of counting to decide whether there are more aspects alike than different. It is also a matter of deciding the weight of each aspect. Involve the class in making a decision in order to write a topic sentence. Tell students to write a topic sentence in response to the prompt.

Students work with peers

Remind students of the importance of referring to the comparison/contrast checklist as they begin to write. Ask partners to choose between the topic sentences each has written or to write an entirely new sentence together. Next, tell them to begin using the "organizational structure" column on the left side of the planning area of their organizer as a guide for completing their constructed response. Working together, while each is writing on his or her own organizer, students should begin writing their constructed response for the first text. Circulate as students are working to answer questions or give feedback. As students finish, call on partners to display their work. Think aloud as you process, and solicit students to process the merits of the work that is displayed.

Students work alone

Now, ask students to work individually to complete the response for the second text. Circulate as students are working to answer questions or give feedback.

Teacher formatively assesses student work

Call on students to display their completed paragraph. Process the merits of the work that is displayed. Formatively assess as many students as you can based on work that is displayed and the processing that students do as they discuss the work.

6.	Teacher returns to the content standard to identify progress in understanding and retaining new content.	In order to identify student progress with the new content, ask students to write an exit ticket in response to this stem: In what ways did the reading, thinking, and writing you did today help you understand the content standard? Explain.
7.	Closure	Ask students to reflect on their current level of understanding of the content standard(s) and the literacy skill(s) they worked with today by using "fist to five" hand signals to the following questions as you display them, read them aloud, and ask for student responses: On a scale of fist to five, where making a fist means not at all and holding up all five fingers means you understand it so completely that you could be the teacher, rate your understanding of the following content standard: _____ On a scale of fist to five, where making a fist means not at all and holding up all five fingers means you understand it so completely that you could be the teacher, rate your level of understanding of the following CCSS literacy skill: _____

Visit **go.solution-tree.com/commoncore** to download and print this figure.

PART IV:
Range of Reading and Text Complexity

A turning away from complex texts is likely to lead to a general impoverishment of knowledge, which, because knowledge is intimately linked with reading comprehension ability, will accelerate the decline in the ability to comprehend complex texts and the decline in the richness of text itself. This bodes ill for the ability of Americans to meet the demands placed upon them by citizenship in a democratic republic and the challenges of a highly competitive global marketplace of goods, services, and ideas.

—COMMON CORE STATE STANDARDS INITIATIVE (2010B)

The 10th standard of the CCR Anchor Standards is a straightforward statement, elegant in its simplicity: "Read and comprehend complex literary and informational texts independently and proficiently." We have focused solely on informational texts in our strategies. However, when it comes to range of reading and text complexity, your students will have to do it all—become proficient at reading Shakespeare as well as the *Economist* or *Nature*. You may already have read Strategy 20, as we suggested in the introduction. If so, then you are already aware that there is only one big strategy for this intimidating standard.

The big idea of this final section of the CCR Anchor Standards, Range of Reading and Text Complexity, is this: *in order to reach the goal stated in Standard 10 for all students,* all students *must do far more reading (especially of informational texts) in both ELA and content classes, and they must do it in texts of increasing complexity.* Standard 10 is about literacy rehearsal, *the sustained practice of various reading and writing processes shown by research to develop the reading and writing proficiencies that enable students to* eventually *read and comprehend complex literary and informational texts independently and proficiently.* Note the word *eventually.* The goal set forth in Standard 10 will not happen overnight or easily. Literacy rehearsal must be a top priority for every teacher, not just those in the English department. Literacy rehearsal with literary informational text must be a priority for every teacher—not just content teachers. English teachers and content teachers will have to pull together to achieve Standard 10. English teachers may have to support content teachers in acquiring the skills to analyze the texts of their discipline so they can show their students how.

Content teachers will need to support the English teachers by selecting more literary informational texts such as historical documents, speeches, scientific research articles, and journalistic pieces as the basis of their strategy instruction. English teachers will need to support content teachers as they learn to model writing in response to reading for their students. Instructional specialists will have to support all teachers as they struggle to scaffold the most basic of the anchor standards: reading closely to determine what the text says explicitly. Literacy rehearsal demands that all teachers refuse to give their students passes to get out of reading and writing in their classrooms.

Literacy Rehearsal

The Gist of Literacy Rehearsal

Teachers are asked to engage their students in the sustained practice of various literacy processes such as those contained in Strategies 1–19 in order to ramp up the rigor of literacy rehearsal in English language arts, history/social studies, science, and technical subjects.

CCCR Anchor Standard 10 for Reading: *Read and comprehend complex literary and informational text independently and proficiently.*

Rehearsing is very common in secondary schools. Sports teams practice routines and build strength in the weight room. The speech and debate teams spend nearly every weekend competing in rehearsals in their league or conference for state and national tournaments. The choral department is in non-stop rehearsals for the school musical. And of course, the dance team and cheerleaders are rehearsing during the summer vacation in order to do well at the annual competition. The moral of this story is this: in order to read and comprehend literary and informational texts independently and proficiently, students must engage in literacy rehearsal.

As beneficial as extracurricular activities are for all students, when did we lose our way and begin to believe that our students can succeed in whatever educational or professional venue they choose without rehearsing for those life competitions as well? We budget, plan, hire staff, supervise, and evaluate all of these extracurricular rehearsals with meticulous care. Then we celebrate their success with press releases and pep rallies. However, we seldom focus for more than a meeting or two on how to identify "what it really takes for students to succeed and what we can do to get them ready" as the subtitle of David Conley's (2005) book *College Knowledge* states. There are, of course, outstanding examples of teachers, departments, and schools that make a habit of literacy rehearsal. However, we advocate the literacy rehearsal habit for every secondary school. No matter where your students may be on the continuum of reading and writing proficiencies, they need sustained practice. The literacy rehearsal needed to achieve Standard 10 of the CCR Anchor Standards for Reading and its associated writing, listening, and speaking skills takes place in a whole-school context in which departments and teams work in professional learning communities to engage in discussion, reflection, problem solving, and sharing around a single topic: ramping up rigor in their classrooms and departments when it comes to content literacy.

Literacy rehearsal differs from activities such as sustained silent reading (SSR) and drop everything and read (DER). These practices encourage students to read books of their own choosing but do not generally qualify as literacy rehearsal. Literacy rehearsal in the broad sense of Standard 10 involves sustained opportunities for reading to learn from both literary and informational texts and then writing to express and explain one's thinking with evidence from text. Literacy rehearsal in a narrower sense, as we have applied it in this book, involves sustained opportunities for reading to learn from expository informational text such as content textbooks and literary informational text (literary nonfiction). Wherever students are engaged in literacy rehearsal, whether in ELA or content classrooms, and whatever they are reading, whether literary or informational texts, literacy rehearsal requires concentration and effort. It involves reading and intensively thinking about a text to determine if the author's reasoning about a claim is valid, and the evidence is relevant and sufficient. It also entails the close, careful, and thoughtful reading of texts to trace the development of an idea or theme or to determine the structure of a text. Literacy rehearsal requires mental, physical, and emotional engagement of both teachers and students. Literacy rehearsal requires drawing conclusions, making inferences, writing summaries, questioning the author, and integrating knowledge and ideas from multiple sources.

Effective Teachers—The Key to Ramping Up Content Literacy

There is only one engine powerful enough to drive a buildingwide commitment to daily literacy rehearsal—effective teachers. However, administrators and literacy leaders should not for a moment conclude that the answer to implementing literacy rehearsal lies in memos, directives, binders, and books. These artifacts have a limited value in bringing about change without paying attention to the people on the receiving end of this deluge of paper. People need support, release time, money, and professional development to tap into their motivation, talents, and desire to be more effective teachers who get results.

The secret to ramping up the rigor of content literacy in your school lies in two categories of people that have some overlap in their memberships: (1) content departments or teams that constitute a professional learning community, and (2) a literacy cohort composed of teacher leaders from various departments, instructional specialists, and an administrative representative to provide ongoing, embedded professional development to staff members.

Following is a brief description of how these two groups function when supported by their administrative team.

Professional Learning Communities (PLCs)

There are dozens of books, workshops, online courses, and webinars to provide the guidance and motivation you need to install the PLC concept in your school if you have not already done so. The key to a successful PLC implementation lies in maintaining a laser-like focus on student learning and vigorously defending any assaults against the allocated meeting time with noninstructional "business." Recall that in the introduction we provided two forms to help PLCs plan before the implementation of a strategy (figure I.6 on page 16) and to evaluate after showing your students how to use the strategy (figure I.7 on page 17).

Strategies 1–19 are, by design, the "101" of content literacy strategies. They are intended to show you and your students the first steps to implementing the CCR Anchor Standards for Reading, not to provide a recipe or prescription for "reading and comprehending complex literary and informational texts independently and proficiently."

The wizardry that can wave a magic wand and produce students who measure up to Standard 10 upon high school graduation only exists in the collective wisdom, experience, energy, creativity, and desire found in a collaborative group of teachers focused on the most critical and challenging goal facing educators today: ramping up expectations and providing daily opportunities for literacy rehearsal at a more challenging level.

A Site-Based Literacy Cohort

The Common Core State Standards have provided you with a set of marching orders. This book gives you the strategies to help show your students how to meet the standards. However, in order to bring about sustained and meaningful change, professional development is needed to help all teachers acquire the expertise they need. Professional learning communities provide a venue for teachers to reflect, question, and plan for implementation. We know that not all teachers will have the background knowledge needed to simply pick up this book and implement tomorrow. They need models of their own before they will be prepared to model for their students. Our professional development model subscribes to the following: "Professional development must be ongoing, deeply embedded in teachers' classroom work with [students], specific to grade levels or academic content, and focused on research-based approaches. It also must help to open classroom doors and create more collaboration among teachers in a school" (Russo, 2004, p. 2).

As we stated in the preface, we did not set out to write a book about how to implement these strategies in a whole school. However, having said that, neither can we leave you at this point without giving you some guidance to do just that: a to-do checklist in the form of a one-year timeline that will lead you and your colleagues through the formation of a literacy cohort—a team of individuals who will work together to develop their expertise in teaching the nineteen strategies in this book and then fan out through the departments and teams of their school to teach their colleagues. If this cohort is especially energized and inspired, they can even engage in model teaching in their classrooms, where colleagues can see exactly how another teacher does it. We have seen the cohort model work in middle and high schools as highly effective teachers assume leadership roles and motivate their colleagues to experiment and ramp up rigor through daily literacy rehearsal in classrooms throughout the school.

Figure 20.1 is a suggested one-year implementation plan for establishing and implementing a literacy cohort on your campus. This group of literacy specialists from every content area will become the literacy leaders who are out in front of their colleagues growing, learning, taking risks, and discovering the joy of becoming a teacher leader.

FIGURE 20.1: Model Timeline for Using a Literacy Cohort to Implement Strategies

Implementation Stages	Suggested Time for Implementation	Specifics of Required Tasks
Stage 1: Identify current school beliefs and practices	One to two hours	Leaders discuss the following. Does our school: Have a team approach to raising student achievement? Believe in the value of peers learning from peers? Have a compelling vision that includes (or can include) literacy? Have the ability to stay focused on and committed to improving the reading and writing skills of all students?

Stage 1: Identify current school beliefs and practices *(continued)*		Have the necessary resources: Leaders with time to monitor and support the cohort and teacher implementation of strategies? Someone with literacy expertise to guide the cohort? Funds for substitutes? Money for professional resources? If our school cannot currently answer yes to these questions, are we willing or able to make the necessary adjustments?
Stage 2: Complete the work necessary for the cohort's start-up	One to three months prior to the beginning of the school year	School leaders identify a building literacy expert or hire an outside consultant, select members of the literacy cohort (two teachers from each content including electives), identify and reserve specific resources, announce the principal's literacy vision for the school, and explain the general purpose of the cohort to the faculty in the "welcome back to school" letter that goes out prior to the start of school.
Stage 3a: Communicate with the faculty	Ten to fifteen minutes with the full faculty at the first meeting of the school year	The principal communicates a vision and sense of urgency and explains the rationale for the creation of the cohort and the broad expectations for the cohort's first year: they will become literacy experts and share their expertise in using identified literacy strategies with their content colleagues. The principal introduces the cohort.
Stage 3b: Start the school year with the cohort and build their expertise; select strategies	During the first month of school	The principal identifies the leaders of the cohort—the steering committee (chairperson, administrative liaison, literacy expert)—and helps create a yearlong calendar for monthly cohort meetings. The cohort creates a purpose statement in alignment with the principal's vision, identifies short and long-term goals and timelines them, discusses how success will be measured, establishes regular communication channels to keep the faculty informed on matters related to the cohort. The literacy expert begins the professional learning experiences that will help cohort members learn three identified strategies and make the strategies content-specific.

continued →

Implementation Stages	Suggested Time for Implementation	Specifics of Required Tasks
Stage 4: Observe the use of strategies, and identify when professional learning/sharing will occur	During the second month of school	Cohort members begin their own rehearsal with the strategies in their classrooms. School leaders and the literacy expert observe cohort members' use of the selected strategies in the instructional practices of their content classrooms; cohort members have release time to make peer visits to other cohort members. The cohort (along with the principal) identifies the context for sharing the first set of strategies—during PLC time, on a teacher workday, during release time—and a schedule is constructed and shared with the faculty.
Stage 5: Prepare cohort members to be facilitators of professional learning	During the second month of school	Cohort members meet for a full-day professional learning and planning session facilitated by the literacy expert. Like-content cohort members will work together to create presentation materials that will include content-specific texts and organizers in alignment to content and grade-level Common Core standards. Presentation products will include: a PowerPoint, participant handouts, and an outline of facilitator notes for presenters to use as they model specific strategies.
Stage 6: Present professional learning to content-area departmental colleagues	During the third month of school	Cohort members will facilitate the planned professional learning session for their content-area departmental colleagues (PLCs), sharing the now content-specific, buildingwide strategies. Feedback is requested from colleagues.
Stage 7: Support the implementation	Six to eight weeks	Cohort members provide support and modeling as their content colleagues plan for and implement the buildingwide literacy strategies. Progress or obstacles to implementation are discussed at PLC meetings. Administrators encourage and monitor the implementation of strategies. The principal models the use of the strategies at schoolwide meetings. The cohort continues to seek feedback from teachers regarding the strategies.
Stage 8: Reflect on the implementation	Prior to the end of the first semester	Cohort members review their timelines, short- and long-term goals, and the level of their growth as literacy experts. The cohort (along with the principal) makes mid-course corrections as necessary. Any additional supports or resources that are needed are identified.

Stage 9: Plan for the next set of strategies— continue the recursive process throughout the rest of the year	Beginning of second semester	Cohort members reflect on the feedback from the faculty regarding the professional learning opportunities. The cohort and school leaders measure their success with the first three strategies introduced during the first semester. Accomplishments are shared with the faculty and celebrated. The principal reiterates a commitment to literacy. Planning begins for the sharing of the next set of strategies. Literacy leaders repeat the earlier processes with the new strategies.
Stage 10: Celebrate and prepare for year 2	End of the school year	School leaders publicly celebrate the work of the cohort and faculty. The principal determines if any adjustments need to be made to members of the cohort or steering committee after meeting with members to debrief and review their level of commitment to the cohort. Resources for year 2 are identified. The principal decides if the cohort needs to meet during the summer in order to plan professional learning for the beginning of the new school year.

Conclusion

Although you may not have thoroughly reviewed or taught all of the strategies at this point, we hope that what you have read has fulfilled the expectations you had when you purchased the book. The following big ideas were foremost in our minds as we wrote, and we hope they will guide you as you seek to implement these strategies with your students:

- There are two keys to unlocking students' abilities to read and comprehend complex literary and informational texts independently and proficiently:
  + Content instruction facilitated by literacy strategy instruction that provides students with the models for the reading-thinking processes they need to understand complex text and master the content standards of a particular discipline—*content literacy*
  + Daily engagement with reading and writing in response to and in the service of reading comprehension—*literacy rehearsal*
- The strategies we have designed are not prescriptions or recipes. They offer suggestions and possibilities. Although each one has a solid research base, they must be enhanced with the creativity, deep

knowledge of content, and instructional expertise of you and your colleagues to make them spring to life in your classroom and achieve the desired results. Implementing content literacy and literacy rehearsal in your school is best done in a professional learning community where *all* teachers and administrators are passionate and assume responsibility for *all* students. Implementing the literacy strategies in this book within the framework of collaborative teams will build instructional capacity, as well as result in increased achievement on the part of your students.

- The professional growth needed to implement content literacy and literacy rehearsal in your school is best delivered by a literacy cohort—a group of teachers serving as literacy leaders and professional developers for their colleagues. Embedded professional development is essential for the systemic and synergistic growth needed to achieve the standards.

- Achieving progress with the CCR Anchor Standards and our strategies will be more like a marathon than a 100-yard dash. There will be periods of time as you work with your colleagues and students that will bring discouragement and frustration. However, persevere. The prize is literacy for all students.

GLOSSARY

analysis—In Standard 1, a close, careful, and thoughtful reading of the text

analyze—In Standard 2, to trace the development of an idea or theme; in Standards 9–11, to figure out how the author develops (writes about) an individual, event, or idea; in Standards 14–15, to determine the structure of the text

argument—An idea that is to be proved

author's approach—The overall way an author writes about something

author's purpose—Why the author is writing a text or what the author hopes to accomplish in the text

author's style—How the author uses language (words, phrases, and sentences) in writing

belief—An acceptance that a statement is true

believe—Think that something is true

cause—Make something happen; something that makes something else happen

central idea—What the text is mainly about

cite—Write down evidence you found in the text

claim—An idea that is to be proved

concept—A concrete idea of what something is

conclusion—A decision you make about what the evidence in the text means; sometimes referred to as "drawing a conclusion"

connotative word—A word used in a nonliteral way

consensus—An agreement you reach with someone by talking about something

content—The subject matter of the text

context—The words and sentences around a word or phrase you don't know

craft—The way an author writes; a unique style

critical thinking—Reading and intensively thinking about a text to determine if the author's reasoning (thinking) about a claim is valid (defensible), and the evidence is relevant (connected), and sufficient (enough)

decide—Make up your mind about something

decision—Making up your mind about something or figuring it out

delineate—Describe (tell about) something explicitly (in detail)

development—The way an author gradually tells more and more about the content in order that the reader can have a better understanding

embed—Put quotation marks around words or phrases from the text that you are inserting into your own writing

embedded quotation—See *textual evidence*

essential statement—A conclusion about what the text means

evaluate—Make up your mind about the value of something

event—A single happening in time, a recurring happening in time, or a historical happening that extends over years or in some cases decades or centuries

evidence—Textual proof that supports your conclusion or inference

explain—Make something clear to someone; give reasons for your decision about what the evidence means

explicit—Clearly stated in the text leaving no doubt as to meaning

feel strongly about—Agree with something and be willing to argue or debate about it with others

figurative language—Words or phrases used to make comparison between individuals, events, and ideas in the text, and similar ideas, events, and individuals not in the text

how—In what way

idea—An opinion, belief, concept, or theme

integrate—To think about various kinds of media to come up with a single idea they have in common

identify—Recognize or point out something in the text

individual(s)—A single person or a group of people with similar characteristics

inference—A type of conclusion based on explicit evidence from the text and the reader's own reasoning and background knowledge

integrate—To think about various kinds of media (or texts) in terms of a single idea

key words—In telegraphic highlighting, words that tell the reader what the text is explicitly about

key supporting details—Important information and ideas that tell about the central idea of the text

know—Be aware of something

navigate—To read text in several kinds of media one after the other with understanding about what they mean and how they connect

opinion—A judgment about something that may or may not be based on fact

oppose—Disagree with something

position—How you feel about something

problem—Something that needs to be fixed

process—Read, write, think, or talk about something

prove—Show or demonstrate the truth of a statement

question—Asking someone for information or raising a doubt about the truth of something

read—Get meaning from text

reasoning—Thinking, understanding, drawing a conclusion, or making an inference

relate—Make or figure out a connection between two or more things

relevant—Connected

show—Point out or prove something

snapshot summary—A sentence or phrase you write that states the central idea of one chunk of text you have read

solution—A way to solve a problem

sufficient—Enough

style—How an author uses language

summarize—Write or tell the meaning of what you have read in your own words

summary—A short statement that tells what the text is most importantly about

support—Agree with something

supporting details—Various important facts in the text that help explain the central idea of the text

technical word—A word that has a specific meaning for the text or the content

telegraphic highlighting—Highlighting the key words in a text

text—In the context of classroom instruction, any printed material you are expected to read and understand

text structure—The way a text is organized by the author

text summary—A sentence that combines or blends several snapshot summary statements to create a summary of the entire text

textual evidence—Phrases or sentences in the text that prove a statement or conclusion

theme—An abstract idea of what something is

thesis—An idea that is to be proved

tool—In reading, something you use to help you solve a problem

trivial information—Information in text that does not answer the question you are asking or support the conclusion you have drawn

valid—Defensible

weight of a word—How important a word is to the overall meaning of the text

what—The topic or content of the text

why—The reason or purpose for something

REFERENCES AND RESOURCES

Adams, M. J. (2009). The challenge of advanced texts: The interdependence of reading and learning. In E. H. Hiebert (Ed.), *Reading more, reading better: Are American students reading enough of the right stuff?* (pp. 163–189). New York: Guilford Press.

Adkins, E., & Adkins, R. (2006). *Chickahominy Indians-Eastern Division: An ethnohistory.* Bloomington, IN: Xlibris Press.

Adler, M. (1940). *How to read a book.* New York: Simon & Schuster.

Ambrose, S. E. (1994). *D-Day, June 6, 1944: The climactic battle of World War II.* New York: Simon & Schuster.

Applebee, A. N. (1986). Problems in process approaches: Toward a reconceptualization of process instruction. In A. R. Petrosky and D. Bartholomae (Eds.), *The teaching of writing.* Chicago: National Society for the Study of Education.

Applebee, A. N., & Langer, J. A. (1983). Instructional scaffolding: Reading and writing as natural language activities. *Language Arts, 60*(2), 168–175.

Apple Dictionary. (2009). Version 2.1.3.

Archer, A. L., Gleason, M., & Vachon, V. (2005). *Multisyllabic word reading strategies: Teacher's guide.* Longmont, CO: Sopris West.

Barnum, D. (2012, February 3.) *Reason for cancer's foothold.* Letter to the Editor of the *Houston Chronicle.* Accessed at www.chron.com /opinion/letters/article/Letters-Reasons-for-cancer-s-foothold -3003893.php on April 1, 2012.

Baumann, J. F., & Kameenui, E. J. (1991). Research on vocabulary instruction: Ode to Voltaire. In J. Flood, J. Jensen, D. Lapp, & J. R. Squires (Eds.), *Handbook of research on teaching the English language arts* (pp. 604–632). New York: Macmillan.

Beck, I. L., McKeown, M. G., Hamilton, R. L., & Kucan, L. (1997). *Questioning the author: An approach for enhancing student engagement with text*. Newark, DE: International Reading Association.

Boscolo, P., & Mason, L. (2001). Writing to learn, writing to transfer. In G. Rijlaarsdam, P. Tynjala, L. Mason, & K. Lonka (Eds.), *Studies in writing: Vol. 7. Writing as a learning tool: Integrating theory and practice* (pp. 83–104). Dordrecht, The Netherlands: Kluwer Academic.

Bereiter, C., & Bird, M. (1985). Use of thinking aloud in identification and teaching of reading comprehension strategies. *Cognition and Instruction, 2*(2), 131–156.

Bereiter, C., & Scardamalia, M. (1987). *The psychology of written composition*. Hillsdale, NJ: Erlbaum.

Boscolo, P., & Mason, L. (2001). Writing to learn, writing to transfer. In G. Rijlaarsdam, P. Tynjala, L. Mason, & K. Lonka (Eds.), *Studies in writing: Vol. 7. Writing as a learning tool: Integrating theory and practice* (pp. 83–104). Dordrecht, The Netherlands: Kluwer Academic.

Brown, A. L., & Day, J. D. (1983). Macrorules for summarizing texts: The development of expertise. *Journal of Verbal Learning and Verbal Behavior, 22*, 1–14.

Bursuck, W. D., & Damer, M. (2007). *Reading instruction for students who are at risk or have disabilities*. New York: Pearson.

Centers for Disease Control and Prevention. (2009). *Annual deaths attributable to cigarette smoking—United States, 2000–2004*. Accessed at www.cdc .gov/tobacco/data_statistics/tables/health/attrdeaths/index.htm on March 12, 2012.

Clark, G. (2011, November 13). Armadillos are armed for survival. *Houston Chronicle*. Accessed at www.chron.com/life/article/Armadillos-are -armed-for-survival-2276361.php on May 31, 2012.

Coleman, D. (2011, April 28). *Bringing the Common Core to life*. Speech presented at New York State Education Department's Bringing the Common Core to Life Conference and Webinar, Albany, NY.

Coleman, D., & Pimentel, S. (2011). *Publishers' criteria for the Common Core State Standards in English language arts and literacy, grades 3–12*. Washington, DC: Common Core State Standards Initiative.

College Entrance Examination Board. (2002). *The AP vertical teams guide for English* (2nd ed.) Princeton, NJ: Author.

Collins, A., Brown, J. S., & Holum, A. (1991). Cognitive apprenticeship: Making thinking visible. *American Educator*, 6–11, 38–41.

Collins, J., Lee, J., Fox, J., & Madigan, T. (2008). *When writing serves reading: Randomized trials of writing intensive reading comprehension (WIRC) in low-performing urban elementary schools.* Unpublished manuscript, State University of New York at Buffalo.

Collins, J., Madigan, T., & Lee, J. (2008). *Using thinksheets to improve higher-level literacy.* Unpublished manuscript, State University of New York at Buffalo.

Common Core State Standards Initiative. (2010a). *Common Core State Standards for English language arts & literacy in history/social studies, science, and technical subjects.* Washington, DC: Author. Accessed at http://corestandards.org/assets/CCSSI_ELA%20Standards.pdf on September 23, 2011.

Common Core State Standards Initiative. (2010b). *Common Core State Standards for English language arts & literacy in history/social studies, science, and technical subjects. Appendix a.* Washington, DC: Author. Accessed at www.corestandards.org/assets/Appendix_A.pdf on March 13, 2012.

Conley, D. T. (2005). *College knowledge: What it really takes for students to succeed and what we can do to get them ready.* San Francisco: Jossey-Bass.

Conley, D. T. (2007). The challenge of college readiness. *Educational Leadership, 64*(7), 23–29.

Covey, S. (1989). *The 7 habits of highly effective peoples: Restoring the character ethic.* New York: Simon & Schuster.

Davey, B. (1983). Think aloud—Modeling the cognitive processes of reading comprehension. *Journal Reading, 27*(1), 44–47.

Dewitz, P., & Dewitz, P. K. (2003). They can read words, but they can't understand: Refining comprehension assessment. *Reading Teacher, 56*(5), 422–435.

Dillon, J. T. (1988). *Questioning and teaching. A manual of practice.* Amsterdam, NY: Teachers College Press.

Dinh, K. (2005, October 16). Vietnam revisited: I was a refugee long before Katrina. *Houston Chronicle.* Accessed at www.chron.com/opinion /outlook/article/Vietnam-revisited-I-was-a-refugee-long-before -1934934.php on April 1, 2012.

Edmonds, R. (1981). Making public schools effective. *Social Policy, 12*(2), 56–60.

Englert, C. S. (1995). Teaching written language skills. In P. Cigilka & W. Berdine (Eds.), *Effective instruction for students with learning difficulties* (304–343). Boston: Allyn & Bacon.

Federal Trade Commission. (2011, July 29). *FTC releases reports on cigarette and smokeless tobacco advertising and promotion.* Accessed at http://ftc .gov/opa/2011/07/tobacco.shtm on March 22, 2012.

Feller, B. (2006, July 3). *Mindless reading seen as fundamental.* Accessed at www.seattlepi.nwsource.com on July 4, 2006.

Frayer, D., Frederick, W. C., & Klausmeier, H. J. (1969). A schema for testing the level of concept mastery (Working Paper No. 16). Madison: University of Wisconsin.

Fussell, P. (1975). *The Great War and modern memory.* New York: Oxford University Press.

Goldstein, R. (2002, October 14). Stephen Ambrose dies at 66. *New York Times.* Accessed at www.nytimes.com/2002/10/14/obituaries /14AMBR.html?scp=1&sq=Stephen%20Ambrose%20Dies%20at%20 66&st=cse on April 1, 2012.

Goodwin, D. K. (1987). *The Fitzgeralds and the Kennedys: An American saga.* New York: Simon & Schuster.

Graves, M. F., Cooke, C. L., & LaBerge, M. J. (1983). Effects of previewing difficult short stories on low-ability junior high school students' comprehension, recall, and attitudes. *Reading Research Quarterly, 18*(3), 262–276.

Gray, W. (1960). The major aspects of reading. In H. Robinson (Ed.), *Sequential development of reading abilities* (Supplementary Educational Monographs No. 90). Chicago: University of Chicago Press.

Guthrie, J. T., & Kirsch, I. S. (1987). Distinctions between reading comprehension and locating information in text. *Journal of Educational Psychology, 79*(3), 220–227.

Herber, H. L., & Herber, J. N. (1993). *Teaching in content areas with reading, writing, and reasoning.* Needham Heights, MA: Allyn & Bacon.

Herber, H. L., & Nelson, J. (1975). Questioning is not the answer. *Journal of Reading, 18*(7), 512–517.

Hord, S. M. (1997). *Professional learning communities: Communities of continuous inquiry and improvement.* Austin, TX: Southwest Educational Development Laboratory.

Johnson, D. D., & von hoff Johnson, B. (1986). Highlighting vocabulary in inferential comprehension instruction. *Journal of Reading, 29*(7), 622–625.

Joyce, B., & Showers, B. (2002). *Student achievement through staff development* (3rd ed.). Alexandria, VA: Association for Supervision and Curriculum Development.

Just, M. A., & Carpenter, P. A. (1987). *The psychology of reading and language comprehension.* Boston: Allyn & Bacon.

Kaufman, K. (2000). Vultures. In S. J. Phillips & P. W. Comus (Eds.), *A natural history of the Sonoran Desert* (p. 377). Tucson, AZ: Arizona-Sonoran Desert Museum Press and Berkeley: University of California Press.

Kirkpatrick, D. D. (2002, April 9). Pulitzer Prizes and plagiarism. *New York Times*, p. A22.

Lazaroff, D. (2000). Powering down. In S. J. Phillips & P. W. Comus (Eds.), *A natural history of the Sonoran Desert* (p. 410). Tucson: Arizona-Sonoran Desert Museum Press and Berkeley: University of California Press.

Leu, D. J., Jr., Kinzer, C. K., Coiro, J., & Cammack, D. (2004). Toward a theory of new literacies emerging from the Internet and other information and communication technologies. In R. B. Ruddell & N. Unrau (Eds.), *Theoretical models and processes of reading* (5th ed., pp. 1570–1613). Newark, DE: International Reading Association.

McEwan, E. K. (2001). *Raising reading achievement in middle and high schools: Five simple-to-follow strategies for principals.* Thousand Oaks, CA: Corwin Press.

McEwan, E. K. (2004). *7 strategies of highly effective readers: Using cognitive research to boost K–8 achievement.* Thousand Oaks, CA: Corwin Press.

McEwan, E. K. (2006). *Raising reading achievement in middle and high schools: Five simple-to-follow strategies* (2nd ed.). Thousand Oaks, CA: Corwin Press.

McEwan, E. K. (2009). *10 traits of highly effective schools: Raising the achievement bar for all students.* Thousand Oaks, CA: Corwin.

McEwan, E. K., & Bresnahan, V. (2008). *Vocabulary, grades 4–8*. Thousand Oaks, CA: Corwin.

McEwan, E. K., Burnett, A., & Lowery, R. (2008). *The reading puzzle: Comprehension, grades 4–8*. Thousand Oaks, CA: Corwin.

McEwan, E. K., Dobberteen, K. W., & Pearce, Q. L. (2008). *The reading puzzle: Fluency, grades 4–8*. Thousand Oaks, CA: Corwin.

McEwan-Adkins, E. K. (2010). *40 reading intervention strategies for K–6 students: Research-based support for RTI*. Bloomington, IN: Solution Tree Press.

McKenna, M. C., & Robinson, R. D. (1990). Content literacy: A definition and implications. *Journal of Reading, 34*(3), 184–186.

McKoon, G., & Ratcliff, R. (1992). Inference during reading. *Psychological Review, 99*, 440–466.

Mehan, H. (1979). *Learning lessons: Social organization in the classroom*. Cambridge, MA: Harvard University Press.

Merlin, P. (2000). The coyote. In S. J. Phillips & P. W. Comus (Eds.), *A natural history of the Sonoran Desert* (p. 37). Tucson, AZ: Arizona-Sonoran Desert Museum Press and Berkeley: University of California Press.

Merton, R. (1968). The Matthew Effect in science. *Science, 159*(3810), 56–63.

Mislevy, R. (1995). *Test theory reconceived*. White paper based on an invited address to the meeting of the National Council of Measurement in Education, Atlanta, GA.

Mossberg, K. (2012, January 27). Giffords case raises awareness of traumatic brain injury. *Houston Chronicle*. Accessed at www.chron.com/opinion/outlook/article/Giffords-case-raises-awareness-of-traumatic-brain-2754566.php on April 1, 2012.

Nagy, W. E. (1988). *Teaching vocabulary to improve reading comprehension*. Washington, DC: ERIC Clearinghouse on Reading and Communication Skills.

National Governors Association Center for Best Practices and Council of Chief State School Officers. (2010). *College and Career Readiness Anchor Standards for Reading in grades 6–12*. Washington, DC: Author.

Nickerson, R. E., Perkins, D. N., & Smith, E. E. (1985). *The teaching of thinking*. New York: Routledge.

Novak, J. D. (1998). *Learning, creating, and using knowledge: Concept maps as facilitative tools in schools and corporations.* Mahwah, NJ: Erlbaum.

Novak, J. D., & Gowin, D. B. (1984). *Learning how to learn.* Cambridge, UK: Cambridge University Press.

Palaima, T. (2011, November 8). Remembering the origins of Veterans Day. *Austin-American Statesman.* Accessed at www.statesman.com/opinion /remembering-origins-of-veterans-day-1957502.html on April 1, 2012.

Pearson, P. D., & Fielding, L. (1991). Comprehension instruction. In R. Barr, M. L. Kamil, P. Mosenthal, & P. D. Pearson (Eds.), *Handbook of reading research* (pp. 815–860). White Plains, NY: Longman.

Potts, T. (2011, December 6). Stories of an attack 70 years ago will live forever. *Houston Chronicle.* Accessed at www.chron.com/opinion /outlook/article/Stories-of-an-attack-70-years-ago-will-live -2350835.php on April 1, 2012.

Pressley, M., & Afflerbach, P. (1995). *Verbal protocols of reading: The nature of constructively responsive reading.* Hillsdale, NJ: Erlbaum.

Pressley, M., & Burkell, J., Cariglia-Bull, T., Lysynchuk, L., McGoldrick, J. A. Schneider, B., et al. (1995). *Cognitive strategy instruction that really improves children's academic performance.* Cambridge, MA: Brookline Books.

Pressley, M., El-Dinary, P. B., & Brown, R. (1992). Skill and not-so-skilled reading: Good information processing and not-so-good information processing. In M. Pressley, K. R. Harris, & J. T. Guthrie (Eds.), *Promoting academic competence and literacy in school* (pp. 91–127). San Diego, CA: Academic Press.

RAND Reading Study Group. (2002). *Toward an R&D program in reading comprehension.* Santa Monica, CA: RAND.

Raphael, T., Kirschner, B. W., & Englert, C. S. (1986). *Students' metacognitive knowledge about writing.* Lansing: Michigan State University, Institute for Research on Teaching.

Russo, A. (2004, July/August). School-based coaching: A revolution in professional development—or just the latest fad? *Harvard Education Letter, 20*(4). Accessed at www.hepg.org/hel/article/269 on July 3, 2012.

Sanchez, A. (2011, October 23). In teen sex education debate, both sides ahead. *Austin American-Statesman.* Accessed at www.statesman.com /opinion/sanchez-in-teen-sex-education-debate-both-sides-1930040 .html on April 1, 2012.

Schmoker, M. (2006). *Results now: How we can achieve unprecedented improvements in teaching and learning.* Alexandria, VA: Association for Supervision and Curriculum Development.

Schooler, J. W., Reichle, E. D., & Halpern, D. V. (2004). Zoning out while reading: Evidence for dissociations between experience and metaconsciousness. In D. T. Levin (Ed.), *Thinking and seeing: Visual metacognition in adults and children* (pp. 203–226). Cambridge, MA: Massachusetts Institute of Technology Press.

Schumaker, J. B., Deshler, D. D., Bulgren, J. A., David, B., Lenz, B. K., & Grossen, B. (2002). Access of adolescents with disabilities to general education curriculum: Myth or reality? *Focus on Exceptional Children, 3*(3), 1–16.

Scientific root words, prefixes, and suffixes. (n.d.). Accessed at www.biologyjunction .com/prefixes%20and%20suffixes.pdf on August 3, 2012.

Shanahan, C., Shanahan, T., & Misischia, C. (2011). Analysis of expert readers in three disciplines: History, mathematics, and chemistry. *Journal of Literacy Research, 43*(4), 393–429.

Stanovich, K. E. (1986). Matthew effects in reading: Some consequences of individual differences in the acquisition of literacy. *Reading Research Quarterly, 21*(4), 360–407.

Surgeon General. (2010). *A report of the surgeon general: How tobacco smoke causes disease: The biology and behavioral basis for smoking-attributable disease fact sheet.* Accessed at www.surgeongeneral.gov/library /tobaccosmoke/factsheeet.html on March 22, 2012.

Thorndike, E. L. (1917). Reading as reasoning: A study of mistakes in paragraph reading. *Reading Research Quarterly, 6*(4), 425–434.

Tierney, R. J., & Readence, J. E. (2000). *Reading strategies and practices: A compendium* (5th ed.). Boston: Allyn & Bacon.

Tovani, C. (2000). *I read it, but I don't get it: Comprehension strategies for adolescent readers.* Portland, ME: Stenhouse.

Trowbridge, R. (2011, December 21). Radical reform of higher education is inevitable. *Houston Chronicle.* Accessed at www.chron.com/opinion /outlook/article/Radical-reform-of-higher-education-is-inevitable -2418714.php on April 1, 2012.

University of Washington Psychology Writing Center. (2005). *Plagiarism and student writing.* Accessed at www.scribd.com/doc/6482296/How-to -Cite on April 12, 2012.

Vygotsky, L. S. (1962). *Thought and language.* Cambridge, MA: MIT Press.

Vygotsky, L. S. (1978). *Mind in society.* Cambridge, MA: Harvard University Press.

Walberg, H. J., & Tsai, S. L. (1983, Fall). Matthew effects in education. *Educational Research Quarterly, 20,* 359–373.

Wills, S. (2011, December 8). Wills: We lost the war on drugs. *Austin-American Statesman.* Accessed at www.statesman.com/opinion/wills-we-lost-the-war-on-drugs-2021249.html on April 1, 2012.

Zwelling, L. A. (2012). Time for some innovative thinking in the war on cancer. *Houston Chronicle.* Accessed at www.chron.com/opinion/outlook/article/Time-for-some-innovative-thinking-in-the-war-on-2884570.php on April 1, 2012.

INDEX

W

How to Teach Thinking Skills Within the Common Core
James A. Bellanca, Robin J. Fogarty, and Brian M. Pete
Empower your students to thrive across the curriculum. Packed with examples and tools, this practical guide prepares teachers across all grade levels and content areas to teach the most critical cognitive skills from the Common Core State Standards.
BKF576

Common Core English Language Arts in a PLC at Work™, Grades 9–12
Douglas Fisher and Nancy Frey
Explore strategies for integrating the Common Core State Standards for English language arts for grades 9–12 in this interdisciplinary resource. You'll also learn how to implement the CCSS within the powerful collaborative framework of PLC at Work™.
BKF586

Rebuilding the Foundation
Edited by Timothy V. Rasinski
Teaching reading is a complex task without a simple formula for developing quality instruction. Rather than build on or alter existing models, this book considers how educators and policymakers might think about rebuilding and reconceptualizing reading education, perhaps from the ground up.
BKF399

40 Reading Intervention Strategies for K–6 Students
Elaine K. McEwan-Adkins
This well-rounded collection of reading intervention strategies, teacher-friendly lesson plans, and adaptable miniroutines will support and inform your RTI efforts. Many of the strategies motivate all students as well as scaffold struggling readers. Increase effectiveness by using the interventions across grade-level teams or schoolwide.
BKF270

Solution Tree | Press
a division of
Solution Tree

Visit solution-tree.com or call 800.733.6786 to order.

Wait! Your professional development journey doesn't have to end with the last pages of this book.

We realize improving student learning doesn't happen overnight. And your school or district shouldn't be left to puzzle out all the details of this process alone.

No matter where you are on the journey, we're committed to helping you get to the next stage.

Take advantage of everything from **custom workshops** to **keynote presentations** and **interactive web and video conferencing**. We can even help you develop an action plan tailored to fit your specific needs.

Let's get the conversation started.

Call 888.763.9045 today.

solution-tree.com